The Idea of Neoliberalism:
The Emperor Has Threadbare Contemporary Clothes

THE IDEA OF
NEOLIBERALISM
THE EMPEROR HAS THREADBARE CONTEMPORARY CLOTHES
JOHN DIXON

Westphalia Press
An Imprint of the Policy Studies Organization
Washington, DC
2017

THE IDEA OF NEOLIBERALISM
All Rights Reserved © 2017 by Policy Studies Organization

Westphalia Press
An imprint of Policy Studies Organization
1527 New Hampshire Ave., NW
Washington, D.C. 20036
info@ipsonet.org

ISBN-10: 1-63391-505-0
ISBN-13: 978-1-63391-505-3

Cover and interior design by Jeffrey Barnes
jbarnesbook.design

Daniel Gutierrez-Sandoval, Executive Director
PSO and Westphalia Press

Updated material and comments on this edition
can be found at the Westphalia Press website:
www.westphaliapress.org

To the late Alex Kouzmin

For Tina, Piers, Aliki, David, and Isabella

CONTENTS

PREFACE

> Neoliberalism is an elusive and contested notion, a hybrid term awkwardly suspended between the lay idiom of political debate and the technical terminology of social science, which, moreover, is often invoked without clear referent. For some, it designates a hard-wired reality ... while others view it as a doctrine. ... It is alternately depicted as a tight, fixed, and monolithic set of principles and programs that tend to homogenize societies, or as a loose, mobile, and plastic constellation of concepts and institutions adaptable to variegated strands of capitalism.
>
> Wacquant (2009, 306)

This book is the outcome of a 40-year intellectual odyssey. It was initiated by my teaching in the mid-1970s of neoclassical economic theory and public choice theory to questioning and skeptical practicing public officials in Canberra, and by the adoption in the early 1980s of the neoliberal reform agenda by the then Australian, center-left, Prime Minister, Bob Hawke. The result is a critical exposition of the idea of neoliberalism.

Neoliberalism, as a set of ideas, represents the 1970s rebirth—rebranding—of classical liberalism that originated in the mid-eighteenth century Scottish Enlightenment associated with the thinking of David Hume, Adam Smith, Adam Ferguson, and Dugald Stewart. Its doctrine is grounded in three foundational principles:

- the absolute supremacy of individual liberty;

- the Lockean idea of a protective democracy; and

- the free-market economic philosophy.

While the holy grail of neoliberalism is not embodied in any coherent corpus of received interpretation—constituting a Neoliberal Manifesto—the ideas underpinning its dogma can be deduced from these foundational principles and its predispositions or standpoints towards:

- ontology—specifically, individualism (only self-caused and self-interested individuals exist in the world of persons); and

- epistemology—specifically, empiricism (privileging factual truths about the world of persons), and rationalism (privileging logical truths about cause of social actions in that world).

This permitted the assembling of a mental construct of neoliberalism, akin to a Weberian pure ideal-type—a "unified analytical construct" (Weber [1903–1917/1949] 1997, 90), with "the highest possible degree of logical integration" (Weber [1914/1922] 1968, 20). This construct enables the demarcation of neoliberalism's worldview—its point-of-view on the social world—the world of persons. It has own its framing assumptions (organizing ideas) and its own blind spots (reality obfuscations). This enables the world of persons to be consistently—but incompletely—described, explained, and understood, on the presumption that it is as neoliberalism purports it to be. This is the methodological tool used to mark out and analyze the incompleteness of the dogma of neoliberalism. Of course, in the Weberian tradition such a mental construct is not an hypothesis (to be empirically verified); it does not *per se* imply an ethical ideal (but they can embody moral propositions); and it does not exhaust reality (thereby permitting variations in praxis, in terms of the social, economic, and political ideas, institutions, policies, and practices inspired and validated by such a mental construct).

This is very eclectic book. It draws upon concepts, frameworks, paradigms, and theories from philosophy, social theory, economics, political science, sociology, social psychology, organizational theory, public administration, and management. This necessitated its distinctive style. First, it has extensive footnotes. These serve three functions: to define (giving the reader all the technical definitions needed to make the text accessible); to elaborate (giving the reader an appreciation of any nuances); and to contextualize (giving all readers an appreciation of how subject matter is situated within a particular academic literature). Second, it has an extensive bibliography. Finally, it has a thematic index of both the text and footnotes.

All authors are inevitably intellectual debtors. My major intellectual debt is obviously to the thousand or so scholars whose work has been cited. My other debts cannot be adequately expressed, let alone repaid. Foremost are my personal and professional debts to the late Alex Kouzmin, with whom I collaborated regularly over 25 years on themes related to the neoliberalism, and to whom this book is dedicated. I must also thank the editorial and production team at Westphalia Press, particularly Rahima Schwenkbeck, who is a delight to work with. Their professionalism is evidenced by the end product. Of course, my overwhelming and utterly un-repayable debt is the very personal one I owe my wife, Christina. She has, yet again, put up with me writing yet another book. Indeed, the years of marriage that she has endured is now less than the number of books and book-length manuscripts she has endured, which is evidence of something after 44 years.

1.

NEOLIBERALISM:
ITS PHILOSOPHICAL FOUNDATIONS

Neoliberalism is in the first instance a theory of political economic practices that proposes that human wellbeing can best be advanced by liberating individual entrepreneurial freedoms and skills within an institutional framework characterized by strong private property rights, free markets and free trade. The role of the state is to create and preserve an institutional framework appropriate to such practices.

Harvey (2005)

INTRODUCTION

The idea of neoliberalism[1] as a social, political, and economic philosophy derives, but significantly deviates, from classical liberalism.[2] This places its origins in the Scottish Enlightenment occurring in the middle decades of the eighteenth century and in the thinking of David Hume, Adam Smith, Adam Ferguson, and Dugald Stewart.[3] As a system of ideas and ideals, neoliberalism (née classical liberalism) has three foundational principles.

The first principle is the absolute supremacy of individual liberty. This privileges the individual—taken to be "a thinking intelligent Being"[4]

---

1   Alexander Rüstow, a German scholar, was in 1938 the first to use the term "neoliberalism," with the connotation that it embraced "the priority of the price mechanism, free enterprise, the system of competition, and a strong and impartial state" (Mirowski and Plehwe 2009, 13-14) and so it endorse state economic intervention. This school of liberalism lost its impetus in the 1960s (Kotz 2015).

2   As does Haymes, Vidal de Haymes, and Miller (2015, 7). See also Kotz 2015; Saad-Filho and Johnston 2005; Steger and Roy 2010.

3   Hayek (1960, chs. 1 and 9) dubbed this practical or pragmatic liberalism, which he considered stood in contradistinction to the more theoretical and radical French rationalist school of liberalism, associated with, among others, Jean-Jacque Rousseau, particularly influential was his *The Social Contract* ([1762] 1973).

4   Locke's ([1689] 2004, II, 27, S. 9) depicts human being as: ... a thinking intelligent

(1689–1690] 2004, II, 27, S. 9)—over the social (Bunge 1996; McCann 2004). Mill ([1859] 1963, 262) held that "the burden of proof is supposed to be with those who are against liberty; who contend for any restriction or prohibition .... The *a priori* assumption is in favor of freedom ...." Thus, individuals are assigned the natural right to live, liberty, and property, and, thereby, the right to be free to pursue their material wellbeing without any obligation to satisfy the needs or wants of others. So, importance is placed on personal responsibility and the intimate linking of liberty, private property, and the free market (see Mack and Gaus 2004).

The second foundational principle is the Lockean idea of a protective democracy (Locke ([1689] 1960; but see also Hobbes [1651] 1948; Nozick 1974; Oakeshott 1975). This limits the role of government to enforcing contractual obligations and defending against any threats to individual rights, so making the state weak, unobtrusive, and small (Hendriks and Zouridis 1999, 126; see also Ellis 1992; Held 1987; Nozick 1974). As Smith (1755) remarked: "Little else is requisite to carry a state to the highest degree of opulence from the lowest barbarism, but peace, easy taxes, and the tolerable administration of justice; all the rest being brought about by the natural course of things"[5] (see also Stewart 1829 324). This proposition is grounded in the Scottish Enlightenment theory of spontaneous order—the self-generating and self-regulating capacity of civil society—first articulated by Hume ([1739–1740] 1978, [1751] 1998); Smith ([1776] 1976); and Ferguson ([1767] 1782; [1776] 1792), then elaborated by Spencer ([1851] 1995) and Menger ([1871] 1994), and finally further refined by Polanyi (1957) and Hayek (1960, 1991).

The third foundational principle reflects the importance of the free-market economic philosophy—an ideological commitment to maximizing a society's material wellbeing (Bromely 1990). This involves:

- Private enterprise being conducted in deregulated markets:

Being, that has reason and reflection, and can consider itself as itself, the same thinking thing in different times and places; which it does only by that consciousness, which is inseparable from thinking, and as it seems to me essential to it. Filling out this depiction is Descartes' ([1641] 1975; [1644] 1983) dualist mind-body dichotomy—the immaterial mind being an entity separate from the physical body (Searle 2004), and Freud's discernment of the importance of unconscious (subconscious or metaconscious) mental states, which are disruptive of conscious mental states (Freud ([1912] 1959)).

5   The source of this quotation was an unpublished paper presented by Adam Smith to his Glasgow club in 1755, a copy of which was acquired by his contemporary, Dugald Stewart (Kennedy 2005, 241-248).

Under classical liberalism, a "free market" was a one free from all forms of economic privilege, monopolies, and artificial scarcities (see Popper 1994). Under neoliberalism it refers to a market free from government intervention.

- Competition, including the liberalization of international trade, under the rubric of globalization[6]: The underlying premised is that countries will only trade only if there are net gains from such trade. However, from a national perspective, foreign trade gives rise to both winners—those industries that have an international comparative (price) advantage, and so can compete in particular foreign and domestic markets with the relatively more expensive foreign domestic producers—and losers—those in industries that do not have an international comparative advantage, and so cannot compete with the less expensive foreign domestic producers, a consequence of which is structural unemployment.

To Ralston Saul ([2005] 2009), the free-market economic philosophy involves the emergence of a "Crucifixion Economics": "... free market assumptions were transposed into a global movement economics and as a tool to weaken government, discourage taxes, force de-regulation and entrench private monopolies" (p. 33). This makes neoliberalism indisposed to the proposition that the state should compensating individuals, communities, and regions in order to correct any negative redistributive effects generated by the market.

Classical liberalism's faith in the marketplace, and so in the belief that government should be weak, unobtrusive, and small—grounded on the presumption that people have personal autonomy and, so can be held personally responsibility for their own fate—was challenged during the nineteenth century Industrial Revolution by the all-to-evident evils and injustices of free market capitalism (Green ([1895] 2006); Mill ([1859] 1963). This loss of faith in the capacity of the free market to empower individuals to take control of their lives was accompanied by a growing faith in government's ability to govern economic affairs, attributable in part to the increasing democratization of Western states (Ritchie 1896, 64). So, classical liberalism faced a threat to two of its sacrosanct principles— personal liberty and protective democracy—posed by the recognition of

---

6   The International Monetary Fund (IMF) (2000) considers that international trade is one of four essential dimensions of globalization, the others being international capital flows, migration flows, knowledge flows.

the flaws in its third sacrosanct principle that justified an interventionist state in order to correct the failures of the free market—the failures of capitalism (Keynes 1972). This gave rise to the social liberalism project.

This liberal variant took root in the last third of the nineteenth century and became mainstream liberal thought for most of the next century. It advocated the acceptance of the collective values of social intervention and cooperation. In Millsians terms, while the state can be an instrument of tyranny in the hands of the majority or the political rulers (so constituting a threat to personal liberty that justifies the imposition of constitutional checks and balances to place limits on its powers), the state has an obligation to intervene in the marketplace, when private actions do harm to others, so as to correct any resultant adverse consequences (Mill [1863] 1968). This re-balancing of liberty (negative freedom) and enablement (positive freedom)[7] in favor of the latter clearly differentiated it from classical liberalism and its heir apparent—neoliberalism.

The re-ascending influence of classical liberalism re-branded—with a vengeance in the last quarter of the twentieth century—as neoliberalism became possible because of the growing sophistication of neoclassical economic theory. This first involved, a century earlier, the demarcation of an economy as a closed, law-abiding determinant system (Colander 2000)—a mathematical abstraction—grounded in a set of *ceteris paribus* (other things being equal) assumptions that isolated it from, and made it independent of, any structural influences in the host society (Edgworth 1881; Jevons [1871] 1888; Marshall [1890] 1920; Menger [1871] 1994; Wicksteed 1910). This permitted the deducing of *a priori* or logical knowledge by analyzing the rational—utility and profit maximizing—behavior of socially isolated, self-determining, and self-interested actors—

7   Berlin (1969) drew the distinction between negative and positive freedom. Negative freedom is the right of self-determination: freedom from control, interference, or exploitation, which is identified with the Hobbesian idea of the absence of constraint or obstacles. It is based on three premises: that individuals require the private space to identify appropriate personal goals and ambitions; that personal goals and ambitions have value only if they are freely chosen; and that voluntary action—reflecting choice and acceptance of personal responsibility—enables individuals to meet important spiritual needs. Positive freedom is the right to be able to take control of one's life: freedom to choose and realize desired outcomes, achieved by collective empowerment, which is identified with Rousseau's ([1762] 1973 notion of moral self-government. It is also based on three premises: that all individuals have capacities or latent, but desirable, qualities; that positive freedom is the realization of these capacities, which may therefore be conceptualized, in the broader sense, as personal autonomy; and that social conditions are the decisive influence on the realization of these capacities.

Sen's (1977) rational fools (see also Dixon 2010, 2016a, 2016b, Dixon, Dogan, and Sanderson 2009).

It was, however, the impeccable logic of public choice theory—epitomized in the seminal work of Buchanan and Tullock (1962)—that ultimately permitted collective action—action by the state—to be re-conceptualized as an economic (exchange) phenomenon. Advanced was the proposition that freely determined individual preferences[8] are the determinants of both private (market) and public (government) actions—the so-called logic of collective action (Olsen 1965). Its conclusion, in the Lockean tradition, is that the state is inherently coercive and intrusive, and is both inefficient and unknowing of its citizens' preferences for government actions. This provided a logical explanation for the very evident public loss of faith in government as means of enhancing human welfare, and a growing faith in the market's ability to do a better job. Neoliberalism's hostility to collectivist ideologies[9]—including social liberalism—is grounded its unequivocal commitment to the absolute supremacy of individual liberty, private property, the free market, and to the assignment of personal responsibility.

The purpose of this chapter is to elucidate neoliberalism's foundational ontological[10] and epistemological[11] premises that determine how it

---

8   These "are the way an actor values alternative outcomes of the decision process being modeled. ... Actors prefer a particular outcome because they believe it will best satisfy some deeper goal" (Roberts Clark 1998, 252 and 254).

9   The distinguishing feature of collectivist ideologies is their emphasis on the protection of the individual by group membership in return for group loyalty, whether grounded in duty (an adherence to binding normative imperatives (Zimmerman 1996); shared value (norms that endorse co-operation within a group, so bonding homogenous groups) (Putnam 2000), or coercion (the threat of force, which creates a situation in which the choice is between doing what is demanded or suffering the threatened unappealing consequences).

10   Ontology seeks to provide a consistent account of the nature and coherence of what exists in the world (Schatzki 2002) and of the status of the categories of phenomena that possess causal efficacy—able to give rise to social actions (Dixon, Dogaan, and Sanderson 2009). In the social sciences the ontological debate has focused on whether social actions can best be ascribed, in reductionist terms, to the internal agential dimensions or free will—agential-causation (agency ontology); or, in holist terms, to the external structural dimensions or determinism—social-causation (structuralist ontology) (Archer 2000).

11   Epistemology is concerned with the investigation of the nature, extent, sources, and legitimacy of knowledge and the truth-value of knowledge claims (see Kirkham 1992). The two long-contending approaches to epistemology in the social sciences are naturalism (grounded in objectivism) and hermeneutics (grounded in subjectivism), which gives rise to Bernstein's (1996) objectivist-relativist trap; the Cartesian

describes, analyses, and explains[12] the social world—Marcel's "world of persons" (1952, 164). These provide the foundations for its distinctive worldview.

Neoliberalism:
Its Ontological And Epistemological Premises

When describing, interpreting, explaining, and evaluating the web of beliefs about the world of persons, two fundamental issues need to be considered (Dixon, Dogan, and Sanderson 2009). The first is ontological (Dale 2002); what exists that can give rise to social actions.[13] Attribution theory seeks to account for how a person explains—attributes reasons for—the behavior of self or others (Jones et al. 1972) by reference to reasons that are internal or external to the person whose behavior is being explained (Heider [1958] 1982).[14] The second is the epistemological: how should the veracity of knowledge claims (proposition or statement) about human affairs be established? At issue is how best to establish genuine knowledge (truths[15] or certainties) (Chisholm 1989; Lucey 1996; Sosa 1994). This requires the application of a truth-standard—a truth-criterion—that enables judgments to be made about what constitutes sufficient justification to warrant a belief being given the status of truth[16] (Kirkham

---

anxiety condition resulting from the suggestion that human events are explainable either objectively—privileging explanation and certainty—or subjectively—privileging understanding and relativity (Rubin 1994; Wright 1971).

12 In contention in the social and behavioral sciences is whether explanation can or should be understood in terms of causation (lawful relations between one material phenomenon and another, so establishing an antecedently sufficient causal chain; reasons (motivations with their overlay of moral justification); or purposes (functions) (see also Campbell, O'Rourke, and Silverstein 2007; Psillos 2002; Wright 1971).

13 In the words of the twelfth-century Persian (Afghan) mystic and poet, Rúmi (1956, 77): "There is a disputation that will continue till Mankind is raised from the dead between the necessitarians [determinists] and the partisans of free will [indeterminists]."

14 Such attribution can be based on the multiple observations of co-variation of the behavior to be explained and the possible causes (co-variation principle) (Kelley 1967; 1973) or on generalized causal propositional beliefs (the causal schemata principle) (Kelley 1972).

15 "To say of what is that it is not, or of what is not that it is, is false, while to say of what that it is, or of what is not that it is not, is true" (Aristotle [350 BCE/1924/1953] 1994–2000, 4, 7).

16 Nietzsche ([1886] 1998, 5) emphasis in original), however raised a more fundamental question: why is truth important? Why is there a will to truth? What is the value of this will? "Given that we want truth: *why do we not prefer* untruth? And

1992). However, as James ([1897] 1979, 15) pointed out, "no concrete test of what is really true has ever been agreed upon."[17] Thomas and Znaniecki (1918–1920) identified the two polar perspectives: establishing the facts that are independent of the perceiving person (*en-so*); and establishing the understandings that are the product of immanent acts in a perceiving human mind, conditioned by a person's mental states, which give rise to interpretations that "take social meaning into account and interpret his [sic] experience not exclusively in terms of his own needs and wishes but also in terms of the traditions, customs, beliefs, and aspirations of his social *milieu*" (p. 230) (*pour-soi*). The dilemma then confronted is well defined by Nagel (1979, 196, see also 1986):

> The problem is one of opposition between subjective and objective points of view. There is a tendency to seek an objective account of everything before admitting its reality. But often what appears to a more subjective point of view cannot be accounted for in this way. So either the objective conception of the world is incomplete, or the subjective involves illusions that should be rejected.[18]

Neoliberalism advances both a definitive ontological view about what exists in the world of persons that has the causal capacity[19] to give rise to so-

---

uncertainty? Even ignorance?" He goes on: "However much value we may ascribe to truth, truthfulness, and altruism, it may be that we need to attribute a higher and more fundamental value to appearances, to the will to illusion, to egoism and desire" (p. 6).

17   "Truth in human relations is of this more intangible and dubious order: hard to seize, harder to communicate" (Stevenson [1879] 1909-1914).

18   Chesterton ([1908] 2007, 97) captured the essence of this problem:
      The real trouble with this world of ours is not that it is an unreasonable world, nor even that it is a reasonable one. The commonest kind of trouble is that it is nearly reasonable, but not quite. Life is not an illogicality; yet it is a trap for logicians. It looks just a little more mathematical and regular than it is; its exactitude is obvious, but its inexactitude is hidden; its wildness lies in wait.

19   In contention in the social and behavioral sciences is whether in the world of persons causal capacity should be understood in terms of determinism (Earman 1986), which, essentially, means that a phenomenon has causes grounded in dependency relationships with one or more other phenomena (hard determinism). Causal or scientific determinism (see Butterfield 1998) posits a strictly mechanistic causal relationship in that every event has an unbroken chain of prior material occurrences—"all events and states of affairs are determined by antecedent causes and laws of nature" (Kane 2005, 284)—Leibniz's ([1704/1764] 1996) Principle of Sufficient Reason). This mechanistic view was originally argued by Leucippus and Democritus (Taylor 1999), who considered that everything happens in accordance with laws of nature (Russell 1946, 86)—in Humean terminology this is "necessity"—"the

cial actions,[20] and definitive epistemological view about what is knowable about that world of persons, how it can best be known, and how can its truthfulness be best established. Its standpoints are firmly grounded in:

- agency ontology—specifically, individualism (only individuals exist in the world of persons and they are *causa sui* (self-caused)), and utilitarianism (social actions are explainable by the actual or expected utility of their consequences); and

- naturalist epistemology—specifically, empiricism (giving rise to factual truths about the world of persons), and rationalism (giving rise to logical truths about causation in that world).

Agency Ontology

This posits that in the world of persons all that exist are individuals whose social actions can best be ascribed to their self-determined set of hopes, aspirations, goals, and preferences (their intentional mental states[21]). These give the reasons for following a particular course of action that they judges to be personally acceptable and required. This enables neoliberalism to provide a consistent—but incomplete—account of the world of persons and the status of the categories of phenomena within it that possess the power of producing a human action.

Agency ontology permits neoliberalism to deny that social wholes exist as anything more than a mereological sum. So, social institutions—societies, communities, groups, organizations, and families that are the constituents of Simmel's ([1922] 1955, 126-127) "web of group affiliations"—are merely the aggregate of their members. Agency ontology is, thus, firmly

---

necessary connexion among events" ([1748/1777] 1902, 75). Contrastingly, probablistic determinism holds that "causes raise the probabilities of their effects, all else being equal" (Hitchcock [1997] 2002). Alternatively, indeterminism holds that "some events [are] entirely [materially] uncaused, or nondeterministically caused [by events], or [are] caused by agents and not deterministically caused by events" (Clarke [2000] 2004).

20   In the words of the twelfth-century Persian (Afghan) mystic and poet, Rúmi (1956, 77): "There is a disputation that will continue till Mankind is raised from the dead between the necessitarians [determinists] and the partisans of free will [indeterminists]"

21   These constitute propositional attitudes that connect a person to a proposition in a way that involves holding particular attitudes (expectancies and value) towards and/or intentions (hopes, aspirations, goals, and preferences) about that proposition (Cresswell 1985; Lycan 1990; Rey 1997).

grounded in ontological individualism and metaphysical individualism.

Ontological Individualism

This is the proposition that only individuals exist in the world of persons. It embraces nominalism, essentialism, reductionism, and social atomism.

Nominalism

This holds that particulars are all that exist, making universals—features that are shared by many different particulars (such as shared language, culture, or values)—merely ideas or concepts that have no independent existence (Armstrong 1978, 1989, 2000; Ockham [c1329] 1974). Indeed, universals cannot exist, because they are only feature that particulars have in common is that they are covered by the same term, therefore it is language, rather than independent reality, that underlies perceived likeness: "a whole which has parts has no reality of its own, but is a mere word, the reality is in the parts" (Roscelin of Compiègn cited in Russell 1946, 457).

Essentialism

This holds that for any specific kind of material object or phenomenon there is a set of characteristics or properties that any such object or phenomenon of that specific kind must have (Hallett 1991). Fuss (1989, x–xii) argues that essentialism

> ... is most commonly understood as a belief in the real, true essence of things, the invariable and fixed properties which define the 'whatness' of a given entity ... Importantly, essentialism is typically defined in opposition to difference ... The opposition is a helpful one in that it reminds us that a complex system of cultural, social, psychical, and historical differences, and not a set of pre-existent human essences, position and constitute the subject. However, the binary articulation of essentialism and difference can also be restrictive, even obfuscating, in that it allows us to ignore or deny the differences within essentialism.

Reductionism

This is the proposition that complex systems can be fully understood in terms of their components—less complex objects or phenomena (Charles and Lennon 1992; Ryan 1970)—"The properties of the mass are dependent upon the attributes of its component parts" (Spencer [1851] 1995, 1) and can be explained by reference to them. Chaos Theory, however, challenges this proposition (Ferguson [1994] 2004, 221).

Social Atomism

This advanced the proposition, in the tradition of the ancient Greek atomist Democritus (Taylor 1999), that knowledge of social institutions is limited to what is knowable about the discrete individuals who are their constituents (Watkins 1957; Weissman 2000).

Metaphysical Individualism

This is the proposition that the existence of a social institution is contingent on the patterns of social relationships of the individuals whose social actions come together to sustain its existence. Thus, social institutions— and the social phenomena [22] they spawn—can be reduced to the social actions of individuals.

Agency ontology permits neoliberalism to posit that only individuals have causal capacity. It embraces free will (self-determinism), indeterminism (incompatibilism), compatibilism (soft determinism), and self- interest.

Self-determinism

This is the proposition that individuals have the free will, so they can freely decide on their social actions. They have the capacity to choose, from an array of alternative courses of action, to perform particular social actions consciously (knowingly and responsibly[23]) and voluntarily

---

22 Markey's (1925-1926, 733) classic definition of social phenomena conceptualized them, behaviorally, as the interaction of human beings:
> Social phenomena are considered as including all behavior which influences or is influenced by organisms sufficiently alive to respond to one another. This includes influences from past generations.

23 Pettit (2001, 12) considers that "to be fully fit to be held responsible for a certain choice is to be such that no matter what you do, you willfully deserve blame should the action be bad and fully deserve praise should the action be good. ... And your action in a given case will be free so far as it materializes in a way that enables you to count as fully fit to be held responsible." Thus, to be held responsible for a choice of action, the action taker must have been aware of the alternatives courses of action at the time of making the decision, must have been capable of evaluating those options,

(unconstrained by the freedom-limiting punitive, oppressive, coercive, compulsive, or manipulative conditioning factors, whether embedded in internal cognitive processes or neurobiological states, or in external social institutions or social phenomena). This means that they "could have chosen or acted otherwise voluntarily" (Kane 1985, 128).

The self-determined human motivations—manifesting as preferences or choices—that give rise to social actions are grounded in intentional mental states (see, for example, Donagan 1987). Such motivations are premised on individuals:

- being capable of self-rule—the ability to think rationally, to exercise self-control, and to be free from debilitating (genetic) pathologies and (unconscious) self-deception and to be able to be free from the external interference of others and, thus able to choose freely their hopes, desires, and choice preferences (deliberative and choice independence) (Arneson 1991; Dworkin 1988); and

- having individual authenticity—the ability to be critically self-reflective, which means having the capacity to reflect upon and endorse a set of desires (procedural and substantive independence) (Benson 1987; Christman 1989; 1991; Frankfurt [1971] 2002; Stoljar 2000).

These cognitions and cognitive processes—as part of the interior mental life of first-person experiences (Searle 2004)—are presumed to take place in an immaterial mind[24] that exists separately from the brain (mentalism)—Descartes' ([1641] 1975, [1644] 1983) mind-body duality—as conscious[25] mental acts undertaken by an autonomous self.[26] This meta-

---

and must not have been the victim of unwelcome duress (pp. 13-14).

24   "The operation of the mind ... is not so much an aspect of our lives, but in a sense, it is our life" (Searle 2004, 6). To Berkeley ([1710] 1962, 38) the mind is "wherein ideas exist ... whereby they are perceived."

25   Consciousness is a single, well-defined, unified field of first-person awareness—the first-person mental experiences that are unobservable and only individually knowable (Thorpe 1962, 21)—that has the qualities of, at least, self-awareness, sentience, sapience, subjectivity, unity, and intentionality (in the sense of being able to attach meaning to an external object, which enables a person to perceive self as separate from its environment (Blackmore 2003; Searle 1983, 2004). Indeed, Kinsbourne (2008, 152), considers that "being conscious is what it is like to have neural circuitry in particular interactive functional states."

26   In the mentalist tradition, Rosenberg (1979) defined the self-concept as "the totality of the individual's thoughts and feelings having reference to himself [sic] as an

physical proposition, which "fell out of favor in scientific circles in the twentieth century"[27] (Al-Khalili and McFadden [2014] 2015, 332), is premised on either the mind existing in a metaphysical realm as a nonphysical substance (entity) that is both autonomous and causally efficacious (substance dualism) (Eccles 1994; Popper and Eccles 1977) or on the brain having both physical and metaphysical (mental) properties (property dualism) (Robinson 2003). Metaphysical realists assert that "the existence of the mind is a contingent fact" (Stroll 2006, 12). In any event, mental states are presumed to be embedded in reasoning and reflecting human minds.

Intentional mental states have two presumed attributes. One is that they can bring about social actions by being able to affect neurobiological states and processes taking place in the brain.[28] How the nonmaterial mind can affect the material brain (mental causation) is an unresolved issue.[29] The other attribute is that intentional mental states are indeterminate. This means that they are unaffected by any internal or external determining condition. So, they are unconstrained by agential determining conditions—whether physiological (related to age, gender, ethnicity, and physiological completeness), neurobiological (related to processes in

object." Allport (1955, 40) called it "proprium," which embraces "all aspects of personality that make for inward unity"—the self as experienced and the functional self. In the behaviorist tradition. Skinner (1971, 199) considered that "a self is a repertoire of behaviors appropriate to a given set of contingencies" (see also Rovane 1998). Neuroscience, however, "suggests that the self is best understood as a sort of illusion that the brain creates (Butler-Bowden 2007, 5).

27 Materialists (physicalists) hold that either the mind supervenes on the brain (material monism) (Firth 2007; Pylyshyn 2007), or that the mind does not exist (eliminativism) (Feyeraband 1963; Rorty 1971). The unresolved issue is, of course, how the brain gives rise to consciousness, which suggest an irreducible, subjective state of awareness that is intrinsically mental (Searle 2004, 91). Somewhat facetiously, McCloskey (1998, 27) remarks:

   It is a postulate of modernism, largely unspoken and therefore unargued, that minds do not exist. The puzzle is that the modernist who examines his [sic] mind when getting dressed in the morning and assumes the existence of other minds when driving to work, claims to deny both as soon as he flicks on the lights at his laboratory.

28 Under the Input-Output Picture of consciousness (Mele 2003; Spiker 1989), intentional mental states shape and govern meaningful action, because the interaction of meaning, purpose, and action places consciousness at the point at which perceptual inputs interface with behavioral output, on the premise that an individual's mental states can be directed onto tangible or intangible objects (Brand and Walton 1976; Searle 1983).

29 Eccles (1994, 5) hypothesizes that "mental events act by a quantal probability field to alter the probability of emission of vesicles from presynaptic vesicular grids."

the brain), or psychological (related to mental properties or states (Buss 1999)). These internal determining conditions can have their origins in:

- inherited genetic make-up (hereditarianism[30]), in relation to particular physiological attributes (physiological freedom-diminishing conditioning factors), to particular genes being responsible for particular behaviors (genetic freedom-diminishing conditioning factors) (Wilson 1975, 1978), to particular inherited neurobiological processes in the brain (neurobiological freedom-diminishing conditioning factors) (Lucas 1970), or to the psychological makeup of mental properties or state in accordance with the laws of psychology (because human actions are in accordance with either their strongest desire (orectic psychological determinism) or their best reason (rational psychological determinism) (psychological freedom-diminishing conditioning factors)) (Berenson 1976; Lucas 1970); [31] or

- unconscious mental states, which Freud ([1912] 1959) conceived as a personal repository of suppressed and forgotten experiences and memories that he considered to be the driver of human behavior over which a person has little control and which defy any sort of introspection[32] (Mollon 2000; Searle 2004) (unconscious freedom-diminishing conditioning factors).

Intentional mental states are also presumed to be unaffected by any societal determining conditions. So, they are unconstrained by any mandated social actions that are the product of a person's obligations towards others (structural freedom-limiting conditioning factors) grounded in:

---

30 The theory of evolution holds that certain traits (attributes and capabilities) give certain individuals a survival advantage. These traits are passed down to more dependents than traits that do not constitute a survival advantage (Wilson 1975, 1978).

31 The physicalist tradition holds that the brain follows the known laws of science. So, people are conceptualized as biological machines. Thus, all mental states and phenomena are contingent upon physical phenomena (Firth 2007; Pylyshyn 2007)—the product of neurobiological states and processes taking place in the brain (Chalmers 1996; Kim 1993; Poland 1994).

32 To Jung ([1934] 1981), however, the unconscious is the repository of inherited religious, spiritual, and mythological symbols and understandings, expressed through universal thought forms or mental images (archetypes) (collective unconscious). To Frankl ([1948] 2000, 31) it can be "differentiated into unconscious instinctuality and unconscious spirituality."

- economic processes and production relations (economic free-dom-limiting conditioning factors) (Marx [1859] 1977);

- the beliefs prevalent in a social whole that have to be adopt-ed in order to sharing something in common so as to become integrated into that group (social freedom-limiting condi-tioning factors) (Durkheim [1895] 1982; Mead 1934; Parsons 1937, 1951);

- culturally specific cognitive structures or artifacts (cultural freedom-limiting conditioning factors) (Benedict [1934] 1989; Lévi-Strauss [1958/1963] 1974);

- language that shapes the way meaning is created and commu-nicated about the world of persons (linguistic freedom-limit-ing conditioning factors) (Harré 1980, 1983);

- interactive discourse processes that underpin the social con-struction of knowledge of the world of persons and affirma-tion of self (discourse freedom-limiting conditioning factors) (Derrida 1976, 1978; Foucault [1966] 1989, [1969] 2002; Lacan 1968; see also Berger and Luckmann 1967); and

- customary behaviors with respect to particular relation-ship that have become culturally obligatory (relational free-dom-limiting conditioning factors) (Ho 1998).

Thus neoliberalism, in the social atomist–reductionist tradition, gives no capacity for freedom-limiting social conditioning factors, to even influ-ence the content of individuals' hopes, aspirations, goals, and preferences. As Mill expressed it ([1859] 1963, VIII, 879): "human beings in society have no properties but those which are derived from, and which may be resolved into, the laws of the nature of individual men" (see also Bentham [1789] 1970, Ch. 1, Sec. 4). The status of social institutions and phenom-ena is, thus, reduced to epiphenomena: "a mere aggregate consequence of individual activities, incapable of acting back to influence individual people" (Archer 1995, 4). So, individuals have compelling free will.

Indeterminism and Incompatibilism

This is the proposition that social actions are the result of human mo-tivations— reasons—without reference to any freedom-limiting social conditioning factors (agent-causation (Chisholm [1964] 2002), because those factors either do not cause social actions (simple indeterministic libertarianism[33]), or do not inevitably cause them (event-causal libertarianism[34]) (Kane [2001] 2002). In the absence of any antecedently sufficient causal chain, social actions can only be exempt from prior-event causality (Campbell, O'Rourke, and Silverstein 2007) (libertarian free-will or metaphysical freedom). This is because they are either not strictly caused (naturalistic libertarianism) or entirely exempt from causation (supernatural libertarianism). Thus, free will is incompatible with strict or hard determinism[35] (incompatibilism), because if determinism is true then free will is an illusion (Slimansky 2002). As a consequence, a person cannot be *causa sui* and so is not a genuinely free agent.[36] Essentially, this means that free will exists because determinism is not true (libertarian incompatibilism).

This proposition, however, creates a dilemma. It is contingent upon the veracity of indeterminism-incompatibilism assumption that agents do not—or cannot choose to—permit either freedom-limiting social conditioning factors to shape the content of their intentional mental states, recognizing, of course, that the disposition to accept such conditions may be the product of cognitive biases that function almost entirely at a sub-intentional level. These biases are grounded in

- unconscious mental states (as intention-determining suppressed and forgotten experiences and memories) (Mollon 2000; Searle 2004);

- neurobiological properties and processes (because all mental states are contingent upon genetically determined physiological and neurological structures and processes) (Lucas 1970, 84-89; Wilson 1975; 1978); or

- psychological laws that determine intentional mental states (Berenson 1976, 116-117; Lucas 1970, 78-83),

---

33 This construction of indeterminism avoids the need to explain how intentional mental states can cause physical actions (mental causation).

34 This construction of indeterminism is consistent with the proposition that reasons for action are its causes, albeit, not inevitably and thus only indeterminately.

35 A deterministic relationship exists when "the occurrence of the determined event is *inevitable* or *necessary*, given the determining conditions" (Kane 2005, 5, emphasis in original).

36 Kane (1985) argues, however, that even if a person's character determines his or her actions, they can still be considered free, provided that person has freely chosen his or her character and remains free to change it at will—can exercise deliberate self-forming willings or actions that bring about character-development.

None of these are, of course, amenable to change by acts of will.

Soft Determinism and Compatibilism

This is the proposition that, following the Humean conceptualization of causation[37]— "causation does not give rise to compulsion or constraint or indeed to any form of necessity" (Stroll 2006)—individuals have the capacity, by exercising their free will, to diminish or reject the capacity of determining conditions to shape the content of their hopes, aspirations, goals, and preferences, and so to influence the course of social action they chooses to follow. As Schopenhauer ([1839] 1999) epigrammed: "A man can surely do what he wills to do, but he cannot determine what he wills" (see also Meyers 1989)

Free will, then, can be exercised in the absence of freedom-limiting conditioning factors (constraints or impediments that prevent actions being taken). Thus, free will is the freedom to act in whatever way a person is inclined *and able to* do in any situation, which means he or she could have chosen to act differently if so willed (Neilson 2002; Skinner 2002). This, however, requires that person to be willing to exercise that freedom of will, on the presumption that what matters is that he or she takes ownership of, or is committed to, whatever he or she has willed—regardless of the sources from which its content was acquired—and that he or she is free to act accordingly (hierarchical motivation) (Frankfurt [1971] 2002).

Self-interest

This is the proposition that social actions are the product of intentional mental states grounded exclusively in self-interest considerations (Elster 1982; Hollis and Nell 1975; Hume [1739–1740] 1978, [1748] 1975; Locke [1689–1690] 2004; Smith [1759] 1976, [1776] 1976). This manifests, in the Epicurean tradition, as the will to acquire hedonistic pleasures and avoid displeasures (Bentham [1789] 1970). According to Hume [1739–40] 1978, II, 3), the starting point for understanding human behavior

---

37 Hume, a skeptical empiricist, argued that an assertion explaining one material phenomenon in terms of another is based on confused logic. To him, causation had three components: priority (a cause must precede its alleged effect), contiguity in time and space (a cause and its alleged effect must be spatio-temporally adjacent), and necessary connection (a cause must make its alleged effect happen) (Searle 2004, 137). On this basis, any proposition maintaining that it is a necessary truth that one material phenomenon must automatically follow another is, no matter how clever, based on a fallacious argument (Hume [1748] 1975, XII, 3).

is *pathos*—passions, desires, tastes, and preferences. This is taken to be beyond logical disagreement and moral dispute, for individuals—and only individuals—can determine and define their requisites for the good life. How these passions are satisfied is the realm of *logos*—reason or instrumental (technical or means-ends) rationality: "Reason alone can never be a motive to any action of will ... reason is and ought only to be the slave of passions and can never pretend to any other office than to serve and obey them" (Sect. 3). Individuals, according to Rand (1965, 1957), have a rational egotistical belief in self-determination. They are presumed to be isolated, self-determining "Robinson Crusoe" agents (Urry et al. 2007, 96), with the necessary self-determined hopes, aspirations, goals, and preferences and with the capacity to choose what is their best (expected utility maximizing[38]) course of action for them to take, unaffected in any way by what others say and do (metaphysical libertarianism) (Kane [2001] 2002; but see Wildavsky 1994).[39] This privileges rational action and public choice theories (Arrow 1954; Buchanan and Tullock 1962; Downs 1967; but see Tversky and Kahneman 1981, 1986). Neoliberalism's premise, then, is that social actions are best attributed to the product of utility calculations, either because individuals actually seek to maximize their own good (psychological egoism)—perhaps in ways that, largely or exclusively, produce virtuous behaviors—because that enhances their wellbeing in the broadest sense (egoistic moral motivation)—or because they should be seeking to maximize their own good (ethical egoism) (Scheffler 1992).

The Agency Ontology's Classical Liberal Traditions

The following agency traditions all share the liberal belief that all individuals have the natural right to liberty and the pursuit of their own happiness.[40]

---

38 Expected utility theory proposes that a rational action is one that yields the highest expected utility of all possible actions, after allowing for the probability of the occurrence of each possible action's outcomes (Fishburn 1982; Savage 1954)

39 Yet as Nietzsche ([1886] 1998, 21) observes: "The yearning for 'freedom of the will' in the superlative metaphysical sense that unfortunately still prevails in the minds of the half-educated, the yearning to bear complete and final responsibility for one's own actions and to relieve God, the world, one's ancestors, coincidence, society from it—this is really nothing less than being the same *causa sui* and, with a daring greater than Münchhausen's [a reference to Raspe's adventure-hero in Baron Münchhausen's Narrative of his *Marvellous Travel and Campaigns in Russia* (1785)] dragging yourself into existence."

40 "The term happiness refers here to the measure of overall hedonic balance, a

Individualism

This tradition, drawing upon liberal humanism (Davis 1997; Mann 1996), holds that humanity is a human quality embedded in all individuals. This inner human core—the voice of humanity—gives meaning to the world and is the source of ethical authority. This proposition is taken to be timeless and universally applicable. The liberty of the individual is, thus, sacrosanct, to be protected from intrusion or coercion. Thus, the collective must justify any imposition of restrictions on personal liberty.

Unqualified Individualism. This postulates that all explanations of social actions must be expressed solely in terms of reasons embedded in agent-caused intentional mental states. This, in the reductionist–atomism tradition and following Hobbes and Menger (Lukes 1968; Udehn 2001), is premised on individual psychology being fully a-social or pre-social—essentially, others play no role in the development of an individual's "concept of self." As Hobbes ([1642] 1949, 8: 1) asserted: "consider men [sic] as if but even now sprung out of the earth, and suddainly [sic] (like Mushromes [sic]) come to full maturity without all kind of engagement to each other." Agent-causation requires individuals to have personal autonomy, making the contents of their intentional mental states completely self-determined (narrow mental content) (Fodor 1987, 1991; Kripke 1979; Loar 1988; White 1991), so the reasons for undertaking social actions become an expression of their authentic self. To achieve such control over their intentional mental states requires individuals to be able to access and understand them, without being able to draw inference from observing them, and without having anything or anyone to mediate between their self-ascribed beliefs and the object of those beliefs (Russell 1917). This presumes that action takers haves the capacity to reflect critically on their intentions, which generates self-knowledge (Cassam 1997; Wright, Smith, and Macdonald 1998) that, with the first-person authority with which they are held (Parrott 2012), privileges a presumption of truth (Jackson 1987).

---

theoretical average across all pleasures and pains" (Parducci 1995, 1). This constitutes an egoistically subjective satisfactory good life—a propitious situation and a positive state of mind. It stands in contrast to the objectively desirable life—*eudaimonia* (literally in Greek, 'having a good guardian spirit', best translated as human flourishing)—which is a good life from everyone's perspective, as sought by Socrates and the Stoics (as a virtuous life), by Aristotle (as a virtuously ethical life of right (rational) actions for greater human wellbeing), by Plato (as perfect goodness), and by Epicurus (as a life characterized by detachment, serenity, and freedom from anguish).

Libertarian Individualism. This holds that agents have the right to full self-ownership—the absolute right to use of their body as they see fit; to transfer those rights to others; and to full payment immunities for the possession and execution of those rights (Vallentyne 2001, 12). These rights, thereby, make all human interactions voluntary, so endorsing the right to act in a self-interested manner (Hayek 1948, 1960, 1991; Humbolt [1791] 1969; Locke [1689–1690] 2004; Milton [1644] 1949; Nock [1924] 1991; Nozick 1974). Hayek (1960) recognized the supreme importance of rightful self-governance. He propounded true individualism, "which regards man not as highly rational and intelligent but as a very irrational and fallible being, whose individual errors are corrected only in the course of a social process, and which aims at making the best of a very imperfect material" (Hayek (1948, 9).[41] A little later he adds: "the famous presumption that each man knows his interests best...is neither plausible nor necessary for the [true] individualist's conclusions" (p. 15).

Utilitarianism

This tradition, grounded in the works of Bernoulli, Bentham, John Stuart Mill, and Spencer, holds that that all explanations of social actions must be expressed solely in terms of states of mind about the actual or utility of its consequences: "Nature has placed mankind under the governance of two sovereign masters, *pain* and *pleasure*. It is for them alone to point out what we ought to do, as well as to determine what we shall do" (Bentham [1789] 1970, 2, emphasis in original). This is utilitarianism's utility principle—"...[the] principle which approves or disapproves of every action whatsoever according to the tendency which it appears to have to augment or diminish the happiness of the party whose interest is in question" (Bentham [1789] 1970, 2) (psychological utilitarianism). Bentham ([1789] 1970, 4) considered that social actions are made explicable by reference to hedonic or utility calculations, which "sum up all the values of all the pleasures on the one side, and those of all the pains on the other." He measured the amount of pain in accordance with seven criteria—intensity, duration, certainty, extent, propinquity, fecundity, and purity—and took into consideration the merits of various kinds of pleasure (such as, those associated with sensation, possession, skill, friendship, reputation, power, and malevolence) and demerits of various kinds of pain (such as those associated with want, disappointment, and regret)

---

41 Libertarian paternalism accepts that people can be nudged into doing what is in their best interest by a re-arrangement of the "choice architecture" that sets their choice decision context (Sunstein and Thaler 2003).

(Bentham [1789] 1970). This calculation is premised on the proposition, following the Epicurean tradition, that individuals seeks to enhance their pleasure and avoid any pain, which Frankl ([1948] 2000, 89) described as the "will to pleasure."

Thus, the maximization of personal wellbeing is the only goal that people are motivated to pursues (psychological hedonism or egoism) and, indeed, should pursue (evaluative hedonism), as established by what they perceives as giving value to any pursuit (reflective hedonism).[42] Personal sacrifices for others—altruism (Scott and Seglow 2007; but see Ridley and Dawkins 1981)—can only be justified by reference to self-interest, which, of course, converts a sacrifice into a gain. Utilitarianism, thus, sustains the supremacy of individual hedonism and egoism.

Neoliberalism's Agency Ontology Premise

Neoliberalism's ontological standpoint is that only their members exist, because societies, communities, groups, organizations, and families are merely sets of shared ideas—shared language, culture, or values. These shared ideas cannot causally affect human intentions and, thus, social actions. This means that knowledge of the world of persons is limited to what is knowable about the discrete individuals who are its constituent members. So, social institutions and social phenomena can be fully understood, completely explained, and accurately predicted by reference to the actions that those individuals that gave rise to, and sustains, them (methodological individualism) (Arrow 1994; Durkheim [1895] 1982, 1947, [1903–1917] 1949, 1997, 1994; Elster 1982; Watkins 1952, 1968).

So, under neoliberalism, the study of the social must be grounded in the agential free-will ontological proposition. This is premised on individuals' social actions being the fundamental building blocks of any social institution or social phenomenon (Durkheim [1895] 1982, 50-59; Weber [1924] 1947; [1948] 1998). Thus, explanations can only follow understanding why people take the social actions that give rise to those phenomenona. Parsons (1937, 43-51) referred to this as "the action frame of reference" in social-scientific explanation—an action-theoretic mechanism (Alexander 1987). As Weber ([1914/1922] 1968, 13) remarked: "collectives must be treated as solely the resultants and modes of organi-

---

42   What brings meaning to a pursuit is the human essence of striving to persevere in being—*conatus* (Spinoza [1677] 2009]. This generates a self-conscious desire in a person (Hampshire 2005). Therefore, when needs are satisfied by the striving of the individual, his or her wellbeing is enhanced in the process (Scruton [1981] 1984, 57).

zation of the particular acts of individual persons, since these alone can be treated as agents in a course of subjectively understandable action." On this proposition, Elster (1982, 463) commented: "To explain social institutions and social change is to show how they arise as the result of the actions and interaction of individuals. This view, often referred to as methodological individualism, is in my view trivially true." This means adopting an enquiry process that proceeds from the micro (by elucidating the self-determined hopes, aspirations, goals, and preferences that explain the social actions of self-interested constituent social actors, on the premise that they have the freedom of choice to determine the content of their intentions and the ability to ensure that those intentions give rise to the expected desired social actions) to the macro (so as to explain the patterns of social interactions that build up social institutions and give rise to social phenomena).

The key issue is, then, the source of the content of the intentional mental states that motivated their social actions that built up social institutions and gave rise to social phenomenon. On this, Parker (2007, 2) cautions that methodological individualism should not be confused or conflated with individual agency, positivism, rationality, and homeostasis. Indeed, Weber ([1914/1922] 1968), although a keen advocate of methodological individualism, did not privilege the individual over the social: "it is a tremendous misunderstanding to think that an 'individualistic' method should involve what is in any conceivable sense an *individualistic* system of values" (Weber [1914/1922] 1968, 18, emphasis in original). Heath (2015), however, observes that as a result of Elster's [1982] arguments,

> ... methodological individualism became synonymous in many quarters with the commitment to rational choice theory. Such an equation generally fails to distinguish what were for Weber two distinct methodological issues: the commitment to providing explanations at an action-theoretic level, and the specific model of rational action that one proposes to use at that level (i.e., the ideal type).

Naturalist Epistemology

This permits neoliberalism to postulate objective truths—genuine knowledge—about the world of persons.[43] This is premised on two truth

---

43 There is, of course, "no direct relationship between proof on the one hand, and what we can or cannot doubt on the other" (Baggini 2002, 36). This means that a proposition can be evidentially (objectively) proven/unproven but psychologically

propositions. The first is that it is a property that can be investigated.[44] The second is that it is a unique extra-linguistic objective fact that is independent of the truth-seeker. Nomothetic methods presume that what makes a knowledge claim true is evidence (evidentialism), which means that believing a truth claim is warranted if and only if the evidence supports so doing[45] (Feldman and Conee 2004) (the correspondence theory of truth)[46].

Naturalist epistemology axiomatically presumes that the world is real, material and objective.

Realism

This is the long-standing proposition, advanced by Plato, that the external world exists when not being experience, and has properties and relations that are entirely independent of any human knowledge of, or beliefs about, their actuality (metaphysical realism), which gives it cognitive authority (Putman 1987, 1988; Rorty 1997; Searle 1995). What the senses perceive about the external world, despite accepted perceptual fallibilities, is true (epistemological realism) and portrays that world accurately (direct, naïve,[47] or classical realism) (Devitt 1984; Hawking and Mlodinow 2011; Wright 1987; see also Blackburn 1993), evidenced by the fact that different people can perceive the same object in the same way in all essentials (Searle 2004, 190-191). Realism does, however, accept the existence of unobservables (scientific realism) (Psillos 1999; Russell 1946).

---

uncertain/certain to a person because he or she believes it to be untrue/true without any doubt. Doubt of course, is a state of mind—a state of indecision or hesitancy about accepting the truthfulness of a proposition.

44 The deflationary theory of truth holds that truth does not have a nature that can be investigated (Kirkham 1992). To ascribe truth to a statement does not attribute a property called "truth" to that statement, rather it asserts nothing more than the statement to which truth is ascribed (Frege [1918] 1997).

45 Under the Platonic conception of knowledge, for a truth proposition to be genuine knowledge requires the evidence proffered as proof to give rise to propositional (absolute) certainty that can never become false. Descartes ([1641] 1975), in this tradition, held that nothing should be believed unless it is absolutely certain that it is true—de omnibus dubitandum (everything is to be doubted)—(Cartesian doubt).

46 The correspondence theory holds that "a belief is true when there is a corresponding fact [an extra-linguistic fact], and is false when there is no corresponding fact" (Russell [1912] 1997, 129) (epistemological realism) (Russell 1946).

47 "Naïve realism leads to physics, and physics, if true, shows that naïve realism is false. Therefore naïve realism, if true, is false; therefore it is false" (Russell 1940, 15).

Realism, in the tradition of Thucydides, Machiavelli and Hobbes, is "a theory concerned to generate a scientific account of 'the facts as they really are' ... [and] excludes the consideration of normative issues from theory in favor of a purely explanatory endeavor, based on the notion of the separation of facts and values" (Murray 1997, 730). A phenomenon can, thus, be explained by reference to objective truth-conditions (Alston 2002; Devitt 1984; Dummett 1963; Wright 1987). Thus, truth depends upon factuality (epistemological realism).

Materialism

This holds that reality is constituted as material objects and phenomena (see Davies and Gribbin 1992): "everything that exists either is 'matter' or depends on matter for its existence" (Nightingale and Cromby 1999, 227). And all material phenomena can be explained as a manifestation or result of those material objects.

Objectivism

This considers that reality is independent of the mind (Bhaskar [1979] 1998, 2-3): "independent of human conception, speculation or fantasy" (see also Stroll 2006). However, as Berkeley ([1710] 1962, 74) observed, the mind construes the material world as it is experienced—as perceived through a distorting mental lens—and there is "no necessary [causal] connexion" between the two, for the perception of an object—the idea of the object—cannot prove that the separate existence of the object "without the mind, or unperceived." This proposition reduces physical objects to mental entities (mentalist monism), thereby denying the possibility of any genuine knowledge of the material world, leaving just beliefs and opinions. Hume ([1748/1751/1777] 1902), however, observed that while there are no rational grounds for believing that there is an objective reality, there is no choice but to act as if it is true. Similarly, Russell ([1912] 1997) conceived objects as logical constructions inferred from sense data (inferential realism). So, "the only object of our awareness is that experienced by the brain," which may be illusory (Searle 2004, 180, see also 181-184). This means that all knowledge of the external world is grounded in potentially problematic sense data (Ayer 1953; Price 1932; Swartz 1965).[48]

---

48   The extreme position—methodological solipsism—holds that the content of a belief about the external world is fully determined by the mental properties or mental states of the believer (Wood 1962).

The doctrine of objectivism, thus, postulates that a knowledge claim is epistemologically objective—a matter of fact—if the evidence for determining its truth value is material in form and, therefore, can be established by generally agreed enquiry procedures involving inductive inference (inferring conclusions about a category of things from observations of particular things in that category) and/or deductive logic (drawing logically valid conclusions from a set of premises). This gives rise to two types of knowledge, differentiated on the basis of how a proposition can be known (Kant [1781–1787] 1956; Mill [1843] 1988).

Synthetic Knowledge

Synthetic propositions contain *a posteriori* (empirical or sensory experience-based) knowledge that has been justified by reference to facts on the basis of inductive reasoning. This involves empirical evidence (Hempel 1966), in the tradition of Galileo, Bacon, Locke, Berkeley, and Hume (Atherton 1999).[49] Synthetic propositions are closely related to Leibniz's ([1714] 1973) truths of fact, or contingent truths (truth propositions that could be factually untrue), as they "would seem to be knowable only *a posteriori*, since it is unclear how pure thought or reason could tell us anything about the actual world" (Baehr 2006). Kant saw it differently; while *a posteriori* knowledge of objects is of importance, it "is of only practical application, since it has not the slightest effect in enlarging theoretical knowledge of these objects as insight into their nature by pure reason" ([1781–87] 1956, 58). Thus, causal explanation through *a posteriori* knowledge is limited to immediate appearances. The problem that dominates is whether an objective understanding of reality is achievable through the explanation and modification of sensory perceptions.

Analytical Knowledge

Analytic propositions contain *a priori* (non-empirical) knowledge that has been justified by reference to being logically deduced from a set of premises (mathematics, semantics, and logic)—rationalism—in the tradition of Plato, Spinoza, Leibniz, and Descartes (Pereboom 1999). This advances "the self-created world of pure thought" (Russell 1946, 93): "There is nothing in the intellect that was not first in the senses, except the intellect" (Leibniz [1704/1764] 1996, II, 111). Analytical knowledge is grounded in the Platonic proposition that the most important truths

---

49 This presumes that how an object is experienced is how it is when it is not being experienced.

THE IDEA OF NEOLIBERALISM

are those available through reason (Plato [390s-347 BCE] 1997, xiv]. This means that they could never become false (Russell 1946, 58). Analytical *a priori* propositions present the product of syllogistic reasoning or self-evident tautologies, the truthfulness of which logically follows from either a set of *a priori* premises or axioms (statements accepted without proof, from which all other statements of a system can be derived, for the sake of studying the consequences that follow from them) or from its very definition (the predicate is in the subject, which means its opposite implies a contradiction). They are beyond the scope of the senses to confirm, and so they present transcendental deductions that can lead to *a priori* truths. Such propositions are closely related to Leibniz's "truths of reason" ([1714] 1973) or logical necessities (propositions that must be true because their opposites are self-contradictory). So, that all analytical propositions are necessary propositions but not all necessary propositions are analytical propositions (Stroll 2006, 32).

Analytical knowledge offers a profound and strong demonstration of causal explanation. The deductive logic of analytic propositions can provide irrefutable grounds for knowledge claims about logical relationships. But the strength of the causal relationships that they identify derives from the coherence of the definitions held within their premises. Thus, the truth of analytic statements rests on mathematical or linguistic definitions. But, in Aristotelian terms, "how do we know the first premises from which deduction must start? ... we must begin with something unproven, which must be known otherwise than by demonstration" (Russell 1946, 222). Unfortunately, mathematical description cannot be equated with empirical regularity, which means analytic statements can be logically valid, because they necessarily follow from the premises, but empirically untrue, because one or more of the premises are empirically false (Williams and May 1996, 25).[50]

On Knowledge of the World of Persons

Central to neoliberalism's epistemological standpoint are, then, rationalism and empiricism. The truth-value of the knowledge so generated depends, however, on the presence of any verifying evidence (verificationism and logical positivism) and on the absence of any falsifying evidence (falsificationism).

---

50 Of syllogistic reasoning, Russell (1946, 456) identified the following defects: "indifference to facts and science, belief in reasoning in matter which only observation can decide, and an undue emphasis on verbal distinctions and subtleties." Nietzsche ([1886] 1998, 13) is more condemning: synthetic *a priori* judgments "should not 'be possible' at all: we have no right to them, in our mouths they are false judgments."

Rationalism

This, in the tradition of Plato, Spinoza, Leibniz, and Descartes (Pereboom 1999), is the search for the truth—armchair truth (Ferguson [1994] 2004, 266)—on the premise that reality is a system of cause and effect that can be deciphered by reason. Reality is, thus, presumed to be rational (has patterns, symmetries, and predictability), accessible (open to investigation), objective (truths independent of the observer), and has unity (lawful without contradictions and with minor unresolved problems). The ultimate proof that theories represent reality lies in their success in explaining observations and predicting future observations.

Under the doctrine of rationalism, inductive reasoning is considered to give rise to inferior explanations compared with those derived by a process of deductive reasoning.[51] Thus, the validity of a conclusion follows from the logical deductions drawn from the postulated premises. On this basis, deductive reasoning produces contingent truths that are reliant on, first, the truthfulness of the premises from which the *a priori* knowledge is deduced; and secondly, the validity of any *ceteris paribus* assumptions, which is only applicable in a closed system. Thus, rationalism maintains that truths about the "really existing intelligible world that underlies the appearance of changing particulars that we experience" (Shand 2002, 69), which can only be discovered through the methodical application of deductive reasoning. This proposition is grounded in Descartes' ([1641] 1961, 123) observation that "it is only the things that I conceive clearly and distinctly which have the power to convince me completely." Thus, only the mind, divorced as it is from the body, can sanction certainty and truth: "I think, therefore, I am" (p. 82).

Under the principles of rationalism, the world of persons is taken to be a deterministic system of cause and effect. So, deductive inference permits theorizing about causal explanation. Theories, however, provide as-if explanations that may be true in so far as they are capable of exact prediction, but contingent in so far as they are ultimately unprovable (Hollis 1994, 59).

---

51 "Experience is not all, and the savant is not passive; he [sic] does not wait for the truth to come and find him, or for a chance meeting to bring him face to face with it. He must go to meet it, and it is for his thinking to reveal to him the way leading thither. For that there is need for an instrument; well, just there begins the difference" (Poincaré [1905] 1907, 318).

Empiricism

This stresses the fundamental role of sensory experience as the foundation of all knowledge. Its contention is that genuine knowledge—truths—rests on the Humean principle of induction (Hollis 1994, 45), "which seeks to reach principles inductively from observations of particular facts" (Russell 1946, 58). As Lock ([1690] 2004, II, Ch. 1, Sec. 19) observed: "No man's knowledge here can go beyond his experience."

Empiricism grounds causal explanation in the sensory perception of incorrigible empirical observation, whereby the world itself provides stimuli that are directly open to human sensory perception and do not require a pre-existent theoretical frame of reference. It offers causal hypotheses—theories—grounded on the empirical demonstration of constant conjunction—regular correlation. So, a particular social phenomenon follows particular social actions by particular social actors. Knowledge, then, is composed of generalizations based on observed regularities that enable prediction, and serve as contingent explanations based on the probability that future correlations between cause and effect would reflect the patterns observed in previous instances. Thus, empiricist epistemology confronts a twin predicament. By inductive inference, empiricism can offer reasonably reliable predictions, but only a contingent correlation of cause and effect, because it cannot show precisely the connection between the two, which means that it cannot identify unambiguous causal relationships (Williams and May 1996, 25). Indeed, "beyond the constant conjunction of similar objects, and the consequent inference from one to the other, we have no notion of any necessity or connexion" (Hume [1748/1751/1777] 1902, 82).

Empiricism, then, has three discernible fundamental suppositions (Scruton 1985, 123):

- Facts are contingent upon sensory experience, for there can be *a priori* proof for any matter of fact, which means that the only source of factual propositions is induction reasoning.

- Facts grounded in sensory experiences can only establish what is known to be true and, by implication, what is not true, so many theories labeled as laws cannot be sustained by the epistemological limitations of inductive inference from which they derive, so they are merely theories with an unblemished predictive history. As Gribbin (2005, 156) remarks: "Note that a theory can never be proved right. The best that can ever be said is that it has passed all the tests applied so far."

- Factual propositions advanced after empirical enquiry are only true by virtue of their inherent ideas, which means that reason is nothing but the relationship between different ideas.

Verificationism

This stresses that a knowledge claim's the truth-value is established by reference to confirming empirical evidence (Hume [1748] 1975; Locke [1689–1690] 2004; Quine 1951). Under the hypothetico-deductive model, the verification process commences with observation, and proceeds making use of theory to hypothesize causal explanations that provide verifiable explanatory propositions, the truthfulness of which can be tested using empirical evidence. So, if the explanatory propositions are consistent with observed outcomes, then they can demonstrate very high rates of successful prediction (Hempel 1966; Lipsey and Chrystal [1953] 1995). This does not, however, bestow upon them the status of confirmed knowledge claims. This use of theory to manage the problem of explanation has been subject to criticisms, especially by the logical positivists, who consider incorrigible verification as the only basis for genuine knowledge.

Logical Positivism. In the tradition of Ayer, Carnap, and Schlick, this stresses that knowledge propositions are meaningful only to the extent that they can be empirically verified (Ayer 1959).[52] Its contention is that the problem of inductive inference, notably its incapacity to identify causal relationships, denied any epistemological legitimacy to the unverifiable theoretical statements that served as probabilistic guides to explanation. Rooted in radical empiricism[53] (phenomenalism[54]), logical positivism re-

---

52 Logical positivism emerged in the early part of the twentieth century in the work of the Vienna Circle of philosophers, mathematicians and natural scientists as a response to the significant influence of Romanticism on nineteenth century German philosophy of science (Frank 1949). Romanticism was an eclectic pan-European movement in the arts and philosophy that began in Germany and England in the 1770s. It is characterized by its emphasis on imagination, feelings, and intuitions (Abrams 1971; Higgins and Solomon 1993). It featured the philosophy of Hegel, Schelling, Schlegel, von Hardenberg, and Schleiermacher. It rebelled against the "barren rationalism of John Locke and the 'Age of Reason', partly ... to discover some principles of unity (or 'Oneness'), some common hidden truth perceived, cherished and guarded by...representatives of the Hermeneutic tradition through the ages" (Newsome 1997, 178-179). Its emphasis was, thus, on an organic concept of nature (Silz 1929) and "upon mind as opposed to matter" (Russell 1946, 730).

53 "To be radical, empiricism must neither admit into its constructions any element that is not directly experienced, nor exclude from them any element that is directly experienced" (James 1912).

54 This postulates that knowledge claims about the physical world can be reduced to

stricted knowledge claims to the analytic propositions of mathematics and the incorrigible evidence of sense experience (Lewis 1946). Thus, Ayer's ([1936] 1975) verification principle holds that a knowledge claim is meaningless either if it is not true by definition or if, in principle, its truth value cannot be empirically established, which requires that all the evidence needed to establish beyond doubt its truth value must be available. So, he drew the conclusion that "all empirical observations are hypotheses because there is no way of absolutely confirming or refuting such propositions" (Shand 2002, 248). However, this led to the contradiction that is central to the uncertainties of induction: "if an induction is worth making, it may be wrong" (Russell 1927, 83).

Logical positivists, thus, linked knowledge to meaning and claimed that only empirically verified statements have epistemological meaning (Carnap [1928] 1969). So, if meaning is derived from knowledge, and knowledge from verification, then statements that cannot be verified, cannot be considered knowledge, and, therefore, cannot have any meaning epistemologically (Ayer [1936] 1975). This forced them to abandon causal explanation, thereby "denying not only that we could identify any form of natural necessity in the world but that, in principle, we could never come to know the real world" (Williams and May 1996, 27). The implication of this extreme empiricism is to require the abandonment of virtually the entire knowledge base of the physical, human, and social sciences. Despite the heroic failure of logical positivism, it inspired a key development in naturalist epistemology: the recognition by Popper of the theoretical nature of observation (Ackermann 1976, 43-64).

Falsificationism

This stresses that only if a knowledge claim can, in principle, be falsified can it be possibly true, and that the truth value of a knowledge claims is established by the absence of disproving empirical evidence (Popper ([1935/1959] 2000, [1962] 1968, 1979; see also Burke 1983). As Ackermann (1976, 18) argues:

> Falsifiability is a logical notion: a sentence or statement is falsifiable if it is incompatible with some clearly defined basic statements representing possible observations. ... Falsification is actually deciding that a falsifiable sentence is false—and this will depend on methodological rules which we adopt

---

claims about possible sensory perceptions of it (Lewis 1946).

and which set out the decisions to be made as to whether a sentence is falsified given that certain observations are made.

The focus of its concern is the refutation of unfalsifiable contentions of self-referential systems of thought (such as Marxism and Freudianism). So, if the proposed theoretical system cannot survive all falsification attempts, then it cannot be considered to have any truth-value. This process does not result in the discovery of the truth; rather it identifies the best available unfalsified theory.

Neoliberalism's Naturalist Epistemology Premise

Neoliberalism holds that what is knowable about the world of persons is limited to what is knowable about its social institutions and social phenomena and their causality. What is knowable about social institutions and social phenomena are the facts grounded on empirical evidence derived by the use of generally agreed enquiry procedures involving inductive inference. What is knowable about their causality is what is knowable about the individuals whose social actions built up its social institutions and gave rise to its social phenomena. What is knowable about those action-takers is their observed social actions. What is knowable about those observed social actions is that they must be rational, because action-takers always act in their own best (expected utility maximizing) interest.[55] Their best interests are presumed not only to be unaffected in any way by what others say and do, but also to be free from the influence of any debilitating pathologies or self-deception. This is all taken to be true beyond doubt because a combination of experience—Russell's ([1912] 1997) knowledge by acquaintance (Jager 1972; but see BonJour 1985)—and reason has made it a foundational belief that does not need further justification (the foundationalism theory of truth) (DePaul 2000; Moser 1989).

CONCLUSION

Classical liberalism has its origins in the Scottish Enlightenment in the third quarter of the eighteenth century. Its emphasis is on personal autonomy, personal responsibility, and the desirability of government being weak, unobtrusive, and small. A century later, the Industrial Revolution in Britain posed a serious threat to those sacrosanct principles, giving

---

55 As Samuelson (1955, 90) surmised, behavior can be "explained in terms of [individuals'] preferences, which are in turn defined only by behavior."

rise to social liberalism project. This became mainstream liberal thought for most of the next century. The re-ascending influence of classical liberalism came in the last quarter of the twentieth century, when it was re-branded as neoliberalism.

Neoliberalism, like its forebear, privileges the individual over the social. Indeed, all that exist with causal capacity in the world of persons are individuals. The causal knowledge of the world of persons is, thus, limited to what is knowable about those persons. Their social actions, which are the building blocks of social institution and social phenomena, are presumed to be solely explainable their self-determined set of hopes, aspirations, goals, and preferences—agent-caused intentional mental states—which are unaffected in any way by any debilitating pathologies, self-deception, and other people, whether individually or collectively. This is made possible because action-takers have complete free will. So, they are focused only on advancing their material wellbeing, because they are always and ever self-interested. The underlying premises are that individual psychology is fully a-social or pre-social and that individuals are presumed to have full personal autonomy. This is axiomatically taken to be a self-justifying truth.

Neoliberalism also privileges the material properties of the world of persons over its ideational properties. This enables it to deny its proximity to the unknowable—by dismissing the relevance of the metaphysical—and to distance its proximity to the unknown—by dismissing knowledge claims that are unverified by reasoning or sense data. This permits elements of the world of persons to be deemed irrelevant to any decision or action—akin to Sen's (1980, 360) "choice basis of description"—because that world can be described and explained—logically modeled—by selecting from all possible true statements about it a subset on the basis of their relevance.

In view of the deficiencies in both inductive inference and deductive logic—both of which can only provide knowledge that is contingent and can only identify causal relationships that are ambiguous—these forms of investigation deserve to relegated to the function of suggesting states of affairs and scenarios in the world of persons that need to be more completely described, understood, and explained before any decision and action inferences are drawn. To neoliberalism, however, the presumption, which profoundly affects its worldview, that world of persons is a logically explainable material cause-and-effect system in which individuals' self-interested intentional mental states are dominant is beyond reproach.

2.

NEOLIBERALISM:
THE NARROWNESS OF ITS WORLDVIEW

Man [sic] not only strives to perceive his environment as a meaningful totality, but he strives to find an interpretation which will reveal him as an individual with a purpose to fulfill...pointing up man's distinctive ability to find meaning not merely in what is, but in what can be.

Crumbaugh (1973, 29)

INTRODUCTION

Neoliberalism's worldview offers a distinctive and coherent conceptualization of a philosophy of life that informs and justifies a way of living in the world of persons as it is envisaged. This permits the comprehending of the actuality of that world, on the basis of its agency ontological (individualism) and naturalist-epistemological (rationalism) standpoints— its naturalist-agency social-reality disposition. This is the lens through which the world of persons is read—investigated, described, understood, explained, and change predict change. It, thus, gives a stable orientation for decisions and actions. This it does by providing distinctive ways of thinking (characteristic ways of acquiring, validating, and using information), feeling (characteristic emotional arousals and responses), and acting (characteristic social behaviors).

The purpose of this chapter is to elucidate neoliberalism's worldview and its foundational premises, grounded in its circumscribed convictions about the world of persons and the individuals that inhabit it. Neoliberalism's narrowness of its worldview is made manifest in its rejection of alternative worldviews, because they are grounded in different— wrong—epistemological and ontological assumptions.

A Worldview as Social Reality Construct

A worldview is a pre-assembled explanatory filter—a scheme of interpretation (Goffman 1974)—that gives reality its organizing idea or frame. This framing enables the "selecting, organizing, interpreting, and making sense of complex social reality to provide guideposts for knowing, analyzing, judging, persuading, and acting" (D'Andrade 1984, 109), [56] so facilitating the weaving of connections among the unfolding of events (Druckman 2001). It provides a "perspective from which an amorphous, ill-defined, problematic situation can be made sense of and acted on" (Rein and Schön 1993, 146). It guides thinking about the world of persons in predictable ways, to predictable conclusions, thereby giving rise to a sense of ontological security that comes with having "a stable mental state derived from a sense of continuity and order in events" (Bilton, Walker, and Gardner 1996, 665).

This gives rise to a worldview's distinctive:

- sets of truths and truth propositions (presumed and arguable truths);

- mode of reasoning (ways of acquiring genuine knowledge);

- model of the individual (an explanation of what it is to be a human being);

- set of human nature suppositions (the basic attitudes of people toward others);

- set of emotional states or feelings that the world of persons should arouse; and

- ethical principle that provide the basis for deciding what constitutes moral conduct.

These constituents become part of the personal construct[57] (Parsons

---

56 Frames can be episodic or thematic (Gross 2008, 171). Episodic frames present an issue by offering a specific example or case study. Thematic frames place issues into their broader context.

57 Insights can be gleaned from Kelly's (1955) personal construct theory. This theorizes the ways in which a person constructs meaning about anticipated events. Personal construct systems comprise core constructs (important firmly held beliefs that are central to self-identity), peripheral constructs (relatively unimportant and changeable constructs), loose constructs (poorly defined and unstable beliefs that lead to erratic and perhaps invalid predictions), nonverbal constructs (unarticulated assumptions), preemptive constructs (constructions the elements of which do not

1995, 375) of those who choose to adhere to a particular worldview. This comprises immutable core values (enduring beliefs adaptive attitudes (learned dispositions), or changeable opinions (unsubstantiated beliefs). Created is an "assumptive world"[58] (Parkes 1971), one that constitutes a "cognitive map" (Young 1979, 33) of the world of persons as postulated by the informing worldview. This enables the world of persons to be explained and understood, on the presumption that it is as it purported it to be (Geertz 1983). So created is a distinctive operational worldview (Argyris and Schön 1978), one that determines how information is filtered, and, ultimately, how decisions get made, and why actions are taken.

Any worldview, however, has its blind spots—those elements of reality that are obscured from careful, systematic, and critical evaluation. This happens because of the constraints embedded in its set of foundational epistemological and ontological standpoints, which blinds those who choose to see the world of persons through this worldview's lens to elements of social reality, because it encourages their

- ignorance (their lack knowledge of them);

- disregardfulness (their unwillingness to acquire knowledge of them); or

- prejudice (their willingness to ignore knowledge of them).

THE NEOLIBERAL INDIVIDUALIST-LIBERTARIAN WORLDVIEW

Neoliberalism's privileging of the naturalist-agency social-reality disposition underpins its worldview. As seen through this lens, the world of persons has only real and material properties that are objectively knowable, conceptualized as a logically decipherable cause-and-effect system in which actors, who are *causa sui*, determine their self-interested inten-

---

apply to other constructions), propositional constructs (permeable constructions), superordinate constructs (freely chosen constructs that control other constructs) and subordinate constructs (constructs controlled by other constructs). These construct categories are the idiosyncratic means by which a person understands and explains the world he or she experiences, and guides his or her practical action in concrete situations and relationships. To the extent that a person can understand another person's internal constructions of reality, he or she can predict what that person will do, and so: be able to adjust his or her own social behavior accordingly.

58 "The assumptive world is the only world we know and it includes everything we know or think we know. It includes our interpretation of the past and our expectations of the future, our plans and our prejudices" (Parkes 1971, 55).

tional mental states, so permitting the deduction of a set of logical truths about social institutions and social phenomena in that world. Social action and social relationships are presumed to be self-determined, because action-takers are presumed to be in full control of their destiny. This means that they have the power to achieve the goals they set themselves, and consider that they have the natural and inalienable right to negotiate their relationships with whomever they wish, and so have the right to determine how they conduct their social actions and relationships.

On the Individual

From an agency–free will perspective, the distinctive set of the explanations of what it is to be a human embedded in neoliberalism is informed by the following propositions:

- individuals are essentially free being (Bentham, Locke, and Mill), seeking liberation from the interference of other individuals (Hayek, Norzick, and Mises); or

- individuals pursue their own happiness as their primary life-goal (Aristippus the Elder, Bentham, Epicurus, Mill, and Sidgwick).

On the Self

In the mentalist tradition, the exercising of free will is done by an autonomous self with an immaterial mind that can cause social actions by triggering the necessary neurobiological states and processes in the physical brain (see, for instance, Libet 1985; Libet et al. 1983; Libet, Freeman, and Sutherland 1999). Rejected is the proposition that the autonomous self is but an illusory self-embedded in a brain, for this would makes social actions contingent upon genetically determined physiological and neurological structures and processes—a proposition that physicalists have long asserted is only rock-bottom explanations of human behavior (Hogben 1933; Lucas 1970; Wilson 1975, 1978).[59] Indeed, physicalists would argue, variously, that a mental phenomenon—including an intentional mental state—could be:

---

59 Indeed, it is now only by an act of faith that the proposition can be advanced that science will be able to assimilate the mental phenomena of self-awareness, consciousness and personality into the its materialist perspective on the mind-brain. Pippard, an eminent physicist, has made the profoundly important point "... it is through our minds that we will know of the brain, and we are more likely to find how they are related by concentrating on the fundamental thing (conscious knowledge) rather than on its derivate (material brain)" (quoted in Ferguson [1994] 2004, 182).

- re-conceptualized as a behavioral phenomenon, as all statements about mental phenomenon are equivalent in meaning to statements about a behavioral disposition (logical behaviorism) (Hempel 1980; Ryle 1949);

- considered identical to, but not reducible to, a physical phenomenon, because mental phenomenon are not regulated by strict physical laws (anomalous monism or predicate dualism) (Davidson 1980);

- defined as the type of brain states that produce the type of functions fulfilled by mental phenomenon (functionalism) (Armstrong 1968; Block 1980; Putman 1980);

- the product of a mental state that are identical to a brain state (identity theory) (Place 1956);

- ascribed to a neurobiological state and process (reductionism) (Chalmers 1996; Kim 1993; 1998; Poland 1994);

- considered to be illusory and, thus, does not exist (eliminativism) (Feyeraband 1963) (material monism).

A basic tenet of neoliberalism is a theory of self that posits that the self is an autonomous self, who is able to engage in social interactions that are always self-determined, voluntary, and consensual. Thus, their relationship with others is the exclusive product of their willingness to choose to be a lone self capable of "closing the self off from unexpected and potentially innovative voices coming from the external and outside domains" (Hermans 2004, 17), thereby making self immune to the complicity of language, culture, community, and other individuals in their construction of their personal and their social self. This set of presumptions permits neoliberalism to privilege self over others, whether individually or collectively, and to sustain the supremacy of individual hedonism and egoism over altruism (Collard 1975). Thus, the self is taken by neoliberalism to be entirely self-constructed, whether that be:

- the known self (self as an object with a uniqueness that differentiated it from others); and

- the knowing self (self as the subject of introspection by self concerned with how self is represented).

These concepts of self all contribute to individuals' sense of self as an autonomous and lone self:

- *Self-concept*: They see themselves to be in full control of their destiny, with a strong commitment to their self-interest.

- *Self-esteem*: Their feelings of self-worth are grounded in being materially successful.

- *Self-sentiment*: Their prime, integrating motivation is to achieve material success, thereby winning recognition and acclaim from other successful people.

- *Self-objectification*: Their perceptions of their capacities and limitations are self-referential.

- *Self-objects*: Materially successful others are to be admired and idealized, but mirrored and copied only when it in their self-interest to do so.

- *Self-image*: They accept that what is honorable about them is that their actions produce mutually beneficial material consequences for themselves and others.

- *Role-making*: Their desired social role is whatever they can negotiate to advance their interests.

- *Presenting-self*: They endeavor to present themselves as being in control of their destiny.

- *Role-playing*: The social impression they wish to portray is that they alone decide of the roles they play.

- *Role response*: They expect to be treated as equals, if not competitors.

The intentional mental states of the autonomous and lone self reflect the primacy of self over others, unless a choice is made to attach significance to other people when self-interest dictates. Their social engagements are, therefore, superficial; involving only limited interaction and minimal emotionality. Emotions (feelings and imagination) are considered to stand in opposition to reason (thoughts and choices)—the latter is taken to be a central, necessary part of self; the former is merely a chance, extraneous matter, assigned by Williamson (1994) to a residual category of tosh or nonsense. But, emotions, according to Elster (1999a, 403), "matter because if we did not have them nothing else would matter. Creatures without emotions would have neither a reason for living, nor, for that matter, for committing suicide. Emotions are the stuff of life."

On Human Nature

Neoliberalism embraces what it considers to be a self-evidently true proposition that people are rationally, consistently, and immutably self-serving and self-centered and thus motivated by self-interest, which is in need of no further justification. Elster (1979) judged that some preferences (desires) may be grounded in strong emotions that have the potential to subvert rationality by a weakness of will: "by virtue of the high levels of arousal and valence they induce, emotions and cravings are among the most powerful sources of denial, self-deception, and rationalization in human life" (Elster 1999b, see also Elster 1999a; Fingerette 1969). But, "if people very strongly desire what they cannot get, they will be unhappy; such desires are irrational." A rational desire is one that is 'freely and consciously willed' and that is optimally adjusted to the feasibility set" (Elster 1986, 15, see also 1989). This gives rise to a desire for the highest attainable level of satisfaction, rather than permitting preferences to be either over-adapted—"sour grapes" (Elster 1982)—or under-adapted—"Ulysses unbound" (Elster 1979).

Further insights into self-centeredness come from the psychological characterization of narcissism (Baumeister 1993; Bushman and Baumeister 1998; Lasch [1979] 1991; Kohut and Wolf 1978; Wolf 1988). Narcissists have a pervasive, narrow-minded, and overly indulgent obsession with the belief that they are great and perfect—Kohut's (1971) grandiose self—a self-view that emphasizes characteristic attributes that enables the attainment of the outcomes they judge to be good for them. These attributes include:

- a desire to formulate relationships only with those willing to give them confirming and admiring feedback, which increase their feeling of self-worth, thereby reinforcing their self-love;

- a hypersensitivity to slights, criticism, and rejection;

- a proclivity to overreact to perceived failures, to perceived threatening situations, or to perceived insulting provocation, responses to which can extend from irritability, to hostility, and even to violence; and

- a low tolerance of boredom, frustration, inadequacy, and strong emotional feelings, due to a lack of ego development.

Narcissists are often successful in the outside world, because they have confidence and do not fear failing, and respond well in a crisis, because it gives them a chance to bring glory upon themselves. They also feel an inner emptiness, fluctuating as they do between self-love and self-hatred.

This self-centered and self-interested conception of human nature is, in the tradition of Bentham, Condorcet, and Hume, presumed to be universal, constant, and predictable. As Hume ([1748/1751/1777] 1902, 83) remarked: "it is universally acknowledged that there is a great uniformity among the actions of men, in all nations and ages, and that human nature remains still the same, in its principles and operations. The same motives always produce the same actions." And as Samuel Johnston observed: "We are all prompted by the same motives, all deceived by the same fallacies, all animated by the same hope, obstructed by danger, entangled by desire, and seduced by pleasure" (cited in Pinker 2002, 142).

Universally, then, individuals are presumed to be desirous, forever calculating—reflecting on their desires and then re-calculating—what is in their best interest, always consistently, because they have a known and consistent set of self-determined preferences upon which basis they base their actions so as to maximize their material wellbeing (Hogarth and Reder 1987, 1-3). By critically reflecting on their intentions they generate the self-knowledge that privileges a presumption of truth (Blackburn 2005; Cassam 1997; Wright, Smith, and Macdonald 1998). This reflection is conducted only in terms of the actual or expected utility of the plurality of subjective human desires and end-states sought. To Hobbes ([1651] 1948, 48), what ends are sought depends on what a person desires. Locke ([1689–1690] 1824, 202, emphasis in original), thereby privileging the taste theory of value:

> The mind has a different relish, as well as the palate; and you will as fruitlessly endeavor to delight all man with riches or glory, (which yet some men place their happiness in,) as you would satisfy all men's hunger with cheese or lobsters; which, though very agreeable and delicious fare to some, are to others extremely nauseous and offensive: and many people would with reason prefer [sic] the griping of an hungry belly, to those dishes, which are a feast to others. Hence it was, I think, that the philosophers of old did in vain enquire, whether the *summum bonum* [the achievement of the highest moral goodness (virtue) and happiness (Kant [1788] 1906)]—consisted in riches, or bodily delights, or virtue, or

contemplation: and they might have as reasonably disputed, whether the best relish were to be found in apples, plums or nuts; and have divided themselves into sects upon it. For ... pleasant tastes depend not on the things themselves, but their agreeableness to this or that particular palate, wherein there is great variety

Mill, an unequivocal utilitarian, argued that some pleasures are of a discernable finer quality than others, so he applied the following condition ([1863] 1968, 14):

... it must be utility in the largest sense, grounded in the permanent interests of man as a progressive being. Those interests I contend authorize the subjection of individual spontaneity to external control, only in respect to those actions of each, which concern the interest of other people.

Mill privileged intellectual gratification over physical sensations, and argues that altruistic social actions could generate utility because it can satisfy individual desires.

Soberingly, as Berlin (1969, 171) observed, this diversity of human desires cannot be collectively ranked, and certainly cannot be simultaneously achieved. The rationing mechanism endorsed by neoliberalism is, of course, the capacity to pay.

On Social Relationships

Social engagements are predicated on individuals choosing how they wish to determine their relationships with others. This can inform those aspects of self that are related the mental representations of others in any self-other relationship (relational self) (Andersen and Chen 2002). Neoliberalism posits that people determine their relationships with others on the basis of what best advances their self-interest. While the reality of "others as objects"—by their self-presentation—is recognized and acknowledges, others are taken to play no necessary role in the development a person's self-concept. Thus, others are irrelevant to development of their personal identities—the characteristics that makes them "the same person across time and change" (Searle 2004, 205), and so the person they are (Harré 1988); and their social identities—the attitudes held and behaviors displayed in common with others (Tajfel 1981, 1982; Tajfel and Turner 1979, 1986), both which signify their personality, which, as Cattell (1965, 117-118) succinctly remarks, "tells what [a person] will do when placed in a given situation." They are also oblivious to others' idiosyncratic physiological characteristics—gender, age, physical incompleteness, or ethnicity—and/or their ideational standpoints—their ideas and beliefs—unless they have chosen to attach significance to other people when self-interest dictates, but not so as to make them significant others in terms of the development of the personal and social identities (McGuire and McGuire 1982; Sandersen and Cole 1990). They would, thus, be satisfied with categorizing and stereotyping insignificant others according to their capacity to exploit or be exploited for material gain, or to frustrate the achievement of their material hopes, aspirations, and goals. Indeed, their classification of others would delineate their preferred relationship with them, which would be a defining feature of their relational self.

On Explaining Social Institutions and Social Phenomena

Neoliberalism posits that facts about social institutions and social phenomena—social facts—can be completely explained or predicted, in a reductionist way, by the reference to the self-determined self-interested motivations of those whose social actions come together to sustain their existence. As Watkins (1957, 106) argued, to do otherwise generates only an "unfinished or half-way explanations." Rejected, of course, is any proposition that denies the explanatory power of free will. This gives rise to two dilemmas.

The first is how to establish the veracity of the indeterminism–incompatibilism assumption that agents do not—or cannot choose to—permit structural determining conditions to shape the content of their intentional mental states. It must be recognized that the disposition to accept such determining conditions may be the product of cognitive biases that function almost entirely at a sub-intentional—subconscious—level, which, of course, are not amenable to change by acts of will.

The second dilemma is that explanations at the level of the autonomous self-interested individual can be further reduced to:

- *Human behavior* (methodological behaviorism): As unobservable mental states—including intention mental states—cannot be distinguished from, or made independent of, bodily material processes, they are empirically unknowable, so only human behavior can be the subject of empirical observation (Skinner 1938, 1953, 1969, 1973; Tolman 1922, 1932; Watson 1913

[1924], 1930; Zuriff 1985).

- *Mental properties and states* (methodological solipsism): (Fonder 1980), because particular mental states—including intention mental states—can be exclusively individuated on the basis of other mental properties or states, which means that they can be fully determined by inherited mental properties and states, including inherited psychological makeup.

- *Neurobiological properties and processes* (methodological neurobiologicalism): because all mental states—including intention mental states—are contingent upon genetically determined physiological and neurological structures and processes (biological and neurobiological determinism, respectively) (Firth 2007; Hogben 1933; Pylyshyn 2007).

ALTERNATIVE ONTOLOGICAL AND EPISTEMOLOGICAL STANDPOINTS REJECTED

The narrowness of neoliberalism's construction of meaning in the world of persons is made manifest in its rejection of knowledge propositions grounded on what it considers to be wrong ontological and epistemological assumptions. It is, thus, blind those elements of the world of persons that can only be interrogated, understood, and explained through the lens of the denied ontological and epistemological perspectives, namely structural ontology and hermeneutic epistemology.

Structural Ontology

This posits that social wholes exist as independent entities As Durkheim ([1895] 1982, xvii) observed: "whenever certain elements combine, and thereby produce, by the fact of their combination, new phenomena, it is plain that these phenomena reside not in the original elements but in the totality formed by their union." Structural ontology embraces ontological holism, metaphysical holism, and methodological holism.

Ontological Holism

This holds that social institutions are formed by or within systems of relations among their constituent individual members[60] (Armstrong 1989;

---

60 Hegel ([1806] 1998, [1807] 1977) saw an integral relationship existing between the personal and the social when he postulated that individuals' minds are an abstraction

Simmel 1910–1911). It is firmly grounded in immanent realism,[61] the proposition that universals are abstractions that permit the grouping of the likenesses of particulars into a single whole, so as to represent that which is necessary to their constitution (Armstrong 1978, 2000).

Metaphysical Holism

This holds that the social institutions exist as more than their mereological sum, in that they consist not only of individuals, but also of their interrelationships:

> All structuralists recognize as fundamental the contrast between structures and aggregates, the former being *wholes*, the latter composites formed of elements that are independent of the complexes into which they enter. ... [The] elements of a structure are subordinated to *laws*, and it is in terms of these laws that the structure qua whole or system is defined. ... These laws confer on the whole as such *overall properties* distinct from the properties of its elements (Piaget 1970, 7, emphasis in original).

These interrelationships give rise to social institutions grounded in shared norms, roles, and practices.

Methodological Holism

This holds that human social life is best, or most appropriately, understood by analysis at the macroscopic level of the social institutions, values, practices, and processes.[62] This can be extended to an analysis of the social context in which action-takers formulate the intentional mental

---

from, and a participant in, the social (group) mind (the independent collective mind of a social group): "I that is a We, and the We that is an I" (Hegel [1807] 1977, 177; see also Taylor 1975). He argued that an organic (rational) community is one in which individual and collective interests are rationally in harmony. This manifests as a state whose citizens choose to obey and support it as the ultimate form of society, thereby making it a divine idea—the social mind incarnate. Hegel considered that conditions of full selfhood could be met only in such a law-governed social situation.

61 This stands in contrast to transcendental realism (Loux 2002), which holds that universals represent an objective reality that exists outside the mind, is prior to, and independent of, particulars.

62 As Parker (2006, 2) points out, however, methodological holism should not be confused or conflated with subjectivism, non-rationality, or historicism (the proposition that history can be resolved into a single narrative direction).

states that give rise to their social actions[63] (see Ryan 1970); illustratively:

- "Most people are shaped to the form of their culture because of the malleability of their original endowment" (Benedict [1934] 1959, 278).

- "We are forced to conclude that human nature is almost unbelievably malleable, responding accurately and contrastingly to contrasting cultural conditions" (Mead [1935] 1963, 280).

- "Much of what is commonly called 'human nature' is merely culture thrown against a screen of nerves, glands, sense organs, muscles etc." (White, quoted in Delger 1991, 209).

Durkheim ([1895] 1982, 105-106) makes the point:

> If we begin with the individual in seeking to explain phenomena, we shall be able to understand nothing of what takes place in the group. Individual natures are merely the indeterminate material that the social factor molds and transforms. Their contribution consists exclusively in very general attitudes, in vague and consequently plastic predispositions.

This means that individuals are considered to have little capacity to determine their lives. It is, moreover, axiomatically taken to be difficult, if not impossible, for one person to transform social institutions and processes (Baert 1998, 11). Therefore, those who undertake to study the world of persons from this ontological position would adopt a process that proceeds from the position of the macro (elucidating the socio-cultural, economic and linguistic factors that on the premise that that have the necessary causal capacity determine the patterns of social interactions that build up and sustain social institutions and give rise to the social phenomena) to the micro (so as to explain the action-takers' intentional mental states that give rise to social actions).

---

63 Zahle (2016) explains: "Methodological individualists who are engaged in the micro foundations [of methodological holism] debate do not insist that holist explanations should be dispensed with ... it is simply held that these explanations are in need of supplementation by accounts of individual-level mechanisms ["to provide a mechanism, to open up the black box and show the nuts and bolts, the cogs and wheels" (Elster 1985, 5)]. Also, there is no objection to the use of holist explanations in which the explanans is stated in terms of social phenomena and the explanandum is described in terms of individuals, their actions, etc. In fact, explanations along these lines are offered as part of the accounts of the individual-level mechanisms when it is specified how a social phenomenon resulted in individuals forming various beliefs and desires, and having certain opportunities."

On the Attribution of Social Action

Structuralism holds that social actions can best be ascribed to group-elaborated (worked out) norms, roles, and practices. These group-endorsed elaborations identify the courses of action a group judge to be acceptable (unacceptable) and required (prohibited), so constituting the prevailing set of group behavior rules or code of conduct (structural determinism). Structuralism presume that these group elaborations either give rise to social actions (hard determinism) by overwhelming voluntarism—whereby individuals are not able to determine their intentional mental states—or, at least, strongly influence the choice of social actions by molding their hopes, aspirations, and goals (soft determinism). Social actions are, thus, taken to be "only comprehensible in relation to his or her [the action-taker's] social formation and existence" (Bryant 1985, 19; see also Robey 1973).[64] They are determined by conditioning factors external to the action-takers that manifest in the way they can participate in society.

Economic Participation

This is premised on the Marxian proposition that social actions have their roots in the relations of production (economic determinism) (Marx [1859] 1977). Because individuals are, essentially, productive beings, who, by their very nature, cooperate in a process of collective freely chosen labor, they are the product of the prevailing mode of production, which, in turn, is the product of the nature of the dominant economic structure—capitalism, socialism, and communisms (Marx and Engels [1848/1888] 2014). As Marx ([1859] 1977, Preface) observed: "The mode of production of material life conditions the general process of social, political and intellectual life. It is not the consciousness of men [sic] that determines their existence, but their social existence that determines their consciousness." Thus, "man is not an abstract being squatting outside the world...the real nature of man is the totality of social relations" (Marx [1845/1969] 2002, 66) but rather "individuals are ... embodiments of particular class-relations and class interests" (Marx [1867] 1993, I, 10). Marx maintained that the economic pressures that shape structural relations in everyday life determine social actions. Under capitalism, these relations are based on conflict between the profit imperatives of an exploitative

---

64 Hence it has been suggested that "structuralism is a set of principles for studying the mental superstructure" (Harris 1979, 166), and that "all our human properties and powers, beyond our biological constitution, [are] the gifts of society" (Archer (2000, 4).

class and workers' interest in improving their economic conditions. The resultant class conflict manifests as a class struggle. This higher dialectic[65] "consists not merely in producing and apprehending the determination as an opposite and limiting factor, but in producing and apprehending the positive content and result which it contains; and it is this alone which makes it a development and immanent progression" (Hegel [1821] 1991, 60). This analysis offers a framework that appraises of the notion of individual identity in the context of collective consciousness (Hobsbawm 1997, 83; see also Durkheim [1895] 1982). Social actions can, thus, be best ascribed to powerful economic pressures (economic determinism[66]).

Social Participation

This is premised the propositions that "the beliefs, tendencies and practices of the group taken collectively" (Durkheim [1895] 1982, 54) are able to shape its members' cognitive structures and, thereby, their social actions. The human mind is taken to be a *tabula rasa* (Aristotle [350 BCE] 2015; Locke [1689-1690] 2004) and, thus, "has no inherent structure and can be inscribed at will by society or ourselves" (Pinker 2002, 2; see also Dahrendorf 1968). Durkheim ([1895] 1982) argued that basic categories of thought—mental representations of the world—arise from social participation[67] (his theory of the social origin of mind) (Bergson 2004). These representations "are not only external to the individual but are, moreover, endowed with coercive power, by virtue of which they impose themselves upon him, independent of his individual will" (Pinker 2002, 2), so they determine the way a person articulates, denotes, and interpret social relationships, thereby inhibiting and stimulating social actions. The key to the transmission of social facts is socialization (Durkin 1995). This process takes place when a person move into social environments that have

---

65   Hegelian dialectical logic holds that any given thesis (an initial situation) contains within itself contradictory aspects—its antithesis (a negation of that initial situation)—which requires a movement towards a resolution—a synthesis (a unification of thesis and synthesis) (Hegel [1816] 1969).

66   Althusser (1962; [1965] 1969), drawing upon Marx and Engels' ambivalence about any reductionist interpretation of their work, advanced the propositions that social institutions at a certain place and stage in their development have economic, political, ideological, and theoretical sets of practices, each with their own relative autonomy, according to the limits set by their place in the totality, and each thus contributing to the structural causality of the social whole (structural Marxism).

67   Durhkeim ([1912] 2001) talked of collective representations—"The ideas, beliefs, and values elaborated by a collectivity and that are not reducible to individual constituents."

their own group rules and norms defined, sanctioned, and propagated by important others, the violation of which attracts penalties. Produced is Durkheim's *conscience collective*—"the body of beliefs and sentiments common to the average member of a society" (Durkheim ([1895] 1982, 126). This creates a sense of group belonging and hence a feeling of moral obligation to live up to its expectations:

> When I fulfill my obligations as brother, husband, or citizen, when I execute my contracts, I perform duties which are defined, externally to myself and my acts, in law and in custom. Even if they conform to my own sentiments and I feel their reality subjectively, such reality is still objective, for I did not create them; I merely inherited them through my education (Durkheim [1895] 1982, 1).

Social actions can, thus, be best ascribed to group values and attitudes an action-taker adopts in order to become integrated into that group (social determinism).

Cultural Participation

This is premised on the belief that underlying all social actions are fundamental universal cognitive structures that are culturally specific in their contents (Lévi-Strauss [1958/1963] 1974). These deep structures produce and reproduce meaning within a culture—a system of symbolic communication expressed in a culture's practices, phenomena, and activities (such as mythology, kinship, food preparation, religious rites, games, literary and non-literary texts, and entertainment). Understanding these deep structures can only be achieved by reducing them to their relevant constituent parts, thereby permitting the discovery of their operating principles (Lévi-Strauss [1958/1963] 1974). This constitutes the deep grammar of a culture, which originates in the human mind of its constituent members as learned language and cultural practices that operate unconsciously on them. Social actions can, thus, best be ascribed to culturally induced cognitions (ideas, beliefs, and a way of life) and patterns of social behavior (customs and practices) that give a person's life meaning and order (see, for example, Alexander 2003) (cultural determinism).

Linguistic Participation

This is premised on the proposition that the use of a particular language shapes the way people think about and behave in the world of persons.[68] Indeed, the real world is, to a large extent, unconsciously built upon the language habits (Sapir 1958, 69). Harré (1983) considered that human reality has a practical (physical) and an expressive (conversational) dimension, of which the latter tends to be dominant: "the fundamental human reality is a conversation" (p. 20), which "... is to be thought of as creating a social world just as causality generates a physical one" (Harré 1983, 65). Harré and Gillett (1994, 36; see also Harré 1988) develop this point: "[The] structures of discourse in which psychological phenomena, such as remembering, displays of emotion, avowals of attitudes, attribution of causality and responsibility, and so on, are created under the control of conventions of right or wrong performance." Social actions can, thus, be best ascribed to the language people use to shape the way he or she thinks about—creates meaning—and behaves in the world of persons (linguistic determinism).

Discourse Participation

As the self is, under post-structuralism, considered to be incoherent, disjointed, and decentered, it is a mere site in which various socio-cultural constructs and discursive formations are created and sustained by the power structures within a given socio-cultural environment (Derrida 1976, 1978; Foucault [1966] 1989, [1969] 2002; Lacan 1968). Thus, the knowledge is inherently fragmented, diverse, tenuous, ambiguous, and culturally specific, and so always changing and contestable. This means that it can never have finality and completeness. Social actions can, thus, be best ascribed to the meaning attached to the social world derived from self-reflexive discourses (discourse determinism).

Participation in Dutiful Social Obligations

This is premised on social relations being established and sustained by the performance of ritualistic social actions (Ho 1998). These are in accordance with a set of socially binding rules of required social behaviors—relational cognitions—with respect to every actor involved, each of whom has been assigned a socially foreordained ranking and priority. These relational rules dictate the relational roles that they are culturally obliged to perform in any and every situation (relational dominance)

---

68   In nineteenth-century Germany, Herder, Hegel, and von Humbolt recognized the importance of language as the medium by which a society shaped its members (Markova 1983).

(Ho, Chan, and Zhang 2001; Ho and Chiu 1998). So, the unit analysis for social analysis is a social relationship (methodological relationalism) (Ho 1998; Ho and Peng 1998; Ho, Chan and Zhang 2001; Ho et al. 2001; see also Ritzer and Gindoff 1992). Social actions can, thus, be best ascribed to the portfolio of culturally reinforced relationship—defining dutiful action—obligations (relational determinism).

Hermeneutic Epistemology

Hermeneutic grounds knowledge of the world of persons in people's conscious perceptions, so it considers that that world lacks fixity and certainty (Brentano [1874] 1995): "the social world must be understood from within, rather than explained from without" (Hollis 1994, 16; see also Baert 1998). The evidence for determining the truth-value of social knowledge claim is subjective—"truth from a human perspective" (Wiggins 1991, 120; see also Foucault 1983; Luntley 1995)—in that how a person interprets social institutions and social phenomena determines the meaning they attach to them (Hollis 1994). Thus, of course, such genuine knowledge may not correspond to material reality (Bretano [1874] 1973: see also Scruton 1984, 255-57).

Hermeneutics contends that knowledge is generated by the transcendental acts in the perceiving mind of a person engaged in reflection and rumination. This knowledge acquisition process is conditioned by his or her mental characteristics or states, which give rise to personal temperaments, interests, tastes, feelings, interpretations, and prejudices, as shaped by the prevalent socio-cultural and linguistic *milieu*. It embraces subjectivism, antirealism, reflexivity, and relativism.

Subjectivism

This doctrine postulates that a knowledge claim is epistemologically subjective if the evidence for determining its truth-value existing only in the human mind, derived from practice, language, and discourse (Winch [1958] 1990). It, thus, extends the meaning of subjective beyond human feelings, beliefs, and interests (Freud [1929] 1971; see also Harding 1986, 1991; Knorr-Cetina 1981; Shepherd 1993).[69] The cognitive processes used involve personal reflection and rumination that draw upon material

---

69   This gives rise to a method of research that is grounded in the experiences of women, which, according to Tickner (1997, 112) "actually strengthens standards of objectivity."

and immaterial evidence and that occur within a particular socio-cultural and linguistic *milieu*. This grounds knowledge either in the individual (when genuine knowledge is a first-person mental discernment that have been substantiated by inductive, deductive, abductive[70] and retroductive[71] reasoning; intuition;[72] common sense;[73] and revealed wisdom[74]) or in the social (when genuine knowledge is a knowledge claim justified by reference to expert authority or testimony;[75] consensus; or tradition) (Hollis 1994; Natanson 1963).

Antirealism

This holds that reality does not exist independently of the mind, and that the truthfulness of a knowledge claim depends upon the circumstances that would justify its assertion (its assertability-conditions) (Alston 2002; Devitt 1984; Wright 1987).

Reflexivity

This holds that knowledge is shaped by knowledge seekers' acts of self-awareness and reflection on their values, experiences, interests, and beliefs (Bartlett and Suber 1987).

---

70 This form of reasoning is a thought process by which a causal hypothesis is inferred from a body of evidence about a phenomenon that would, if correct, provide the best explanation for that evidence (inference to best explanation) (Lipton [1991] 2004). It, thus, identifies the best explanation for a phenomenon, given all the evidence under consideration (Kapitan 1992).

71 This form of reasoning involves drawing causal inferences from a body of evidence related to one phenomenon, to explain the cause of another phenomenon (Pierce [1898] 1993). It is contingent upon observed concomitances, which may be merely coincidental.

72 Bergson saw intuition as an "instinct that has become disinterested, self-conscious, and capable of reflecting upon its object and of enlarging it indefinitely" (quoted in Russell 1946, 821). Shand (2002, 46) notes, however, "intuitions are without exception sensuous, and therefore, no speculative knowledge is possible which reaches further than possible experience."

73 In the tradition of eighteenth-century Scottish realist philosophy, common sense—the beliefs that come naturally to mind to all people, as responsible agents, based on memory, reason, moral sense, and taste—carries its own authority, despite accepted perceptual fallibilities, because people, proceeding cautiously, are capable of knowing the world (Grave 1960; Moore 1959).

74 This is Aquinas' ([1259-1264] 1905) truths of revelation: "Wisdom ... conferred by God as a particular endowment" (Rofe 2001). See also Dylles 1983.

75 As Welbourne (2001, 125) observed, "the concept of knowledge enters our repertoire of concepts on the back of testimony." See also Coady 1992.

Relativism

This holds "that there are no grounds for postulating or investigating a reality independent of the knower; that there is no ultimate truth and, therefore, no grounds for presuming that any one truth claim is 'better' than any other" (Nightingale and Cromby 1999, 227). So, the multiculturalation of meaning gives rise to a multiplicity of interpretations, reflecting the diversity of cultural contexts (Gergen and Thatchenkey 1998).

On Social Knowledge

Knowledge is taken to be unique to an individual, grounded in his or her conscious perceptions mediated by intentionality—being able to attach meaning to an object (Brentano [1874] 1995). This connection of thought to object requires acts of reflexive interpretation, so as to ensure the appropriate contextualization of meaning (Blumer 1969, Garfinkel [1967] 1984; Wittgenstein 1953). To Blumer (1969), drawing upon Mead's (1925, 1934, 1938) proposition that self-awareness arises through the process of role-taking (social behaviorism) (Cook 1977), an individual takes meaning about the world-of-everyday-life by making sense of what others say through symbolic communications. This involves the interaction of language, identity, and societal values, achieved by means of interactive processes that underpin the construction, negotiation, presentation, and affirmation of self (symbolic interactionalism). To Garfinkel ([1967] 1984), an individual makes sense of what others say by reflecting on actual, ordinary activities (practical actions, practical circumstances commonsense knowledge of social structures, and practical reasoning) (ethnomethodology) (Byron 2004). To Wittgenstein (1953), deriving meaning about the world of persons, and making sense of what others say, is the product of the complex of interwoven speech and action that are ordered in praxis in a way that makes sense to the participants (language games).

If the world of persons can only be understood subjectively, then, by implication, one person's truth is just as valid as another's (perspectivism), and so each person can create reality in a metaphysical domain that is incapable of being addressed by the naturalist methods of enquiry. The dichotomy between truth and reality is deemed an irrelevance and the problems of objectivity do not arise (Bunge 1996, 330), because facts flowing from naturalist methodologies do not contribute much to understanding. In this scenario, as Kant ([1781–1787] 1956) and also O'Neill (1989) reasoned, any ultimate reality cannot be known. This imposes restrictions on "the scope of human reason" (Callinicos 1999, 31).[76]

What, then, is knowable is relative—both across time and across individuals (epistemic relativism)—which means that people in different groups (societies) have very different approaches to reasoning and to belief confirmation and belief systems (Baghramian 2004; Hollis and Lukes 1982; Stich 1990).

Epistemological Hermeneutics

This stresses, in the tradition of Schleiermacher and Dilthey, the discerning of the meaning of an individual's subjectivity through comparison and contrast with the meaning of others' subjectivity. So, the subjectivity of the individual is not directly accessible and can only be approached through the individual in a social setting: "we never directly grasp individuality, but grasp only its difference from others and ourselves" (Ricoeur 1981, 47). Thus, Schleiermacher's [1805–1810] 1977) epistemology can be characterized as structured subjectivity. This universal methodology for the investigation of interpretation requires a recognition of objective (critical) grammatical or cultural structures that enables the divination of individual subjectivity, through comparison with the meanings commonly held by others within a given culture, which enables the investigator "to understand an author as well as and even better than he understands himself" (Ricoeur 1981, 46).

Dilthey ([1910] 2000) located the distinctiveness of the human sciences in "a primordial capacity to transpose oneself into the mental life of others" —through language—such that "man [sic] is not radically alien to man because he offers signs of his own existence" (Ricoeur 1981, 49). It is this social dimension of human consciousness that allows the unique relationship between object and subject within the human and social sciences. Dilthey claimed that the very possibility of individual self-knowledge rests on the capacity for self-interpretation. Thus, individual self-interpretations (knowledge claims) of the world of persons and the social actions of others are the product of historically structured signs and

---

76   The Berkeleyan notion of subjectivism (Berkeley ([1710] 1962), which relied on God as the source of ideas or sensations in the mind, was reinterpreted by Husserl, who sought to isolate pure consciousness by means of a methodology that excluded reflexive and speculative thought from descriptions of mental conditions (Husserl [1929] 1981). Subsequently, Sartre rejected both an objectivist and subjectivist philosophy in developing a position of human intentionality of consciousness (Sartre [1960] 1976).

expressions that become collectively meaningful (genuine knowledge) through mutual recognition.

Existential Epistemology

Schopenhauer, in the metaphysical idealist tradition, grounded knowledge in the self-knowledge of human beings. To him, the world is a manifestation of will—"the world is my idea" (Schopenhauer [1818/1844] 1969, 1) and "no will: no idea, no world" (Schopenhauer [1851] 1970, 56). Under his doctrine of the primacy of will, the real world is the self who has an idea, as all knowledge is based on immediate personal experience.

Knowledge—self-knowledge—is embedded in the lived existence of subjectively aware human beings. Indeed, Heidegger saw the need to analyze the problem of self-knowledge arising from the self in the everyday world being unconscious of its own existence. To him, self-knowledge required the recognition of past determinants, the acknowledgement of present concerns, and alertness to future possibilities. Thus, the world of persons contains a multitude of subjective truths grounded in first-person mental discernments, which render the notion of objective truth paradoxical, and thereby problematic (Warnock 1970, 8-9; see also Ortega y Gasset [1929–31] 2002).

This existential imperative shapes its epistemology, for no clear distinction can be made between evaluation and description: as Nietzsche ([1883–1888/1895] 1967, 78) observed, "perceptions are altogether permeated with valuations (useful or harmful, hence acceptable or unacceptable)." He sought to explain the myth of objectivity in terms of the essential human need to dominate the social and physical environment: "our cognitive apparatus is an abstracting and falsifying mechanism directed not toward knowledge, but toward mastery and possession" (Nietzsche [1883–1888/1895] 1967, 120).

Sartre's conviction was that people must create their own meaning in what they see as a meaningless world ([1943] 1957). He sought to strip away both sentimental and objective speculations about reality. Knowledge of the word of persons, then, is, ultimately, unique to the individual.

Phenomenology

This stresses, in the tradition of Brentano, Husserl, Heidegger, Merleau-Ponty, Schütz, and Sartre (Hammond, Howarth, and Keat 1991), that objects are objects of experience, akin to Kant's phenomena. This makes reality relative and subjective. Understanding, thus, necessitates an investigation of the relationship between the objective and subjective realms, achieved by understanding the process by which an individual conceives and interprets aspects of his or her experience of the world of persons as distinct and meaningful, on the basis of his or her experience of it constituted in and by consciousness. This requires explication of the structures of conscious experience (Embree et al. 1996; Moran 2000; Thévenaz 1962).

Brentano ([1874] 1995) held that knowledge is provided by conscious perceptions that are mediated by intentionality. Husserl (([1931] 1960, 15) considered intentionality to be "[t]he terminological expression ... for designating the basic character of being as consciousness, as consciousness of something ... ." Indeed, he ([1929] 1981) focused on understanding of the essence of a phenomenon experienced through conceptualization and self-reflection. Thus, phenomenology's unit analysis became the mental act (methodological solipsism), which can reveal the essence of knowledge (Scruton 1985, 258). Phenomenological inquiry is concerned only with the human experience.

In this paradigm, the world is knowable by a person through meanings that describe the appearances of objects so, at this level, he or she perceives certain and necessary truths. Thus, a person can participate in a world informed by sense data that can assume some degree of intersubjectivity (Crossley 1996) through language, culture, and a pattern of common sense that has evolved from the commonalities of social experience (Husserl [1907] 1966, [1928] 1931, [1928] 1964).

Knowledge is, thus, always indeterminate, tentative, and incomplete, with the seeker of truth always inclined to question assumptions by returning repeatedly to his or her lived experience (Schütz [1932] 1967, 83, see also 73-74). Knowledge, then, is not only unique to the individual, but also unique to the individual at a specific point in time. It is, thus, both subjective and relative.

Linguistic Epistemology

While the hermeneutic tradition generally recognized the epistemological salience of language, linguistic epistemology per se only emerged with the work of Wittgenstein ([1922] 1961, 1953, [1956] 1978). He emphasized the importance of the relationship between language and reality

(Devitt and Sterelny [1987] 1998). He argued that the objective rules of language are prerequisite of knowledge itself: "That the world is my world shows itself in the fact that the limits of my language (of the only language I can understand) mean the limits of my world" (Wittgenstein [1922] 1961, 5.62). Language gives pictures of the world and consists of pictures of reality. The limits of language are the limits of thought: "What can be said at all can be said clearly, and what we cannot talk about we must pass over in silence" (Wittgenstein [1922] 1961, iv). Furthermore, the linguistic rules that shape knowledge acquisition are intersubjective and, therefore, "the very existence of concepts depends on group-life" (Winch [1958] 1990, 44).

These language rules vary from culture-to-culture and from time-to-time. The later Wittgenstein (1953) came to privileged ordinary language—thought is limited by language—and made the intelligibility of language rules the key both to meaning—meaning of a word is grounded in its use in the language, which links it to behavior and context—and to epistemological certainty. Linguistic epistemology stresses the importance of understanding (and learning) the rules of language that govern the social meaning associated with any social action (Wittgenstein [1922] 1961; 1953).

ALTERNATIVE SOCIAL-REALITY STANDPOINTS REJECTED

As neoliberal individualist-libertarian worldview is grounded on agency ontology (individualism) and naturalist epistemology (rationalism), it rejects the alternative social-reality lens through which the world of persons can be read because they are grounded on wrong ontological and epistemological standpoints) (Dixon 2003; Dixon, Dogan, and Sanderson 2009).

The Naturalist-Structuralist Social-Reality Standpoint

As seen through this social-reality lens, the world of persons is an objectively knowable real and material domain (naturalist epistemology), comprising a collection of social institutions in which ranked individuals construct meaning about the world around them, and their place in it, by reference to their shared beliefs, which define the nature of acceptable practices within their social order (structural ontology). Thus, social institutions (structures) exercise power over agency, so placing constraints on free will, which makes social actions predictable by reference to the pre-existing values, traditions, and practices held in common with others. This, thereby, necessitates in any social analysis the elucidating the socio-cultural, economic, religious, and relational influences that shape the patterns of social interactions, which build up the social relationships that give rise to the social institutions and social phenomena. This is the foundation of the collectivist-hierarchical worldview.

The Hermeneutic-Structuralist Social-Reality Standpoint

As seen through this social-reality lens, the world of persons is a subjective domain, knowable, only as it is socially constructed (hermeneutic epistemology), comprising a collection of social institutions in which unranked individuals collectively construct meaning about the world around them, and their place in it, through discourse (structural ontology). These discursive processes exercise power over agency, so placing constraints on free will. This makes social actions predictable by reference to the negotiated values and beliefs negotiated and held in common with others. This, thereby, necessitates in any social analysis the elucidation of the influences that mold the discourse content that shape the patterns of social interactions, which build up social relationships that give rise to the social institutions and social phenomena. This is the foundation of the collectivist-egalitarian worldview.

The Hermeneutic-Agency Social-Reality Standpoint

As seen through this social-reality lens, the world of persons is a subjective domain, contestably knowable as what individuals have the will to believe to be true (hermeneutic epistemology), comprising a collection of unknowable individuals who individually construct meaning about the world around them, and their place in it (agency ontology). As self-determining agents, they engage endlessly with their subjective interpretation of others' discernments of them, so these perceptions exercise power over agency, so placing a self-imposed constraint on their free will. Their intentional mental states are molded by their search—or their fear of searching—for their sense of uniqueness, purpose in life, and self-fulfillment—the need to live in the way they find most valid and fulfilling. This requires them to have what Camus ([1942] 2005, 55, emphasis in original) called "the freedom to *be*," which is a challenge.[77] So, human

---

77 To some people this existential freedom is seen to be within their reach. Throwing off their "sickness of the soul" (Maslow 1971, 44)—a barrier to their achievement

behavior is unpredictable, because individual causation is conditional on the thoughts, beliefs, expectations, attitudes, and perceptions connected to inner feelings—as a first-person mental discernment (Maslow [1962] 1968; Rogers 1961)—being experienced as a sense of estrangement from self and others (BonJour 2002). This, thereby, necessitates in any social analysis the exploration of the relationship between the objective and subjective realms, achieved by drawing out the process by which individuals conceive and interpret aspects of their conscious experience of the world of persons as distinct and meaningful, so as to ascertain, among other things, who they perceive themselves to be, who they wish to become, and why they fear becoming who they want to become. This is the foundation of the individualist-existential worldview.

THE ALTERNATIVE UNDERSTANDINGS OF
THE WORLD OF PERSONS

What, then, are the particular understandings of the world of persons—its social institutions and social phenomena—that the neoliberal individualist-libertarian worldview rejects?

On Social Institutions and Social Phenomena

As the neoliberal individualist-libertarian worldview posits that social institutions and social phenomena do not exist independently of their constituent members and have no causal capacity, it rejects all the following contending propositions about them:

- Social institutions and social phenomena exist as more than their mereological sum. They have causal capacity on their

---

of self-actualization—is reachable by challenging convention, so that they are not just a reflection of the group. This is a prerequisite for taking ownership of self (Rogers 1961) and for seeking self-realization, thereby discovering and realizing life's true purpose. To others, existential freedom is seen to be beyond their reach, as they are beleaguered by a sense of metaphysical pathos about the human situation and by the reality of Nietzsche's ([1883] 1967) law of eternal recurrence—life's trials and tribulations are inevitably and eternally lived over and over again. They assert—in fear of the consequences of non-conformity and as an antidote to worry—or even believe—as a skeptic)— that bad luck, fate or the powers that be have led them to where they are now: alienated and marginalized from social life. They lack an "appetite for life" (Wilson [1956/1967] 2001, 118). Suffering Maslow's Jonah complex, they fear freedom and the success that may follow it, which exposes them to absolute vulnerability and solitude (Maslow [1962] 1968: 59) constituent individual members' intentional mental states, by means of the structural conditioning factors that manifest in the way they participate in society, and thus on their social actions (the collectivist-hierarchical worldview).

- Social institutions and social phenomena exist beyond their physical attributes and manifestations, as they have a metaphysical dimension—the product of transcendental acts of perceiving human minds of their constituent individual members (ideationalism)—which has causal capacity because meaning of these transcendental mental acts are made understandable:

  - by discourse, the content of which shapes how they conduct their social actions (the collectivist-egalitarian worldview) or

  - by introspection, so as to interpret their implications, which shape how they conduct their social actions (the individualist-existential worldview).

On Being Human

As the neoliberal individualist-libertarian worldview holds that individuals are essentially free beings pursuing their own self-interest, it rejects the following contending propositions about what it means to be a human being:

- Individuals are essentially logical moral beings with the capacity to rise above their feelings and passions, who are always striving for harmony that begins with self and radiates outwards to the family and others, achieved by means of correct behavior, loyalty and sincerity (the collectivist-hierarchical worldview).

- Individuals are cultural artifacts, the product of self-reflexive and inherently culturally specific discourses making them transient interpretations, the product of the interwoven speech and action by a process of "discursive socialization"[78] (Archer

---

78 This makes a person "the linguistically socialized product of having acquired a theory of self" (Archer 2000, 105): "all the recognizable properties of human beings come from joining in 'society's conversations'" (Archer 2000, 87; see also Harré 1983, 20). Thus, the self "is dissolved into discursive structures" (Archer 2000, 34) and life is but a "a tissue of contingent relationships, a web which stretches backward and forward through past and future time" (Rorty 1986, 14-15), making the self a

2000, 87, 98; see also Bourdieu and Wacquant 1992) (the collectivist-egalitarian worldview).

- Individuals are shaped by the necessity of enduring the challenge of human existence in a life devoid of meaning. This makes them essentially unique beings, who are free to choose who they are and who they do, and do not, want to become, achieved by knowing the real truth about themselves gained from intuitive insights) (the individualist-existential worldview).

On Human Nature

As the neoliberal individualist-libertarian worldview privileges the proposition that individuals are consistently and immutably self-serving, self-centered and, self-interested, it rejects all the following contending propositions about human nature:

- Individuals have a basic instinct for seeking pleasure and avoiding pain, but their redemption—the realizing of their excellence or perfection in those human states (such as acquiring knowledge and achievements) or properties (such as accepting other-regarding duties) that are central to human nature—comes from them doing what is morally right, achieved by conforming to the requisite pre-existing group norms. This is best accomplished by the habit of self-control—mastery over bodily passion—thereby becoming Socrates' perfect Orphic saints (Russell 1946: 111), so as "to avoid mental disturbances when excessive emotions fail to obey reason" (Cicero [44 BC] 1971: 34). This enables everyone to attain the Platonic wise, brave, self-controlled, and, thus, well-ordered self (Plato [c380s BC] 1952, which means that within everybody reason has to struggle to regulate and resolve contrary and conflicting emotions (the collectivist-hierarchical worldview).

- Individuals are inherently good with a capacity for real moral progress, with human nature being the product of a person's negotiated social formations, which are shaped, in varying degrees, by culture and circumstance—and, thus, are other-refer-

---

"a network of beliefs, desires and emotions with nothing behind it—no substrata behind the attributes—[albeit one that is] constantly reweaving itself" in the face of environmental pressures (Rorty 1985, 217).

ential—thereby making human nature informed by comparisons with others (the collectivist-egalitarian worldview).

- Individuals are self-referential, because self is the center of existence, but with a sense of resigned acceptance of human finitude, so it is up to them to define their own identity in the course of living out their lives in in a perpetual struggle to recognize their own unique consciousness (Laing 1960) and to gain supremacy over the forces of social constraint, so as to find the most authentic and fulfilling way possible (the individualist-existential worldview).

On Social Actions

As the neoliberal individualist-libertarian worldview holds that social actions are best attributes to self-interest, it rejects all the following contending propositions about what gives rise to social actions:

- Social actions are the product of prevailing group rules or codes of conduct, made socially acceptable because they are grounded on acceptable group-elaborated (worked out) norms, roles, and practices that identify the courses of action judged to:

  - be socially mandated by custom and tradition (the collectivist-hierarchical worldview); or

  - signal a laudable shared commitment with like-minded others (the collectivist-egalitarian worldview).

- Social actions are the product of an individual's search—or their fear of searching—for their sense of uniqueness—who they are, their purpose in life—who they wish to become, and their self-fulfillment—becoming who they want to become (the individualist-existential worldview).

On Social Roles and Relationships

As the neoliberal individualist-libertarian worldview posits that individuals choose their relationships on the basis of what is in their best self-interest, it rejects all the following contending propositions about social relationships.

- Social roles and relationships are predicated on socio-culturally entrenched codes of conduct that have been defined, sanctioned, and propagated exclusively by important others (the collectivist-hierarchical worldview).

- Social roles and relationships are predicated on egalitarian discourse processes defining, sanctioning, and propagating appropriate social conduct (the collectivist-egalitarian worldview).

- Social roles and relationships are predicated on first-person perceptions of others grounded on their subjective interpretation of others' discernments of them, based on past experience, because human nature is knowable only with hindsight (the individualist-existential worldview).

On Social Engagement

As the neoliberal individualist-libertarian worldview advances the proposition that individuals' social engagement are the outcome of bargaining with others for the position that will best promote their individual self-interest, it rejects all the following contending propositions about social engagement.

- Social engagement are the outcome of allowing important others to mediate their engagement outcomes and social relationships, because they share common values, traditions, and customs, made accepted because of a sense of loyalty and duty, which makes the expected modes of social engagement *de rigeur* (the collectivist-hierarchical worldview).

- Social engagement are the outcome of negotiating desired engagement outcomes and social relationships with like-minded others, because they share similarly beliefs and values, made acceptable because the negotiated social engagements signify their laudable common commitments to like-minded others (the collectivist-egalitarian worldview).

- Social engagement can be the outcome of making engagement with others contingent upon remembering past interpersonal experiences with them that suggest dependability, made acceptable because it permits social engagements to be conducted warily, which is important given that people are generally unknowable and unpredictable, and in ways that they believe others expect of them (the individualist-existential worldview).

NEOLIBERALISM:
THE NARROWNESS OF ITS FOUNDATIONAL PROPOSITIONS

Neoliberalism's foundational worldview propositions are grounded in its circumscribed construction of the world of persons.

Truth

As the neoliberal individualist-libertarian worldview privileges the objective truth, evidenced by deductive reasoning or sensory experience it readily denies the validity of other contending truth-standards (truth-criteria):

- Truth can be evidenced by exclusive reference to sufficiently valid reasons that are grounded in cognitive processes of innate intellectual awareness (direct apprehension) (Moore 1903), or of reasoning that has produced a high proportion of true beliefs (reliabilism) (Alston 1989; Goldman 1986; Shope 1983).

- Truth can be evidenced by unanimous agreement by all who have sufficient relevant knowledge or experience to judge its veracity (consensual pragmatism) (Peirce 1877).

- Truth can be evidenced by the success of the practical consequences of a knowledge proposition (instrumental pragmatism) (Dewey [1895–1898] 1972; James [1897] 1979, [1907] 1995, [1909] 1979; Peirce 1877; Schiller [1903] 1912, [1907] 1912).

Reasoning

As the neoliberal individualist-libertarian worldview privileges reasoning identified with propositional (factual) knowledge (Tsoukas 1998), and with the narrative of progress (Gergen and Thatchenkey 1998), so making reasoning purposeful, intentional, causal, and hence intrinsically teleological (Muirhead 1932; Woodfield 1976), it readily denies the applicability of other contending forms of reasoning:

- Reasoning identified with bounded rationality (Simon [1945] 1960, [1945] 1976, [1945] 1982, 1956, 1957), which is focused on working out acceptable solutions in the absence of complete information[79] (the collectivist-hierarchical worldview).

79   Any uncertainties grounded in the lack of knowledge of future events are

- Reasoning identified with communicative rationality (Habermas 1968, 1971, 1975, [1981] 1984, [1981] 1987), which involves a values-based reasoning process that makes good argument and the validity of normative judgments the final authority (Bakhtin [1934–1941] 1981; Gergen and Thatchenkey 1998; Habermas 1986, 1996)[80] (the collectivist-egalitarian worldview).

- Reasoning identified with sense making (Weick 1995), which involves rolling or serial hindsight and is driven by plausibility rather than truthfulness, on the premised of the primacy of non-rationality[81] (Portes 1972) (the individualist-existential worldview).

Problem Solving

As the neoliberal individualist-libertarian worldview holds that problems solving involves identifying the best means of achieving unexceptionable ends,[82] it readily denies the validity of other contending approaches to problem solving:

- Problem solving that involves searching for alternative solutions that can be prioritized by the powers-that-be in accord

---

converted to factual risk probabilities by experts drawing upon empirical evidence to give them some degree of likelihood (Bernstein 1996; Rescher 1994; Shrader-Frechette 1985)

80 This mode of reasoning is informed by critical theory (Adorno and Horkheimer [1947] 1972; Held 1980; How 2003). This holds that: "[r]eason includes not only our capacity for logical inference, but also our ability to conduct inquiry, to solve problems, to evaluate, to criticize, to deliberate about how we should act, and to reach an understanding of ourselves, other people, and the world" (Lakoff and Johnson 1999, 3-4). The truth is always considered to be provisional, which makes its meaning contingent, and privileges Hegalian dialectical rationality. This logic of contradiction enables contradictions—embedded in a thesis and an antithesis—to become a new synthesis—thereby conserving both the thesis and the antithesis while simultaneously abolishing them.

81 Under this notion "the canons of rationality, validity, truth, and efficiency are simply beside the point—irrelevant!" (Shweder 1984, 38). As Gray (2002, 20) notes:

To think of science as the search for truth is to renew a mystical faith, the faith of Plato and Augustine, that truth rules the world, that truth is divine.

So, surprise dominates; intelligence cannot improve ignorance; and goals and values are luxuries.

82 These are so crucial, such as maximizing human welfare, they that they inevitably justify the means used to achieve them, despite any risks involved.

with their satisfactoriness—such as their likely cost, efficiency, and values contestability (the collectivist-hierarchical worldview).

- Problem solving that involves evaluating the desirability of the likely distributional impact of both the contending means and the contentious ends, as intense values-based disagreement about both is anticipated (the collectivist-egalitarian worldview).

- Problem solving that involves sense making, driven by plausibility, with all possible solutions being kept open to maximize opportunities for escaping fate by, at least, preventing the worst outcome or minimizing any damage (the individualist-existential worldview).

Risk Taking

As the neoliberal individualist-libertarian worldview holds that risks need to be conceptualized, defined, measured, evaluated by entrepreneurs, and their ethical acceptability needs to be judged by their net desirable consequences,[83] it readily denies the validity of other contending perceptions of risk taking.

- Risks can be taken only if the critical choices about how they are defined, measured, evaluated, and accommodated are made by experts who must, however, be unencumbered by moral considerations that need to settled upon by the powers-that-be, who would then expect successful risk-taking (the collectivist-hierarchical worldview)

- Risks are to be taken only if the conditions (if any) under which it is ethically acceptable to impose risks on others are specified and agreed to by those effected, which minimizes and highly politicizes risk-taking, so the risks need to be defined, measured, and evaluated by those with an interest in or con-

---

83 Successful risk taking is expected, as entrepreneurial talent and new technology are considered capable of mitigating any unforeseen consequences of risk taking. In the event of failure, blame is assigned either to bad luck—justified on the ethical premise that retrospective responsibility for the consequences of an action should be limited to that which is under the control of the action-taker (Lucas 1993; Zimmerman 1988)—or to rogues—justified on the utilitarian grounds of the consequential reduction in happiness cause by their behavior (Klein 1990).

cern about the expected possible adverse consequences (the collectivist-egalitarian worldview).

- Risks are to be avoided, because the consequence of risk taking are unknowable, and cannot be evaluated as a set of risk probabilities (Taleb 2007), so all that can be done is either to avoid uncertainties—to minimize any adverse consequences—or, if they cannot be avoided, to shrug them off fatalistically (the individualist-existential worldview).

Decision-Making

As the neoliberal individualist-libertarian worldview posits that the intent of decision-making is to make the best solutions will do,[84] so as create the best opportunity for material improvement, it readily denies the validity of other contending perceptions of decision-making.

- Satisfactory decision-making, premised on the accepted need for decision-making to be constrained by hierarchically determined values and beliefs, based on interpretation of the available, albeit incomplete, objective information[85] (Simon [1945] 1960, 1956; Gigerenzer 1991; Gigerenzer and Goldstein 1996) (the collectivist-hierarchical worldview).

- Consensus decision-making, the intent of which is to produce a meaningful interpretation of subjective, socially constructed information that facilitates a compromise decision on value-related problems, on the premise that disagreement about ends is inevitable (the collectivist-egalitarian worldview).

- decision-making, the intent of which is to make plausible sense of reality (Weick 1995), so facilitating the making of no, or at least, incremental decisions, which can involve a garbage-can decision-making process[86] (March and Olsen 1976) or perhaps

---

84 As Schwartz's (2004) maximizers, these decision makers have unrealistically high expectations, always trying to make the best possible choice, but they experiences the existential anxiety that follows the realization that they are free to select from a multitude of available choices, which leads to stress and even depression bordering on the clinical range.

85 As Schwartz's (2004) satisficers, these decision makers are willing to live with decisions that are good enough, which means he or she can make choices without excessive agonizing and without being plagued by post-decision regrets.

86 This process can be characterized as "a collection of choices looking for problems,

even decision-making by lottery (Hood 1998) (the individual-ist-existential worldview).

Trust

As the neoliberal individualist-libertarian worldview privileges the prop-osition that determining the trustworthiness of others—particularist trust[87]—involves an assessment of the probable material costs and bene-fits of extending trust[88] (Gambetta 1988), it readily denies the efficacy of other contending bases for the granting of trust.

- Trust can be extended only when the trustors are confident than those to whom trust is to be extended share moral beliefs that reinforce the obligation to be honest[89] (moralistic trust) (Uslaner 2002) (the collectivist-hierarchical worldview).

- Trust can be extended only when trustors are confident that there has been a building up sufficient mutual expectations of reciprocity—goodwill (Ring and van de Ven 1992, 1994)—to signal their trustworthiness[90] in a way that is mutually under-stood and accepted (Bacharach and Gambetta 1977, 2001) (the collectivist-egalitarian worldview).

- Trust should be extended only when trustors are confident that their trust-inducing personal experiences with those to be trusted are justified that extension of trust (the individual-ist-existential worldview).

---

issues and feelings looking for decision situations in which they may be aired, solu-tions looking for issues to which they may be answers, and decision makers looking for work" (Cohen, March, and Olsen 1972, 2).

87 A distinction can be drawn between particularist trust—the particular trust one person has of another person (believing in his or her honesty and reliability and in the validity of his or her knowledge claims—and generalist trust) the general trust one person has of everyone else, individually as well as collectively in institutions (Allister 1995; Mayer, Davis, and Schoorman 1995).

88 Thus, trustworthiness is reducible to a risk probability (knowledge-based trust) (Yamigishi and Yamigishi 1994), based on the observed actions of the person to be trusted (Luhmann 1979, 1988; Offe 1999), which makes the trust decision essentially a strategic one.

89 Thus, those to whom trust is to be extended must adhere to a fundamentally com-mon set of innate moral values, premised on a belief that no one should try to take advantage of anyone else (Silver 1989, 276).

90 This requires the symbols used to signal trustworthiness have a shared common meaning acquired by mutual participation in an intersubjective communication process that socially constructs roles, norms, and expectations.

Power and Compliance

As the neoliberal individualist-libertarian worldview holds that making people comply by doing what they would not otherwise have chosen to do requires use of exchange power (Boulder 1990), resource or reward power (French and Raven 1959), or economic power (Hales 2001),[91] it readily denies the efficacy of other contending ways of achieving compliance.

- The use of legitimate power (French and Raven 1959), threat power (Boulder 1990), or expert or knowledge power (French and Raven 1959; Hales 2001) to solicit compliance on the basis of a cognitive commitment derived from logical calculations made in the context of structural processes (such as rules and procedures prescribed by those in or with authority) (the collectivist-hierarchical worldview).

- The use of personal or referent power (French and Raven 1959), integrative power (Boulder 1990), or normative power (Hales 2001) to solicit compliance on the basis of a sense of moral commitment to obey instructions that accord with jointly affirmed norms (the collectivist-egalitarian worldview).

- The use of destructive threat power (Boulder 1990) or physical or coercive power (French and Raven 1959) to solicit coercive (alienated) compliance (Etzioni 1961) (the individualist-existential worldview).

Ethics and Morality

The neoliberal individualist-libertarian worldview privileges consequential ethics[92] (Darwall 2003; Gouinlock 1972), which makes the ethicality

---

91 The use of such power is expected to induce instrumental compliance, based on an economic calculation of the compliance costs and benefits involved (Etzioni 1961), which means that rules and contracts have to specify rewards that oblige duties (Onuf 1989, 87, but see also 197 and 217). This sense of avarice may, however, be constrained by any limits people are willing to impose, unilaterally, upon the advancement their own material wellbeing.

92 This means judging the morality of social actions by the value of their actual, or even intended, effects in terms of producing the greatest happiness (pleasure) for the greatest number of people, that is, the most good (act-consequentialism, or, in utilitarian terms, act-utilitarianism), even if this is not the intention, which, perhaps, it should not be (a precept of indirect act-consequentialism). Moreover, social actions can also be moral either if they are in accordance with the preferences of those assessing the rightness of those social actions (preference-utilitarianism) or if they follow a set of rules general acceptance of which would best promote the most good

of a social action the end result of a hedonistic or utility calculation (ethical hedonism (Austin [1832] 1995; Bentham [1789] 1970; Mill [1863] 1968; Peirce ([1878] 1992)) that determines the overall goodness/badness of its consequences, on the premised that its detrimental and beneficial material consequences can be predicted, it readily denies the validity of other contending ethical precepts by which the ethicality of social actions can be judged.

- Their intrinsic moral rightness (deontological ethics) (Fried 1978; Ross 1930) in accord with the categorical moral imperatives embedded in moral rules proclaimed by duly authorized moral rule-givers, on the premise that rule-followers accept their dutiful moral obligations[93] (Kant ([1788] 1906) (the collectivist-hierarchical worldview).

- The virtuousness of the decision makers or action-takers (Nicomachean virtue ethics) (Aristotle [350 BCE] 2004; see also Crisp and Slote 1997; MacIntyre 1981; Meilaender 1984), on the premise that if individuals have excellence of character—being naturally predisposed to act in the virtuous way,[94] for virtuous reasons—they will habitually decide upon and take virtuous actions, because they will feel pleasure in doing so, thereby becoming flourishing people[95] (the collectivist-egalitarian worldview).

(rule-consequentialism or, in utilitarian terms, rule-utilitarianism) (Scarre 1996; Scheffler 1988).

93 This acceptance follows rule-followers agreement to conform to the rule-giver's expectations, because they have granted him or her (living or dead) moral authority grounded "in respect, honour or (as the Romans called it) piety" (Scruton [1981] 1984, 23; see also Zimmerman 1996, 1998).

94 What justifies a virtuous person's choice of the right course of social action is the shared moral experience and consciousness in a particular socio-cultural *milieu*, which makes relative both morality and its derivative, virtuous social actions (moral relativism) (Foot 1978).

95 Flourishing people develop and exercise their various natural capacities (developmentalism (Kraut 2007))—whether they are physical, sensory, cognitive, affective or social—which is the ultimate human purpose. They would attained Maslow's (1970, 1971) self-actualization or full humanness, achieved by engaging and experiencing life with full absorption; by making life-choices that advance personal growth; by listening to self's inner voice; by taking responsibility for thoughts and feelings; by making most of personal abilities; by uncovering and dispelling psychological defenses; and by seeing people in their best light. They would also have achieved authentic happiness (Seligman 2003) as a result of complete character development, which is the product of cultivating and nurturing the personal strengths of, among other things, originality, valor, integrity, loyalty, kindness and fairness.

- Their accordance with self-referential moral opinions[96] (Cicero [44 BCE] 1971), which express moral (emotional) responses[97] to moral problems and represent particular moral points of view (emotivism) (Hägerström 1964; Stevenson 1944, 1963; Urmson 1968) (the individualist-existential worldview).

The Good Society

According to the neoliberal individualist-libertarian worldview's vision, a good society is the one that stresses the importance of all members of society authoring and accepting responsibility for their own lives. It, thereby, values:

- *Liberty*: So acknowledging the individual's natural right to live, liberty, and property, for, according to Locke ([1690] 1965, 287 emphasis in original), it is natural for individuals to live in "a *State of perfect Freedom* to order their Actions ... as they think fit ... without asking leave, or depending on the Will of any other Man."

- *Self-determination*: So privileging individuals as having the freedom to will whatever they wish to will (Kane 1996; Rand 1965).

- *Personal autonomy and responsibility*: So linking liberty, private property, and the free market to enable individuals to attain whatever they will, for which they must accept personal responsibility, especially for the person they choose to become.

- *Meliorism*: So linking neoliberalism to modernity and to the proposition that the improvement in society's material wellbeing is depends on human effort.

---

96 This makes ethical precepts merely personal opinions; matters of self-determined personal taste: "a virtue has to be our invention, our more personal defence and necessity ... each one of us should devise his own virtue, his own categorical imperatives" (Nietzsche [1888] 1969, 12, see also 1887).

97 These responses reveal moral sentiments—feelings that are essential for moral agency (Gibbard 1990; Hume [1748/1777] 1902, 285-294; Taylor 1985)—premised on moral truths being simply unknowable (moral skepticism) (Bambrough 1979). Haidt (2003) has identified four categories of moral emotions: other-condemning (such as contempt, anger and disgust); other-praising (such as gratitude and moral awe); other-suffering (such as sympathy, compassion and empathy); and self-consciousness (such as guilt, shame and embarrassment).

- *Popular sovereignty*: So emphasizing neoliberalism's link to democracy and to the idea that the authority of government needs to be sustained by the consent of its citizens (contractarianism) [98]; and

- *A minimalist state*: So drawing upon the proposition that a society has the capacity to be self-generating and self-regulating, which justifies government being focused only on "the protection of individual rights, life, liberty and estate" (Locke, cited in Held 1987), so permitting private ends to be peacefully pursued, thereby making the primary governance concern the maximizing of negative freedom, achieved by minimizing any positive freedoms that constrain freedom of choice and action.

This good society perspective is grounded on two foundational normative propositions. The first is that individual sovereignty and personal responsibility are preferable to collective paternalism, even if this effectively means the acceptance of inequalities, provided they are the results of market exchange processes that are fair, free, and voluntary (Nozick 1974). The second is that social justice is all individuals have the same natural and civil rights; are rewarded in accordance with their contribution to society's wellbeing; and are required to look after themselves. So, the neoliberal individualist-libertarian worldview readily denies the acceptability of alternative perspectives of the good society.

- A good society is one where the best interest of its members is advanced by them attaining and sustaining integration into their society. This is one in which everyone has a known place, as social status and social role are both hierarchically determined. Self-interest is thus subordinated to the collective interest, as determined by important others. So, cooperation prevails. Justice is served when all individuals understand: "To do one's own business and not to be a busybody is justice" (Plato [c360 BCE] 1955, IV, 433); when rewards are best distributed according to a set of normative expectations that avoid or diminish felt injustice (rank-order equality) (Eckhoff 1974); and

---

98 "Contractarianism, which stems from Hobbesian line of social contract thought, holds that persons are primarily self-interested, and that a rational assessment of the best strategy for attaining the maximization of their self-interest will lead them to act morally (where the moral norms are determined by the maximization of joint interest) and to consent to governmental authority" (Cudd 2013; see also Vallentyne 1991; Hampton 1986).

when the state has an obligation to intervene and correct any adverse consequences of private actions that do harm to self and others (the collectivist-hierarchical worldview).

- A good society is one where the best interest of its members is advanced by them engaging with others with whom they share a common beliefs, understandings, and values—so giving them a sense of who they are.[99] This group identification encourages cooperation through prosocial behavior.[100] So, their social roles are negotiated, which enables self-interest to be discovered collectively, and free will to be exercised individually in the context of shared meanings about what constitutes virtuous decisions and actions. Justice is served when all individuals act virtuously, as informed by their conscience, which "is in all circumstances an infallible guide to right action" (Russell 1946, 719); when the rewards received do not create illegitimate distinctions between them, as they are all moral equals; and when everyone is treated by the collective with dignity and in accord with principles of social solidarity[101] (the collectivist-egalitarian worldview).

---

99   Insights into the underlying psychology can be gleaned for Hoffer's ([1951] 1989) study of group identification. A person, for example, joins a revolutionary mass movement to take on "holy causes" that allows him or her to become a complete and secure self: "True believers are not intent on bolstering and advancing a cherished self, but are those craving to be rid of an unwanted self. They are followers, not because of a desire for self-advancement, but because it can satisfy their passion for self-renunciation!" (p. 12). Taking on a cause creates a sense of belonging and camaraderie that generates new pride, purpose, confidence, and hope.

100 The elements of a prosocial personality include (Davis 1994; Graziano and Eisenberg 1997; Lerner 1980; Oliner and Oliner 1988; Penner et al. 1995; Rotter 1966; Staub 1974): a high degree of social responsibility; a belief in a world in which people get what they deserve (a just-world belief); and a disposition towards empathy. Adler ([1922] 1924, [1929] 1969, [1933] 1973, [1938] 1943) emphasized the importance of cooperative effort to a person striving for his or her ultimate personality-defining and behavior-directing purpose in life—for perfection or completion. This necessitates him or her acting in accordance with his or her social interest, conceptualized as "a striving for a form of community which must be thought of as everlasting, as it could be thought of if mankind has reached its goal of perfection" (Adler [1933] 1973, 34-35). Essentially, by striving for the goals of others, a person also helps him or herself: "We remain open to the other and welcome him [sic] as a host would welcome a guest, according to his own meaning, whose life is respected as equally valid as one's own" (Brennan 1969, 10).

101 This is the acceptance of mutual dependence that advances a commitment to positive freedom and gives rise to social cohesion.

- The good society is one in which the best interest of its members is advanced when the powers-that-be—whether in government, communities, or business—have only minimal control over their lives; are empathetic to the existential human condition;[102] and tolerant of idiosyncratic individuals exercising their freedom to choose their own fate. So, both social status and social roles are self-determined, because life is lived in an ever-changing state of consciousness, as individuals struggle with their interpretations of others' discernments of them, which ameliorates their capacity to recognize their own unique consciousness. They also struggle to recognize and avoid bad faith—the self-deception that inhibits their search for an authentic life[103] (Sartre [1943] 1957; see also Guignon 2004). Self-interest is, inevitably, subordinated to providence and luck. Justice is served when all individuals accept that interpersonal envy is pointless, because equity is unachievable, so inequality of outcomes are inevitable; when nobody receives the rewards that are the product of exploitation; and when everyone embraces and supports the socially marginalize and alienated, who are unable accept responsibility for what they have made of themselves, as they consider themselves to be

---

102 This is the fate of individuals intent on standing in isolation with an ingrained sense of aloneness and unsureness about whom they are (Ortega y Gasset [1935] 2001)—Wilson's ([1956] 1957, 11 and 118) "hole-in-the-corner man" or "man outside." This total solitude generates detachment—"a sense of strangeness, of unreality" (Wilson ([1956] 1957, 15)—and disconnection—"non-acceptance of life, of human life lived by human beings in a human society ... such a life is a dream, it is not real" (p. 18)—that focuses awareness of the existential human condition—the human soul in its direst straits—with all its paradoxes, ambiguities and absurdities: "there is no significance in human life beyond what humans themselves invest in it" (Davies 1992, 21; see also Janicaud 2005).

103 A Sartrian anecdote exemplifies the meaning of bad faith: "the sincere man tries to convince the homosexual that he should openly acknowledge his inclinations and so leave behind his persistent delusion, rooted in bad faith that he is not a committed pederast but only an admirer of 'a certain conception of the beautiful' (Sartre [1943] 1957, 63). But the champion of sincerity demands that the homosexual objectify himself, turning himself into a thing whereby he must adopt the attitudes and manners of a typical homosexual thereby renouncing the true creation of his own self. This action may then lead to a sympathetic understanding from others who, if only in part, forgive the miscreant. Therefore, this expression of sincerity is an act of bad faith, as the homosexual is denied the freedom to be any other way than the imaginary homosexual being (p. 65). The sincere man has tried to derive merit from his own self-gratification and has abused the parameters of sincerity by manipulating its structure to convince another to be what they are not.

unable to determine their own fate (the individualist-existential worldview).

Conclusion

Neoliberalism worldview offers a distinctive and coherent conceptualization of a philosophy of life that informs and justifies a way of living in the world of persons as it is envisaged, on the basis of its agency-ontological and naturalist-epistemological standpoints—its social-reality disposition. This is the lens through which the world of persons is read—investigated, described, understood, explained, and change predicted. It provides a way of comprehending its actuality. It has, however, its blind spots, because of the constraints embedded in its foundational epistemological and ontological standpoints. This blinds those who see the world of persons through this lens to elements of social reality because of their ignorance, dis-regardfulness, or prejudice.

The narrowness of neoliberalism's individualist-libertarian worldview is highlighted by its rejection of alternative cognitions of the world of persons and alternative worldviews, because they are grounded in different—wrong—epistemological and ontological assumptions. Its agency (individualism) ontology permits the assertion that individuals have complete free will. By so doing, they deny—and thus ignore and dismiss—the causal impact on intentions, actions, and relationships of determining conditions internal to the individual (inherited genetic make-up and unconscious mental states) or external (shared values and beliefs). Its naturalist (rationalism) epistemology permits the assertion that the world of persons is real, material, and objectively explainable as a cause-effect system. By so doing, they deny—and, thus, ignore and dismiss—that it has a knowable metaphysical (ideational) dimension (manifesting as commonly held shared values and beliefs) that, arguably, has causal capacity. Grounded on its naturalist-agency social-reality disposition are neoliberalism's foundational propositions, which distinguish and differentiate its circumscribed—but right—construction of the world of persons. To neoliberalism, its individualist-libertarian worldview, with all its accouterments, is beyond reproach.

3.
NEOLIBERALISM:
MARKET FUNDAMENTALISM

Men follow their sentiments and their self-interest, but it pleases them to imagine that they follow reason. And so they look for, and always find, some theory which, *a posteriori*, makes their actions appear to be logical. If that theory could be demolished scientifically, the only result would be that another theory would be substituted for the first one, and for the same. [104]

Pareto ([1906/1927] 1971, 95)

INTRODUCTION

Market fundamentalism is the belief—a quasi-religious belief—that unregulated free markets—*laissez-faire* capitalism—can solve economic and social problems. Given neoliberalism foundational belief in the presumed efficacy of voluntary action, it is not surprising that it accepts the pre-eminence of market fundamentalism as an integral element of its politico-economic project—the realization of *laissez faire* economic arrangements that permit the untrammeled pursuit of individual self-interest. This reflects the general assumption that the market is emancipatory (but see Block and Somers 2014). Indeed, it is considered the best

> ... possible shell for self-reliance and industriousness. If not interfered with, its self-regulatory mechanisms will ensure that all who want to work will be employed, and thus be able to secure their own welfare. Private life may be wrought with insecurity, danger, and pitfalls; and poverty or helplessness is in principle not unlikely to occur. Yet, this is not the fault of

---

104 In a similar vein, the cosmologist, Professor Max Tegmark, also a graduate of the Stockholm School of Economics, who makes the insightful comment: "Alas, I grew disillusioned [with economics], concluding that economics was largely a form of intellectual prostitution where you got rewarded for saying what the powers that be want to hear" (Tegmark [2014] 2015, 10).

the system, but solely a consequence of an individual's lack of foresight and thrift (Esping-Andersen 1990, 42).

The supremacy of the marketplace is based on an adherence to the values of utilitarian individualism[105]. This has long been under extensive attack by moral philosophers (Gorovitz 1977; Smart and Williams 1973) because of, among other things, its lack of a moral dimension (Blaug 1993) and because it judges morality on the basis of consequences (consequential ethics) and ultimate purposes (teleological ethics) (Kouzmin and Dixon 2005). Hence, it is not possible to distinguish among competing values and preferences—so, the preferences for honesty on a par with a taste for peanut butter (Macpherson 1984, 243).

The purpose of this chapter is to explicate neoclassical economic theory in order to understand how a free market economy is intended to operate. This leads into a discussion of its underpinning economic theory of human behavior. Permitted, then, is the articulation of the circumstances that lead to the failure of the market to allocate resources efficiently and equitably, and to the failure of government to be able to address these market failures. Finally, Neoliberalism's salient economic convictions are identified.

NEOCLASSICAL ECONOMIC THEORY

Neoliberalism accepts, axiomatically, the impeccable logic of neoclassical economic theory, because both are grounded in agency (individualism) ontology and naturalist (rationalism) epistemology. Neoclassical economic theory (Veblen 1900) entered the mainstream of economics thinking in the final third of the nineteenth century.[106] This was a time when the economists' intellectual mindset—driven by a sense of Newtonian physics envy[107]—emphasized the desire for analytical (mathematical) rig-

---

105 This is "[a] form of individualism that takes as given basic human appetites and fears ... and sees human life as an effort by individuals to maximize their self-interest relative to these given ends. Utilitarian individualism views society as arising from a contract that individuals enter into only in order to advance their self-interest. ... Utilitarian individualism has an affinity to a basically economic understanding of existence" (Bellah et al. [1985] 2007, 335-337).

106 The intellectual birth of neoclassical economics is marked by the marginal revolution. Marginalism, as a method of economic analysis, permitted economic phenomena to be conceptualized and analyzed mathematical functions (such as, utility, consumption, and production functions). It has its origins in the thinking of Thünen (1826) and Gossen (1854).

107 The use of the physics metaphor reflects the inspirational effect of the Newtonian—clockwork (deterministic)—perspective of the universe on the

or that gives rise to a deterministic (and thus predictable) system. So, the marketplace was conceptualized as a law-abiding cause-and-effect system (Colander 2000; Ingrao and Israel 1990). In the words of Nadeau (2013), "the atomized immaterial minds of economic actors operate within a field of force (utility) in which the 'natural laws' of economics are presumed to legislate over the choices made by the actors." This was, according to Nadeau (2013),

> ... predicated on assumptions about the relationship between parts (economic actors and firms) and wholes (the market systems) articulated by the creators of neoclassical economics. These assumptions were metaphysical in origins and assumed the guise of scientific truths after the creators of neoclassical economics incorporated them into a mathematical formalism borrowed from mid-nineteenth century physics. This myth was perpetuated in theories that disguised the metaphysical foundations of the assumptions under an increasingly more complex maze of mathematical formalism.

The neoclassical economic model is grounded on a set of *ceteris paribus* assumptions that demarcate the market economy as a closed system.[108] This permitted *a priori* knowledge can be deduced by analyzing the market transactions of self-determining, self-interested, and rational—but under-socialized—utility or profit-maximizing economic actors (Edgworth 1881; Jevons [1871] 1888; Marshall [1890] 1920; Menger [1871] 1994, Walrus 1874; Wicksteed 1910). The underlying proposition is that economic behavior can be represented by how people would (ought to) behave if they were rational and self-interested (see Dixon 2017 for a detailed discussion).

---

mathematician-economists in the latter part of the nineteenth century—Jevons [1871], Menger [1871] 1994, Walras (1974), Edgeworth (1881), Marshall ([1890] 1920), and Wicksteed (1910)—who began the mathematical formalization of a system of economic thought (but see Veblin ([1900] 2011).

108 The economists' desire to endogenize the key exogenous variables embedded in the neoclassical economic model, in order to take into account "the economic significance of nonmarket institution" (Bates 1989, 159)—governmental and social institutions and sociopolitical phenomena—has resulted in the extension of the domain of public choice theory into constitutional economics (Buchanan 1990). The aspiration is for "the scope of economics to be permanently enlarged to include studies in other social sciences...[and so] enable us [economists] to understand better the working of the economic system" (Coarse 1994, 46). For thoughtful critiques of public choice theory's contribution to political science see Green and Shapiro 1994 and Udehn 1996).

To the early neoclassical economists, then, the economy was considered comprehensible because they saw it as being governed by two foundational natural "laws" of economics—"laws of demand" (the quantity demanded of a commodity is inversely related to its price) and "the law of supply" (the quantity of a commodity supplied is directly related to its price). These "laws" were taken to be akin to the "laws of nature",[109] given the status of law even though both defied empirical investigation, so making it impossible to prove their veracity. Their "lawfulness," however, was accepted out of necessity, as they were the only behavioral rules that made logical sense and that permitted economic behavior to be modeled. So, the natural "laws" of economic were axiomatically taken to be self-justifying truth claims, accepted to be beyond doubt as foundational beliefs that needed no further justification. They have long been accepted as providing an appropriate of basis for economic theory that offers hypothetical explanations grounded in exchange (*quid pro quo*) transactions (Becker 1976, but see Dixon 2017; Hollis and Neil 1975; Sen 1987). Thus, with apologies to Aquinas [1266–1273/1948] 1990, 392), "this doctrine does not argue in proof of its principles, which are the articles of faith, but from them it goes on to prove something else." As Weintraub (2007) points out, these ontological and epistemological premises "are not open to discussion in that they define the shared understandings of those who call themselves neoclassical economists, or economists without any adjective."

The behavioral axioms embedded in neoclassical economics have given rise to a methodology that has long been accepted as a sacred tenet of its holy grail by generations of inductees into its mathematical mysteries.[110] It is, of course, a methodology that permitted the building of an analytically elegant mathematical model—a static[111] general equilibrium model

---

109 The idea of laws of nature goes back to Pythagoras and Archimedes in ancient Greece and re-emerged in its modern form in the seventeenth century (Kepler, Galileo, Descartes, and Newton). Descartes ([1637] 1951; [1641] 1961) considered these natural laws to be valid in all places and at all times, and to be based upon generalizations derived from observed regularities that hold without exception and provide predictions. Laws of nature give rise to causal chains that determine inevitable effect—scientific determinism. They are the mathematical reflection of an external reality that exists independently of the observer who perceives it. Their status as laws is, thus, assigned after being tested against how reality really is through repeatable direct experience, not by assignment on the basis of their self self-justifying truth-value.

110 Powers (1992, 13) captures the addictive influence of mathematics: "We experience mathematics as a source of Absolute Authority as a repository of Absolute Truth, uncompromised by mere human interest." (See also Lawson 2012.)

111 Blaug [1962] 1996, xvii) laments neoclassical economics "obsessive preoccupation

that explored the deductive logic of maximization to rendered the final economic verdict on economic efficiency (Arrow and Debreu 1954; see also Debreu 1959; Weintraub 1985). This offers a window—albeit a tinted one—into the working of the economy.[112]

Whether neoclassical economic theory meets the scientific standards by which a theory should be judged is a moot point. Hawking and Mlodinow (2011, 68-69) have identified four such standards:

- elegance (simple, without contradictions, and lawful);[113]

- lack of arbitrary or adjustable factors that enable the theory to match observations (fudge factors);

- consistency with, and power to explain, all existing observations; and

- capacity to make detailed prediction that can, in principle, verify and falsify it.[114]

While neoclassical economic theory satisfies the first and the second condition, it falls well short of satisfying the third and fourth standards. Any theory that cannot meet these demanding conditions is not a strong theory. Nevertheless, neoclassical economic theory can still be a plausible theory, because of its logical consistency. There can be no doubting that any theory can facilitate the gaining of heuristic insights,[115] but if it cannot be tested then how can anyone be sure that it describes, explains, and predicts economic reality, after all reality does not bend to theory. It is, thus, just a legitimate point of view—flight-of-fancy?—theory. Perhaps one destined, in time, to be yet another Huxleyan beautiful theory killed by an ugly fact—the veracity of the quintessential economic actor, described

---

with static equilibrium theory.

112 Some leading economists have challenged the usefulness of general equilibrium theory as a guide to the actual behavior of market economies and as an ideal benchmark (see, particularly, Hahn and Petri 2004).

113 Dirac (1963, 47), a renowned physicist, judged: "It seems that if one is working from the point of view of getting beauty in one's equations, and if one has a really sound instinct, one is on a sure line of success."

114 For an extensive discussion of falsification in economics, particularly neoclassical economics see Blaug [1962] 1996, 689ff.,

115 These insights give rise to heuristics—decision rules-of-thumb—that form part of a heuristic process that facilitates the making of judgments (Kahneman, Slovic, and Tversky 1982; Kahneman and Tversky 1979; Tversky and Kahneman 1974; 1981; 1986).

by Veblen ([1898] 1919, 73) as the "lightning calculator of pleasures and pains, who oscillates like a homogeneous globule of desire of happiness under the impulse of stimuli that shift about the area, but leave him [sic] intact." He—as surely must be the case—exists only as an archetype in the minds of adherents to the holy grail of neoclassical economic theory.

Indeed, neoclassical theory proffers analytical knowledge propositions about economic reality as it ought to be—rational, open to mathematical investigation, observer independent, and lawful. It seeks to explain economic phenomena in a manner that satisfies a disposition toward analytical simplicity and neatness, using a logical (deterministic) chain of cause-and-effect, on the premise that the ultimate true economic reality is—must be—simple, logical, and beautiful, rather than convoluted, contradictory, and ugly. The question begged, of course, is whether there are any reasons to believe that economic reality is as neoclassical economics purport it to be. As Hawking and Mlodinow (2011, 47) remark:

> Economics is ... an effective theory ["a framework created to model certain observed phenomena without describing all the underlying processes" (p. 46)], based on the notion of free will plus the assumption that people evaluate their possible alternative courses of action and choose the best. That effective theory is only moderately successful in predicting [economic] behavior because, as we all know, decisions are often not rational or based on a defective analysis of the consequences of the choice.

Economists, in the neoclassical tradition, are engaged chiefly in deriving the logical implications of their theory. Their notions of value neutrality and their preference for avoiding value judgments, sustain their rational behavior assumption and their predisposition toward instrumental rationality—the need for knowledge that is capable of demonstrating, after all alternative courses of action have been systematically examined and weighed, the most efficient means of pursuing economic efficiency considered to be an indubitable economic goal.

Neoliberalism is, thus, informed by a metaphysical economic theory that defines a hypothetical—point-of-view—economic model, the cornerstone of which is economic efficiency.

Economic Efficiency

This relates to the efficiency of the allocation of resources and of the distribution of outputs, as judged by the Pareto optimality efficiency standard (Coleman 1990).

Pareto Optimality Efficiency Standard

This is the theoretical standard applied to judge whether resources have been allocated so as to maximize the economic wellbeing. The Pareto optimality standard holds that a society's material wellbeing is maximized if, at any time, no individual can be made better off without reducing the material wellbeing of another individual. Thus, a Pareto efficiency improvement occurs if, and only if, it is impossible by the reallocation of resources or the redistribution of the outputs produced, to make one person better off without making someone else worse off (Friedman [1986] 1990).[116] To achieve this, economic efficiency standard requires:

- *The optimal allocation of scarce resources*: This is the configuration of resource utilization patterns that maximize the production of commodities (goods and services) from a given amount of resource inputs (production efficiency), achieved when it is not possible increase production of any commodity without reducing the quantity produced of another commodity.

- *The optimal distribution that output*: This is the configuration of consumption patterns that maximize the total utility or satisfaction derived from the maximized level and configuration of production) (exchange efficiency), achieved when it is not possible increase the total utility by selling any commodity at a higher price to a different buyer (on the premise the price theory of value).

Pareto Efficiency and Distributive Justice

The Pareto efficiency standard is distributionally conservative (Sen 1970),

---

116 A related economic efficiency standard—the Kaldor-Hicks efficiency criteria (Hicks 1939; Kaldor 1939; but see Scitovsky 1941)—combines the Pareto efficiency standard with the compensation principle. This holds that an efficiency improvement occurs if and only if there is net gain in material wellbeing of a society after those whose material wellbeing has been increased are able to compensate fully those whose material wellbeing has been diminished. This notional compensation to losers does not, in fact, have to be paid. In the event of full compensation being paid, and given a costless payment transaction, then the Kaldor-Hicks improvement becomes a Pareto efficiency improvement. This efficiency standard underpins the logic of cost-benefit analysis—the conceptualization, measurement, and comparison of the benefits and costs of a program to determine its economic desirability.

in that it requires that no individual can have his or her material wellbeing increased if that results in the material wellbeing of another individual being reduced. This means that neoclassical economics is blind to any individual characteristics or circumstances that may justify a redistribution of income between individuals in order to correct any need-based distributive injustices. So, a society could be moving toward greater economic efficiency but still have—or, indeed, have more—need-based distributive injustice. As neoliberalism privilege economic efficiency over need-based distributive, it can say nothing about the latter beyond its opportunity cost in terms of economic efficiency forgone.

The Pareto Optimality Key Assumptions

Pareto efficiency requires a set of assumption in order to articulate a definitive and precise standard.

Perfect Competition

This assumption specifies that a Pareto-efficient market is one in which there are enough competing buyers and sellers who are well informed enough to ensure that market price of every commodity is beyond the control of one or a few buyers and sellers. The metaphor implied is the eighteenth century—pre-Industrial Revolution—marketplace, one that would have been familiar to Adam Smith. Drawing upon this axiom, the neoclassical economic proposition is that increasing competition is a means of achieving an improvement in economic efficiency, applicable in both market and non-market setting.

The Price Theory of Value

This theory objectifies (quantifies) the subjective (objectively unmeasurable) concept of consumer satisfaction, or utility, by equating a commodity's utility-value with its price (Friedman [1986] 1990). This is premised on the rational buyer—as the "lone, atomistic and opportunistic bargain-hunter ... who knows the price of everything but the value of nothing" [117] (Archer 2000 4)—always being able and willing to "drive the best bargain, such that he never pays more that he [sic] needs and never settles for less satisfaction than he can get" (Archer 2000 53). So, the neo-

---

117 "What is a cynic?"
   "A man who knows the price of everything and the value of nothing"
   Oscar Wilde ([1892] 1917).

classical economic proposition is that charging of a higher price for any commodity will improve distributive (utility-generating) efficiency.[118]

Rational Actors

The assumption demarcates a distinctive Weberian ideal-type individual (Weber [1903–1917/1949] 1997)—Model of Man[119] (Dixon Dogan, and Sanderson 2009; Hollis 1977; Simon 1957; see also Dahrendorf 1968; Dumont 1970)—a *homo economicus*[120] (Dixon 2010, 2016a, 2016b). This ideal type was articulated quite clearly by Edgeworth (1881, 16, but see 52, 104): "The first principle of Economics is that every agent [buyers (consumers) and sellers (producers)] is actuated only be self-interest."[121] Thus, any actions taken in an exchange transaction are assumed to acts of self-interest (Edgeworth 1881; but see Collard 1975). So, an exchange transaction—mediated as it is in neoclassical economic theory by the intervention of the "heavenly auctioneer" (Kaldor 1939, 13)—involves each economic actor doing as well as they can—maximizing subject to all relevant constraints (Weintraub 2007; see also Mises [1949] 1996). As Sen (1977, 332) points out, however, "[i]t is possible to define a person's interests in such a way that no matter what he does he can be furthering his own interests in every isolated act of choice." Thus, all economic actors are taken to be able to make choices that produce the best possible outcomes for them, given complete and certain knowledge of, and the ability to compute, the consequences of all alternative diverse and heterogeneous courses of action. Indeed, this cognitive assumption mean that any and all *ex ante* decisions made by buyers and sellers necessarily—by definition—gives rise to the best possible—perfectly rational—outcomes for them. It also says nothing about the nature, quality, or morality of their preferences, so the trading in mind-altering drugs, children, or ele-

---

118 Alternatively, no value can be placed on commodities provided in a nonmarket environment for which no price is charged.

119 A Model of Man represent distinctive metaphysical perspective on what it means to be human. It denotes a contending foundation for meaning construction, as sets of cognitions that are coherent and logically consistent. As a stick figure, it is constantly only and ever what it is, a stick figure. If, indeed, an abstract Model of Man becomes concrete—as if it actually describes real people rather than scripted hypothetical role-playing actors—there is always the danger of reification, a phenomenon that Whitehead (1925, 75 and 77) referred to as the fallacy of misplaced concreteness.

120 In Kirchgässner's (2008) sympathetic technical explication of *homo economicus* role in the social sciences, he prefers the correct Latin form *homo oeconomicus*.

121 It was Spinoza who observed: "No virtue can be conceived as prior to this endeavor to preserve one's own being" (cited in Russell 1946, 596; see also Hampshire 2005).

phant tasks are treated no differently to trading in milk, bread, and cheese. Drawing upon this presumption, the neoclassical economic proposition is that individual preferences are the determinants of economic actions.

Thus, any exchange transaction conducted always and necessarily gives rise to the best outcomes for the economic actors involved, because they are the result of them exercising their free will. This is made possible because they have full self-ownership (Hayek 1948, 1960; Humbolt [1791] 1969; Nozick 1974), which make all their social actions voluntary, reflecting their capacity to be unconstrained from any internal or external freedom-limiting determining conditions, and their right to act in a self-interested manner (Rand 1965). Self-interest (Hume [1739–1740] 1978, [1748/1751/1777] 1902; Smith [1759] 1976, [1776] 1976), then, means that exchange transactions are the product of utility calculations, reflecting a numerical representation of ordered preference sets (Sen 1977, 1987), on the premise that economic agents are capable of identifying their preferred exchange outcomes from their entire ordered preference set. Such preference sets embody goal completeness, goal selfregardingness, and goal priorities, reflecting *homo economicus*'s self-centered welfare, self-welfare goal, and self-goal choices (Sen 1985, 342-343, 347). Indeed, "[a] person is given *one* preference ordering, and as and when the need arises, this is supposed to reflect his [sic] interests, represent his welfare, summarize his idea of what should be done, and describe his actual choices and behavior" (Sen 1977, 335, emphasis in original). *Homo economicus* have come to be typified as "rational and egoistic with a short-term mentality" (Mohammadian 2011, 305). As the "heavenly auctioneer" mediates every exchange transactions, economic actors are not required to interact personally during any exchange process. All they need to be able to do is to respond to price signals.[122] The rational actors embedded in neoclassical economic theory are, thus, individuated exclusively on the basis of their binary personal preference ranking for different uses of their resource endowment (see, for instance, Arrow and

---

122 Marketplaces in neoclassical economics are, according to Kaldor (1939, 13, emphasis added) "highly artificial abstractions from the real world but the truth that the theory conveys—that prices provide the guide to all economic action—*must* be fundamentally true, and its main implication that free markets secure the best results *must* also be true. ... But the basic assumptions in all this—that prices are very important in the working if a market economy—is rarely, if ever questioned. Yet it is precisely this over-emphasis on the role of the price system that I regard as the major shortcoming of modern neoclassical economics, particularly the Walrasian version of it." In essence: "sellers are price-makers and quantity-takers, and not, as Walrasian equilibrium theory supposes, price-takers and quantity-makers" (Kaldor 1985, 31).

Debreu 1954). So, they are all strangers to each other. *Homo economicus* is a perfectly adequate depiction of the behavior of anonymous buyers and sellers individuals-as-strangers—for the purpose of the answering neoclassical economic theory's hypothetical question: can a positive price vector be determined that will equate the aggregate quantities demanded and supplied of each commodity, item by item, in an economy? But is this "thin" *homo economicus* an adequate typification of a person engaged in exchange transactions in both a market and non-market setting?

THIN HOMO ECONOMICUS: THE CRISIS OF PERSONAL IDENTITY

The ontology of "thin" *homo economicus* has been anthropomorphized by Midgley (2003, 91) as

> [a]n isolated will guided by an intelligence, arbitrarily connected to a rather unsatisfactory array of feeling, and lodged, by chance, in an equally unsatisfactory body. Externally, this human being stands alone. Each individual's relations to all others was optional, to be arranged at will by contract. It depends on the calculation of the intellect about self-interest and on the views of that interest freely chosen by will.

They are, thus, blind to any individuating properties embodied in self and others. This deficiency in the theorizing of the individual in economics has become the focus of a contemporary esoteric discourse around Davis (2003, 2008, 2011), suggesting that the under-theorized *homo economicus* have a personal identity crisis. Of particular interest is Davis's focus on their problematic sense of self-identity—their individuation (in essence, does an unobservable ordered preference set alone demarcate one individual from another?) and their problematic self-continuity—their re-identification (essentially, can an individual who has changed his or her ordered preference set be re-identified as the same individual?). Self-continuity is contingent upon three factors: physiological continuity, conscious state continuity, and sense-of-self continuity (Martin and Barresi 2003; Noonan 2003; Perry 1975; Rorty 1976; Searle 2004).

Physiological Continuity

This is the spatio-temporal continuity of a recognizable body. The issue here is that economic theory does not require *homo economicus* to have a differentiated physical body. All that matters is that their behavior in an exchange transaction can be observed, which reveal their response to price signals, thereby revealing their preferences. As their ordered preference sets is the sole basis of their self-identity, they are blind to their own idiosyncratic physiological facticities. This makes problematic their individuation—because their ordered preference sets provides only a very narrow basis for their individuation, because they are only intermittently knowable to others-as-strangers from their transient transactional behaviors—and their re-identification—because, in the absence of an identifiable physiological continuity, any changes in that preference set make them a different person, except to themselves.

Conscious State Continuity

This is the continuous first-person awareness, because of the memory of consciously experienced past unique personal experiences. But, of course, in the absence of an idiosyncratic body, *homo economicus*'s flow of memorable personal experiences would, no doubt, be disjointed, limited to memories of the occasional instance of very successful or, indeed, very unsuccessful, wheeler-dealings in their exchange transactions with impersonal others-as-strangers. The issue here is that economic theory does not require *homo economicus* to have conscious state continuity, as they only have to be a discontinuous logical responder to price signals in particular markets while engaged in a particular market transaction at a particular point in time. Economic theory does not permit them to reflect on their past experience to learn how to get the best possible deal in a future interpersonal exchange transaction process. In between exchange transactions they cease, in Cartesian terms, to evidence any continued conscious existence.

Sense-of-Self Continuity

This is the continuous first-person sense of what it is to be "me." But being a mind without a differentiated physical body, *homo economicus*'s sense-of-self continuity depends entirely upon the continuity of their ordered preference set. Economic theory requires *homo economicus* to have only an ordered preference set that "represent [their] welfare" (Sen 1977, 335) at the time of engaging in an exchange transaction process. Their sense of self-continuity is thus also problematic.

HOMO ECONOMICUS ELABORATED

The agency (individualism) ontological and naturalist (rationalism) epistemological foundations of neoclassical economic theory permit an elaboration of *homo economicus* (Dixon 2003; 2010; 2016a; 2016b; Dixon, Dogan, and Sanderson 2009). To them, *my world is what is logically true about the world.* They are the actors whose life's ends are self-determined—*I will do whatever I judge to be in my self-interest*—and the means of their achievement are knowable—*my priorities are determined by what I expect of myself; my future concerns are determined by what I decide is important for me*; and *what I am committed to is depends on what is in my best interest.* They, thus, would consider themselves to be essentially free individuals, free from any debilitating (genetic) pathologies and (unconscious) self-deception, and from any external interference of others, whether individually or collectively.

Homo economicus would, of course, have a self (Rosenberg 1979), albeit one that is under socialized, being autonomous and reference-free (Davis 2003, 2008, 2011): a lone self, with a reluctance to establish social relationships that would demarcate features of their relational self, thereby elaborating their self-identity (Erikson 1963, 1964). This aloneness sustains the supremacy of individual hedonism, a proposition that prompted Sen (1977, 336) to conclude: "The purely economic man ['decked in the glory of his one all-purpose preference ordering'] is indeed close to being a social moron."

Indeed, *homo economicus* are "assiduous builder[s] of networks for private gain" (Douglas 1994, 47): their place in the world of persons is, thus, self-determined—*I am what I want to be.* This makes them blind to others' physiological or ideational attributes, disinterested in their acquired social and cultural capital, and oblivious to the social impressions they portray to them. They would not be able to discriminate between Mills and Clark's (1982) exchange relationships (involving superficial social relationships in which people strive for maximum rewards) and communal relationships (involving close or intimate social relationship in which people are governed by emotional concerns). In both instances, their social actions, interactions, and the resultant social relationships would be driven by instrumental concerns grounded in their egoistic motivations. Becker (1976, 131) counters this by advancing the proposition that "forward-looking individuals consider how their choices affect the probability of developing rewarding emotional relations", but, if course, not so as to affect their intentional mental states and thus their preference sets.

Indeed, as *homo economicus* see no need to establish relationships that elaborate their social identity, their disposition is to negotiate with "other individuals" (Watkins 1968)—as individuals-as-strangers—so as to build the necessary exchange relationships that will best be advanced their interests. To this end, they only need to know how others can advance or hinder their interests. Their granting of trust would follow an assessment of the costs and benefits of so doing (Gambetta 1988). They are, thus, quintessentially, always and entirely centered on being ever vigilant about promoting their self-interest by taking only social actions that produce the greatest beneficial outcome for them.

Homo economicus are continually striving to discover knowledge that will unearth opportunities for advancement. Their meta-life-goal is to accumulate wealth, for they have a need for "the achievement of things ... so that they are recognized and acclaimed by others" (Cutting and Kouzmin 1997, 90-91; see also Hollis 1989, 179)). Riso (1987, 26) concludes that such people are "out of touch with [their] feelings, projecting an image which substitutes for genuine feelings." Wealth is their currency of self-hood, which makes them prone to anxiety about their inability to continue acquiring the wealth that is their primary source of self-esteem. Their moral worth can, therefore, only be measured by the social actions undertaken that have produced personally favorable material outcomes. This, then, establishes the form of the social interactions that they believe to be necessary in order to satisfy their self-determined wishes and desires.

Homo economicus judge that the net rewards of any social engagement would be maximized if they bargaining for their position in all social relationship. The time and resources investment in social relations are expected to generate a return (Lin 2001) and to justify their freeriding on the personally beneficial social actions of others-as-strangers. They consider that the acceptance of overriding pre-eminence of self, self-interest, personal freedom, and freedom of choice in any social relationship is preliminary to any social-role engagement. This means that they are intent on negotiating their incorporation into a social unit and their acceptance of any social roles that that implies. The right to maximum freedom to negotiate with whomever they wish is taken to be inalienable.

Homo economicus's inalienable right to negotiate their exchange relationships gives them a preference for a very low level of group incorporation.

This is because they reject the idea of any constraints being imposed by others-as-strangers on either their decision sovereignty or their freedom to act. Such social relationships, they would presume, are with actors who are also in full control of their destiny and continually striving to unearth opportunities for material self-gain, and so are competitors.

Psychologists describe relationships between strangers as secondary, because they are relatively short-lived, involve limited interaction and minimal emotionality, and have clear rules governing interaction and well-defined social roles (Reber 1995). They could well be Orlofsky's (1976) stereotyped individuals who have many superficial and utilitarian relationships without any emotional commitment.

Homo economicus, therefore, seeks out "ego-focused groups," a feature of which is their "exploitability (through inherent fluidity)" (Schwarz and Thompson 1990, 66). These they conceptualized as aggregations of atomistic individuals-as-strangers, characterized by the weakness of collective's claims over its members, by a disinterested in rituals because there is no need to reaffirm the social reality of group life (Douglas 1970), and by no one having a preordained place, thereby privileging negotiations, competition, and contractual relationships. Indeed, as Messner (1997, 176) notes: "There is in principle no difference between contract and organization: organizations are interpreted as the sum of contractual arrangements." So, they demand maximum freedom to negotiate with whom they please, accepting no effective group boundaries and no constraints on their social interactions.

The group that *homo economicus* expects to engage with is, then, one in which the only commitment is only to one's self, and no one has a preordained place—*I determined my place in the group on the basis of my self-interest, and that determines my fate.* Indeed, whether they are willing to share and collaborate with others, and so engage in collective actions, depends on the strength of their belief that their material wellbeing is contingent upon such cooperative interdependence—"generous emotional dispositions account for the voluntary creation of public goods and for angry men" (Archer 2000, 67)—which means that "the relevant features of the social context are, so to speak, built into the individual" (Lukes 1968, 125). If, however, self-interest prevails and, as a consequence competition overwhelms cooperation, then there is a possibility that a hypercompetitive attitude is adopted toward others, all of whom come to be considered as malevolent and untrustworthy (Horney 1937, 1945).

A hypercompetitive attitude manifests as incessant and indiscriminate competition for the purpose of attaining personal superiority (power) over other people: "The psychic result ... is a diffuse hostile tension between individuals" (Horney 1937, 285-286), characterized by the presence of dogmatism, manipulation, exploitation, aggression, derisiveness, even humiliation. When this attitude permeates every area of that person's life, it is fertile ground for neurotic psychiatric disorders characterized by anxiety, depression, or hypochondria. Adler ([1933] 1973) described this striving for personal superiority as a destructive lifestyle that leads to such neuroses. Social psychologists refer to situations where the interest of self and others are in conflict as social dilemmas (Komorita and Parks 1995).

In terms of Riesman's (1950) inner-other directedness dichotomy, *homo economicus* would have an inner-directedness orientation, preferring to act independently and in accordance with their personal moral codes that are grounded in goodness of action. Yet, as Hollis (1989, 179; see also Davis 2003) insightfully remarks: "A rational agent's ultimate reference group cannot be himself alone. He needs some group to identify with in relationships whose flourishing is a measure of his flourishing." In essence, *homo economicus* are seeking to achieve material success in order to be recognized as successful by other materially successful people, but not so as to make them significant others in terms of the development of their personal and social identities.

On Levenson's (1981, 49-52) locus-of-control spectrum, *homo economicus* would definitely be at the internalist end—among those who accept responsibility for their social actions and consider that they are in control of their lives. Material wealth is, thus, the *homo economicus's* currency of selfhood, which makes them prone to anxiety about their inability to acquire material wealth

Central to the credibility of *homo economicus* is, then, the veracity of two firmly held beliefs. The first is that people can, in the Hobbesian tradition, author their lives in their own self-interest through choice:

> The right of nature ... is the liberty each man hath, to use his own power, as wills himself, for the preservation of his own nature, that is to say, of his own life; and consequently, of doing anything, which in his own judgment, and reason, he shall conceive to be the aptest means thereunto (Hobbes [1651] 1962, 103).

So, any social engagement is predicated on determining their roles and relationships with others in ways that advances their self-interest. The second belief is that individuals can and do, in the Machiavellian and Baconian tradition, act intentionally to change their future. Indeed, Adler ([1929] 1969, 1) considered that a person can only be understood teleological, in terms of his or her ultimate purpose in life, whether consciously determined or not. This, he saw, explained "that mysterious creative power of life—that power which expresses itself in the desire to develop, to strive and to achieve and even to compensate for defects in one direction by striving for success in another." *Homo economicus* are, thus, continually striving to advance their immediate material wellbeing in a world that is a real, material, and objectively knowable cause-and-effect system.

On the Universal Applicability of Homo Economicus as an Ideal-type Individual

As an archetype *homo economicus* does not do justice either

- to the profuseness of ways people interconnect meaning, purpose, and action as they strive to perceive the world of persons as a meaningful totality, both as it is and as it might be;

- to the profundity of their emotional responses to people and situations; or

- to the proliferousness of their capabilities in their various social and economic roles.

THE CONDUCT OF EXCHANGE TRANSACTIONS: A FRAMEWORK WITH APPLICATIONS

How the actors engage in *quid pro quo* exchange transactions—whether in a market or non-market setting[123]—depends upon what is happening in their minds (Simmel 1900): how they interconnect meaning, purpose, and action. The challenge that confronts them is to make sense of the market or non-market arena in which the exchange transaction takes place (the transactional arena), and the attitudes expressed and actions taken by others present, thereby "becoming aware of a possibility [for

---

123 Simmel (1900, 82) long ago recognized that exchange was a fundamental element of all human interactions that shapes human life.

action in it] against the background of reality" (Wertheimer 1961, 141). This allows them to take the meaning from that arena (acquire patterns of thought—truths and understandings—and emotions aroused)—their *habitus* (Bourdieu 1990). From this comes their set of self-evidently (unquestionably) true beliefs about it—their *doxa* (Bourdieu 1990).

So, before embarking on any exchange transaction, individuals must have two cognitions. The first is a set of exchange expectations or goals—their desired exchange outcomes and their preferred way of conducting themselves in a particular transactional arena. Their desired exchange outcomes are grounded in their intentional mental states—their preference sets that reflect their interests, represent their welfare, summarizes their idea of what should be done, and describe their actual choices (Sen 1977, 335). Their preferred mode of transactional conduct is contingent upon how they decide to engage with others in that transactional arena. To any transactional arena, the actors bring:

- *How they see themselves*: This is their self-concept,[124] which is grounded on their physiological facticities, their sense of identity, and a set of Jungian "masks" (Strauss 1959) that enable them to play the roles necessary to meet other people's demands of them (Haselbach 1994, 45-46) in a particular transactional arenas.

- *How they see themselves in that arena*: This is their desired social role in that particular arena—the social impressions they wish to portray to others, perhaps contingent upon the role expectations others have of them (Goffman 1959, 1961, 1963).

---

124 In terms of their bodily self (bodily experiences and senses—Hume's ([1739-40] 1978) bundle-of-perceptions perspective); their self-identity (characteristics that give a sense of uniqueness combined with a sense of continuity and sameness); their desired self (desired personal characteristics); their self-extension (sense of identification with external objects, both physical and human); their self-objects (mental representation of significant others to be copied, admired, idealized and mirrored); their self-sentiment (prime, integrating motivations); their self-esteem (feelings of self-worth); self-objectification (ability to perceive their own capacities and limitations); their presenting self (way of presenting self to others); their self-image (learned role expectations and future role aspirations), which may not be consistent with his or her social image (what others perceive about them) or social self (what they reveals to others); their self-as-rational-coper (awareness of their problem-solving and goal-achieving capacities); their self-as-knower (capacity to unify self); and their true self (self-concept that is in harmony with their experiential feelings) (Allport 1955; Baumeister 1993; Bermúdez, Marcel, and Eilan 1995; Cattell 1965; Kohut 1971; McGuire and McGuire 1982; Rogers 1961; Rosenberg 1979; Shoemaker 1963).

- *What they believe has causal capacity in the transactional arena*: This is their belief about what exists that can impose behavioral constraints on them, be they agential (genetic, physiological or psychological), structural (economic, socio-cultural, linguistic, or dialogical), and/or relational (interpersonal) determining conditions.

- *Their perceptions of the other actors' attributes*: These can be associated with gender, age, physical completeness, and ethnicity—some of which are attributable to neurobiological structures and processes that are the product of their inherited genetic make-up (Buss 1999)—and with their ideational standpoints (their ideas and beliefs).

The second cognition is a firm belief that their exchange goals can be meet by engaging in a transaction process in their particular preferred way. This is grounded in their understanding of the fundamental qualities of the transactional arena in which the transaction process will take place; the motivations of the actors engaged in the transactional process; and the envisaged transactional process or course of the exchange interactions. These considerations become important when a mutually beneficial closure of an exchange transaction involves the achievement of exchange outcomes that are shaped by the transactional process, as determined by the actors' physiology and ideational standpoints, and/or by their network of interpersonal relationships, all of which can impose constraints on whether and how they conduct the exchange transaction. Their firm belief has to be that their exchange goals can best be met by engaging in a transaction process in their particular preferred way.

Homo Economicus's Preferred Mode of Exchange

When viewed through the naturalist-agency lens, exchange transactions are opportunities for *homo economicus* to advance their immediate material wellbeing. When engaging in a transactional process, their sense of being "a lone self" permits their self-interest to dominate. Indeed, they have the capacity to exercise their free will, with no acknowledged complicity of other people and in isolation of any social, cultural, or linguistic influences. Their exchange goals are, thus, governed exclusively by their self-determined intentional mental states that underpin their preference sets. They conduct their exchange transactions in an arena perceived to be material in form, with objectively factual qualities, one that is conceptualized as a cause-and-effect system that is decipherable by the application of deductive reasoning, giving rise to truths of logic. As understood through this lens, exchange transactions are conducted on a voluntary and impersonal basis. So, the desired transactional outcomes and the preferred mode of transactional conduct are both the product of hedonistic self-interest calculations.

On the Universal Applicability of Homo Economicus

The universal applicability *homo economicus*'s any exchange transaction is brought into question by their two salient attributes:

- their autonomy and self-centeredness (having self-determined and self-interested intentional mental states); and

- their indifference to the human attributes of others (whether physiological or ideational), since all the others involved are strangers, who play no role in the development of their individual and social selves.

The analytical aptness of *homo economicus* comes into question when the analytical objective is to explain exchange transactions occurring in a non-market setting—such as an organizational, group, or family. In these settings, the presumption that the exchange transactions are only between individuals-as-strangers is naïve because the people involved may have mutually recognized social relationships because they have previously engaged in focused social interactions (Giddens 2001, 92). This means that others have become individuals-as-familiars—acquaintances, colleagues, friends, or even intimates (Orlofsky 1976), each with distinguishing human attributes that reflect their personal and social identities. So, where the actors' desired exchange outcomes and preferred exchange processes are shaped by determining conditions—whether external (economic, social, cultural, linguistic, discursive, or interpersonal), or internal (genetic, physiological and psychological make-up)—the free will premise underpinning *homo economicus*'s decisions and actions is compromised.

Alternative exchange process preferences can be deduced as speculations about how the Models of Man embedded in other worldview would prefer to conduct exchange transactions (Dixon 2017). These alternative exchange transaction modes cannot, of course, be accommodated in neoclassical economic theory.

Homo Hierarchus's Preferred Mode of Exchange

Homo hierarchus is the archetypal individual (Model of Man) who sees the world of persons through the naturalist-structuralist lens. They would consider exchange transactions to be opportunities for the building of relationships with important others who can advance their future interests. When engaging in a transactional process, their sense of social self requires them to classify all others involved by their importance to self. Once so categorized, their duties and obligations towards them become clear. Trust is extended only on the basis of a commonly held set of innate moral values (Uslaner 2002).

For the closure of an exchange transaction, the key issue for *homo hierarchus* is that the final exchange outcome is acceptable to important others. This requires that they understand what important others expected of them, by drawing inferences from their comments and observed behaviors; that they have resolved any ethical issues by reference to what is right or wrong (Fried 1978); and that the closure decision, once agreed upon, is taken to imply all the objective information they need to make a satisfactory decision in accordance with hypothetical consent (Schwarz and Thompson 1990) to whatever unknown past or present actions have brought about the mutually beneficial *quid pro quo* exchange.

Thus, *homo hierarchus's* conduct in the transactional process reflects both their self-regarding aspirations and their other-regarding duties. Their aim is to ensure that a satisfactory exchange outcome is produced and that the transactional process, itself, builds their relationships with important others. This, they anticipate, will enhance their immediate social status—their currency of selfhood—and, by adding to their personal stock of social capital, their performance in subsequent exchange transactions in this arena. Created is a set of social proprieties behind which they can safely entrench themselves, satisfied for a little longer that their behavior is beyond reproach, thereby allaying their fears of a lowering of their social status.

Homo Sociologicus's Preferred Mode of Exchange

Homo sociologicus is the archetypal individual (Model of Man) who sees the world of persons through the hermeneutic-structuralist lens. They would consider exchange transactions to be opportunities for designing and delivering avowed commitments to like-minded others who can advance their future interests. When engaging in a transactional process, their sense of being a dialogical self (Hermans 2004) preoccupies them with delivering those avowed commitments. Trust is extended only on the basis of sufficient goodwill being built up through discourse (Ring and van de Ven 1992, 1994).

For the closure of an exchange transaction, the key issue for *homo socio-logicus* is that the final exchange outcome is a worthy one. This requires that they have all the information they need to make a decision that would be in accord with the commitments they share with the like-minded others; that they have resolved any ethical issues by reference to what a worthy person would think or do (Aristotle [350 BCE] 2004); and that the closure decision, even when agreed upon, does not imply their consent to whatever unknown past or present actions have brought about the mutually beneficial *quid pro quo* exchange, which can only be achieved if everyone concerned or affected by those actions gives their direct consent.

Thus, *homo sociologicus*'s conduct in the transactional process reflects the commitments they have expressed to like-minded others. Thus, the process needs to ensure that a worthy exchange outcome is produced, and that the process, itself, builds their relationships with like-minded others. This, they expect, will give them recognition and acclaim for honoring their social vows—their currency of selfhood—and, by adding to their personal stock of social and cultural capital, enhance their performance in subsequent exchange transactions in that arena. Created is a sense of self-righteousness behind which they can safely entrench themselves, satisfied for a little longer that their behavior is beyond reproach, thereby allaying their social rejection anxieties.

Homo Existentialis's Preferred Mode of Exchange

Homo existentialis is the archetypal individual (Model of Man) who sees the world of persons through the hermeneutic-agency lens. They would consider exchange transactions to be opportunities for building their relationships with dependable others they considered able to advance their future interests. When engaging in a transactional process, they are uneasy and doubt-ridden "becoming selves" preoccupied with scanning their stock of taken-for-granted knowledge, derived from past experiences and honed instincts—their natural attitudes (Husserl [1931] 1960)—to decide how best to conduct this exchange transaction. Trust is extended only on the basis of trust-inducing personal experience.

For the closure of an exchange transaction, the key issue for *homo ex-*

istentialis is that the final exchange outcome be the most plausible one for them. This requires that they have all the information they need to make decisions that their experience and honed instincts tells them are most plausible; that they have been resolved any ethical issues by reference to what they consider to be in accord with their personal moral code (Bambrough 1979, 14); and that a closure decision, once agreed, does not imply consent (Schwarz and Thompson 1990) to whatever unknown past or present actions have brought about the mutually beneficial *quid pro quo* exchange, because no past actions can be justified simply by unaffected others agreeing to them.

Thus, *homo existentialis*'s conduct in the transactional process reflects their need to wearily and cautiously do what they think is most plausible. This means engaging, inspirationally, in random search behaviors—"how do I know what I think until I see how I act" (Weick 1979, 56)—to determine the most plausible exchange goals they can expect to achieve. Indeed, this may reflect spur-of-the-moment decisions (Kane 1985, 16) and actions that are the product of unconscious responses Thus, the process needs to ensure that a plausible exchange outcome is produced, and that the exchange transaction builds their relationships with dependable others they judge to be able to advance their interests in the future. This, they consider, vindicates their weary and cautious approach, so justifying their social cynicism—their currency of selfhood—while enhancing their performance in subsequent exchange transactions in this arena. Created is a sense self-satisfaction, behind which they can safely entrench themselves, satisfied for a little longer that they are, indeed, survivors against all odds.

The Economic Theory of Government

The economic rationale for the minimalist role of the state has its foundations in the concepts of market failure and government failure.

Market Failure

This is a situation where markets cannot achieve the maximum material wellbeing possible for a society (economic inefficiency), where consumer do not know what is in their best interest (flawed consumer sovereignty), or where the market cannot achieve a just distribution of income (needs-based distributive injustice).

Economic Inefficiency

This is the market's failure to achieve the Pareto optimality efficiency standard because it is not being able to use the given and limited set of resources of a society to maximize output and to distribute that output to maximize the material wellbeing of that society's members. This can be attributed to a variety of factors.

- *Imperfect Competition*: This occurs when there are not enough sellers (monopoly, monopolistic competition, oligopoly market situations) and buyers (monopsony or oligopsony market situations) to ensure that market price of every commodity (including labor and capital) is beyond the control of one or a few buyers and sellers,[125] so preventing rent-seeking behavior.[126] This results in prices being sub-optimal relative to the Pareto-efficient price vector.

- *Externalities*: These are the external costs (negative externalities) and external benefits (positive externalities) that are the byproduct of the production or consumption of a commodity (Caplan 2008):

  - *External costs*: These arise when costs are incurred by people as a byproduct of:

    - a supplier's production process (production external costs) that go uncompensated and are, thus, not included as a production cost; or

    - a buyer's consumption process (consumption external costs) that go uncompensated are, thus, not included as a consumption cost.

  This results in the over-production or over-consumption of the commodity concerned relative to its Pareto-efficient level of production and consumption.

---

125 As Smith's [1776] 1976, Pt II) pointedly remarked: "People of the same trade seldom meet together, even for merriment and diversion, but the conversation ends in a conspiracy against the public, or in some contrivance to raise prices."

126 Rent-seeking involves the efforts by economic agents to obtain economic rent (a premium income paid to a factor of production that is in excess of that needed to keep it employed in its current use) attained by manipulating the market (by restricting competition) or the sociopolitical environment (such as, by lobbying for government subsidies or for the imposition of regulations on competitors) in which the economic activity takes place (Krueger 1974; Tullock 1967).

- *External benefits*: These arise when benefits are provided to people, as a byproduct of:

  - a supplier's production process (production external benefits) for which they do not pay, and are, thus, not included as revenue; or

  - a buyer's consumption process (consumption external benefits) for which they do not pay, and are, thus, not included in his or her utility reckoning.

  This results in the under-production or under-consumption of the commodity concerned relative to its Pareto-efficient level of production and consumption.

- *Public Goods*: These are commodities that are jointly consumed by multiple consumers, without detriment, which makes their consumption non-rivalrous, so no one cannot be excluded from their consumption (pure public goods). This means that no price can be charged before consumption can take place, so the market has no incentive to provide such commodities (Cowen 1993).

- *Lack of Property Rights*: This occurs when there is an absence of resource property rights, which enables producers to access freely a resource—*making it* a common property resource. The absence of a property right can be because it is too expensive, or physically impossible, to establish such an ownership right. So, because these resources are freely available, the market is incentivized to overuse them in production processes relative to their Pareto-efficient usage if market prices were paid.

- *Information Asymmetry*: This occurs when in a market exchange transaction one party has more information than the other party, because it is not in the interests of the former to share complete information with the latter. So, either a buyer or a seller is not well informed enough to ensure that market price is not beyond the control of the other party. This results in prices being suboptimal relative to the Pareto-efficient price vector.

According to the theory of second best,[127] these sub-optimal market out-

---

127 The theory of the second best (Lipsey and Lancaster 1956) holds if one Pareto

comes cannot be readily corrected by public intervention, without the prospect of further reducing economic efficiency (Lipsey and Lancaster 1956; but see Arrow [1969] 1983).

Flawed Consumer Sovereignty

This occurs when consumers do not know what is in their best interest because of ignorance or short sightedness. So, if utility value of a commodity is, according to experts, either

- underestimated, then its consumption levels would be below that which those experts think they should be (*merit goods*); or

- overestimated, then its consumption levels would be above that experts which think they should be (*de-merit goods*).

Public intervention to rectify these inferior outcomes of flawed consumer sovereignty would be Pareto inefficiency, so the opportunity cost of that intervention is the forgone economic efficiency, which is an economic deterrent to any public intervention.

Needs-based Distributive Injustice

This is market's inability to achieve an equitable distribution of income, determined in accordance with a needs-based distributive justice principle. Such a principle has three key dimensions: What should be subject to redistribution (such as the consumption goods and services, income, wealth, or opportunities)? Who or what should subjects of the distribution (natural persons or groups of persons (such as, families and communities)? On what basis should the redistributed be made (such as, equally to all in a given category of need or according to individual needs)?

Any redistributive public intervention to correct these needs-based distributive injustices would be Pareto inefficiency, so the opportunity cost of that intervention is the forgone economic efficiency, which is an economic deterrent to any redistributive public intervention.

---

optimality condition cannot be satisfied because of market failure, the next-best solution may cause further moves away from Pareto optimality. The implication being that any public intervention intended to correct a market failure, so as to increase economic efficiency, may actually further decrease economic efficiency.

Government Failure

Neoclassical economics, as with its offspring, public choice theory, has acquired the classical Benthamite distaste for the public sector. The behavioral presumption made is that each actor on the politico-administrative stage is "a maximizer of some value and who acts to obtain it in a purposeful and non-randomized manner" (Simon [1945] 1982) cited in Doron 1992, 339). Thus, they will always be self-serving whenever there is an incentive and an opportunity to be so. The seminal Downsian economic theory of government (Downs 1957, 11) models the implications of the rational behavior premise

> ... on the assumption that every government seeks to maximize political support.[128] We further assume that the government exists in a democratic society where periodic elections are held, that its primary goal is re-election, and that election is the goal of those parties now out of power. At each election, the party which receives the most votes (though not necessarily a majority) controls the entire government until the next election, with no intermediate votes either by the people as a whole or by a parliament.

Riker (1982, 98) elaborated: "citizens are rational in the sense that they seek to maximize utility from governmental actions and ... [political] parties are rational in the sense that they seek to maximize votes." So, politicians would be irrational in that they did not seek re-election so as to fulfill their goal of changing their society according to their ideals or to pursuit their economic interests. This means that altruism, like heroism, is re-cast as a complex expression of self-interest (Hirshleifer 1977; Margolis 1982). The public sector is, thus, constantly under suspicion of being inefficient, wasteful, and, so, not giving value for money, because the absence of any automatic disciplining mechanism—market forces—permits rent-seeking behavior by bureaucrats, their clients, and politicians who govern them (Terrell 1993). This behavioral presumption is a fundamental tenet of the neo-institutional economics, which defines an organization as a stable collection of interrelated rules and incentives (Dunsire 1988; Weimer 1995) and postulates a theoretical framework for

---

128 Riker (1962, 33), challenged this proposition:

Downs assumed that political parties (a kind of coalition) seek to maximize votes (membership). As against this, I shall attempt to show that they seek to maximize only up to the point of subjective certainty of winning. After that point they seek to minimize, that is, to maintain themselves at the size (as subjectively estimated) of a minimum winning coalition.

institutional design in terms of contracting between parties, the governance of such contracting, and the conferring of property rights.

The ontological roots of neo-institutional economics lie in transaction-cost theory (Coase 1937, 1994; Commons 1931; Williamson 1979, 1985, 1993) and in agency theory (Alchian and Demsetz 1972; Jensen and Meckling 1976). Transaction-cost theory considers an organization to be an information-gathering and information-processing mechanism created to obviate the need to re-negotiate, continually, market-transaction contracts that are unavoidably incomplete due to environmental uncertainty (Bryson and Ring 1990; Williamson 1985). Agency theory sees an organization as a governance mechanism over-sighting the hierarchical contractual relationship between the "principal" (such as an owner in the private sector or politicians in the public sector), who is the risk-taker in an environment facing exogenous uncertainty (Fama 1980; Fama and Jensen 1983a, 1983b; Jensen and Meckling 1976). He or she, however, delegate decision-making discretion to an "agent" (such as a manager), who controls access to information, so creating the potential for organizationally inefficient information asymmetry, which arises when some members of an organization have information they can withhold from others (Moe 1984, 1991, 1995).

This principal-agent problem is considered to be especially significant in public sector organizations. This is because the non-transferability of ownership discourages politicians—as "principals" or even multiple "principals" who may have conflicting and unstable political demands (Moe 1991))—from specialization in their ownership responsibilities resulting in less-effective monitoring of organizational management (De Alessi 1983). Emerging from these conceptualizations of an organization is a concern about opportunism in public administration, the product of the self-serving—rent seeking, even deceitful and dishonest—behavior by bureaucrats, their clients, and their masters—politicians (Johnston and Kouzmin 1998). This opportunism is created either because environmental uncertainty makes contracts incomplete or because "principals" cannot effectively monitor the behavior of their "agents", who do not share identical interests with them, and who have information that is not accessible to them. This line of reasoning gives rise to the proposition that there is the inherent tendency for bureaucrats to make decisions and to implement policies in ways that that are consistent with their own self-interest (Downs 1967, 77-78).

NEOLIBERALISM'S SALIENT ECONOMIC CONVICTIONS

The neoliberal economic worldview privileges the following salient convictions and readily denies alternative perspectives.

On Time and the Future

The short term inevitably dominates the long term. As Keynes famously remarked, "The long run is a misleading guide to current affairs. In the long run we are all dead" (Keynes 1923, 27). The future is forever changing. It abounds with opportunities awaiting entrepreneurial exploitation that would leave the future better off. So, the neoliberal individualist-libertarian worldview readily denies contending perspectives on time and the future.

- A balance must be achieved between the short and the long term, as the continuity of the past, present, and future is important, so the future should not be seriously threatened (the collectivist-hierarchical worldview).

- The long term must dominate the short term, because the future is expected to undergo a radical change for the worse (the collectivist-egalitarian worldview).

- The future is unknowable and, thus, chance and fate determine the sequence of future events (the individualist-existential worldview).

On Nature

Nature is benign and forgiving, and, thus, natural resources are to be exploited. So, the neoliberal individualist-libertarian worldview readily denies contending perspectives on nature

- Nature is bountiful within limits, but perverse and vulnerable, so exploitation has to be planned or coordinated by the state to conserve natural resources for future generations (the collectivist-hierarchical worldview).

- Nature is ephemeral, fragile, and unforgiving, so natural resources must be diligently and carefully managed by those committed to long-term environmental sustainability (the collectivist-egalitarian worldview).

- Nature is erratic and capricious, so the conservation and management of natural resources is problematic, leaving their future in the hands of luck and fate (the individualist-existential worldview).

On Technology

Technology, including information technology, is a source of exploitable opportunities and a means of mitigating unforeseen consequences and of reducing costs. So, the neoliberal individualist-libertarian worldview readily denies contending perspectives on technology.

- Technology should be used by those seeking to guide and manage society, because it is a means by which the behavior of individuals, and groups of individuals, can be monitored and regulated. But, information technology should be subject to tight controls, so as to avoid the spread of contradictory and incompatible information, which can threaten the legitimate, expert, and knowledge power-base of the hierarchy.

- Technology should be considered a source of unacceptable environmental and social risks. While information technology facilitates both communications with both insiders and the conversion of outsiders, it should be subject to tight controls so as to avoid values-disconfirming information being more readily available, so threatening the collective cohesion (the collectivist-egalitarian worldview).

- Technology should be considered a source of power for the unknowable powers-that-be, and so should be tightly controlled, especially information technology, which is a means by which powers-that-be can achieve social control[129] (the individualist-existential worldview).

On Economic Growth

Economic growth is most desirable, because there would be more material goods and services available to satisfy people's wants. So, the neoliberal

---

129 Social control relates to the establishment and enforcement of a standard of behavior, put forth by social institutions in response to social and economic behaviors that are deviant, problematic, threatening, or undesirable, in order to maintain conformity to established norms and rules (see Mead 1925).

individualist-libertarian worldview readily denies contending perspectives on economic growth.

- Economic growth is acceptable only if it is planned or coordinated by the state to conserve resources and to ensure that there adequate public resources to enable the state to meet all the necessary state-assessed human needs and to engage in the necessary conspicuous public displays that build citizenship bonds (the collectivist-hierarchical worldview).

- Economic growth must be discouraged because it threatens long-term environmental sustainability and generates undesirable interpersonal differences (the collectivist-egalitarian worldview).

- Economic growth is unacceptable as it is, inevitably, the result of unknowing powers-that-be exploiting the ordinary people (the individualist-existential worldview).

On Wealth Creation

Wealth creation by the private sector is most desirable, because there would be more wealth for deserving risk-taking entrepreneurs, the benefits of which trickle down to others. So, the neoliberal individualist-libertarian worldview readily denies contending perspectives on wealth creation.

- Wealth creation is acceptable, but only if any public contributions or sacrifices made in the process lead to public gain by enhancing public resources (the collectivist-hierarchical worldview).

- Wealth creation is unacceptable because it creates interpersonal differences, which makes the maintenance of equality of outcome problematic (the collectivist-egalitarian worldview).

- Wealth creation is unacceptable, as it is, inevitably, the result of unknowing powers-that-be exploiting the ordinary people (the individualist-existential worldview).

On Scarcity

Scarcity justifies the use of the market to allocate the available resources so as to ensure that the maximum achievable level of material wellbeing is generated. So, the neoliberal individualist-libertarian worldview readily denies contending perspectives on scarcity.

- Scarcity justifies administrative resource allocation by direct bureaucratic fiat so as to ensure that there adequate public resources to meet all the necessary state-assessed human needs and to engage in the necessary conspicuous public displays that build citizenship bonds (the collectivist-hierarchical worldview).

- Scarcity justifies voluntary collective action to change inegalitarian lifestyles in order to ensure that resources last as long as possible (the collectivist-egalitarian worldview).

- Scarcity is a capricious burden that must be borne as fate decrees, and so justifying no societal response by unknowing powers-that-be (the individualist-existential worldview).

On Reconciling Human Wants and Scarce Resources

While wants are unlimited and resources are limited, both—and the gap between them—are considered manageable by the market. Wants are exclusive sourced within the individual, and they must be revealed the process of seeking to satisfy them (so becoming consumer demands). The market is, then, able to ration commodities on the basis of the capacity to pay. So, the neoliberal individualist-libertarian worldview readily denies contending perspectives on reconciling human wants and scarce resources.

- In the face of scarcity, the state, using its expert knowledge, is in the best position to determine what human needs should be met from available scarce resources and the coercive power of the state should be used to ensure that any necessary individual sacrifices are made in the collective interest (the collectivist-hierarchical worldview).

- In the face of scarcity, the only acceptable option is for individuals collectively—as virtuous and socially responsible individuals—to decrease voluntarily their consumption demands to a level below that which can be resourced, on the grounds that "thrift is more elegant, more appropriate than vulgar display" (Douglas 1994, 228) (the collectivist-egalitarian worldview).

- In the face of scarcity, given the world operates without rhyme nor reason, there is no point in trying to manage the gap between needs (demand) and resources (supply), so all that can be done is to live in hope of good fortune, but survive by coping with whatever fate decrees (the individualist-existential worldview).

On Balancing Government Budgets

Government, following the principles of monetarism (McCallum 2007), must balance its budget—by reducing government expenditure—because current government expenditure should be paid from current government revenue—without the imposition of additional tax burdens.[130] This avoids increasing the size of the public sector, and its share of capital ownership, by increasing public borrowing.[131] Moreover, public debt acquisition raises the real rate of interest, as government borrowing has to compete with private borrowing, a consequence of which is a crowding-out (reducing) of private investment, because a higher rate of return is required for private investment to be profitable. This subsequently slows down the rate of private capital accumulation and, thus, economic growth. This means that government should use its borrowed funds only to invest in projects with a similar rate of return as private investment. And the repayment of public debt places an unreasonable burden on future generations of taxpayers who had no say in its acquisition. So, the neoliberal individualist-libertarian worldview readily denies contending perspectives on government budgets.

- Budget deficits enable governments to stimulate demand and thus the economy—Keynesian economic theory (Keynes [1936] 2007)—so as to create jobs and, thus, sustain social harmony and social stability (the collectivist-hierarchical worldview).

---

130   As Tobin (2007) explains:

  In monetarists' view, government budgets have important supply-side effects for good or ill but have no demand-side role unless they trigger changes in monetary policy. In Keynesian theory, fiscal policy is a distinct demand-side instrument. The government affects aggregate demand directly by its own expenditures and indirectly by its taxes.

131   The alternative is to finance any budget deficit by increasing the amount of money in circulation, but this is inflationary and only possible if government has retained control of monetary policy.

- Budget deficits financed by public debt enable an intertemporal income redistribution (from future taxpayers to present government beneficiaries) that permits government to provide social support to needy segments of society without overburdening current taxpayers, while are the same time slowing down undesirable economic growth by crowding-out private investment (the collectivist-egalitarian worldview).

- Achieving balanced budget should not be at the expense of the ordinary person carry the burden, by having lower public support provided for those in need or by paying higher taxes. This would only be to the benefit the rich, who would then not be require to make greater tax contributions, and who can more readily access the capital market, so enabling them to become even richer (the individualist-existential worldview).

CONCLUSION

Drawing upon neoclassical economic theory and its offspring public choice theory, neoliberalism privileges of the marketplace as the best means by which a society can maximize its material wellbeing (attain economic efficiency). Although it is recognized that there are circumstances when the marketplace can fail to meet that that aspiration (market failure), it proffers reasons why government is unable to correct those failures and to advance the material interest of its citizens (government failure). This justifies neoliberalism's assertion that the public sector is intrusive, inefficient, and wasteful.

In coming to this conclusion, neoclassical economic theory uses a theory of the individual under which individuation is exclusively on the basis of binary personal preference ranking—so giving rise to a Weberian ideal-type *homo economicus*—thereby demarcating all others as strangers distinguishable only by their preference rankings. This conflates all human relationships into exchange relationships between individuals-as-strangers who have no mutually recognized social relationships. Neoclassical economic theory accepts the appropriateness of applying this relationship premise to exchange transactions even where the presumption must be that there is a mutually recognized social relationship between transacting agents, as acquaintances and friends (in groups), colleagues (in organizations), and intimates (in families)—so giving rise to exchange transactions between individuals-as-familiars.

As a theoretical construct of the individual, *homo economicus* is far too under socialized (totally abstracted from all the all the social dimensions of life) and too epistemologically prejudiced (willing to dismiss any contending knowledge claim the truth-value of which cannot be objectively determined) to do justice to the ways people interconnect meaning, purpose, and action; to their emotional responses to people and situations; and to their capabilities in their various social roles.

To neoliberalism, market fundamentalism and all its behavioral appurtenances are beyond reproach.

4.
Neoliberalism:
Market Governance

Since the days of Adam Smith the market has not only been appreciated in its own right as an institution of self-coordination but also as an antidote against narrow-minded mercantilism and state-centric parochialism.

Willke and Willke (2012, 87)

Introduction

Neoliberalism questions the governance legitimacy and efficacy of sovereign national governments—democratic or otherwise (Andrews and Kouzmin 1998; 1999)—by asserting that the market could, should, and does much better than the state. The call has been to privatize the public sector and, effectively, to suppress democratic accountabilities (Klein 2007). This emerged as the normative public sector framework for "southern-gradient economies" whilst being implemented as the New Public Management in "northern-gradient economies" (Kouzmin 2002).

The purpose of this chapter is to identify neoliberalism's distinctive set of descriptive and normative propositions about how society and its institutions should be governed: its perspectives on societal governance and the public interest; on the market sphere and business risk-taking; and on public sphere (on government, the polity, citizenship rights and obligations, public policy, and public provision). It concludes by critically articulating neoliberalism's public sector reform vision.

Societal Governance

This is the "mode of social co-ordination or order" adopted by a society (Mayntz 1993, 11; see also Kajer 2004; Kooiman 2000, 2003; Miller 1989; Thompson et al. 1991).

Market Governance

The neoliberal individualist-libertarian worldview, with its utilitarian orientation, endorses market self-regulation[132] (Polanyi 1957). This presumes that the most efficient way of running society is by granting, enforcing, and protecting the fundamental right of all people to use, in minimally regulated markets, whatever private property they own as they see fit so as to satisfy their wants. Then, buyers and sellers would be free to negotiate enforceable contracts and to conduct their transactions in accordance with their contractual obligations, within the rule of the law (the laws of property, tort, and contract) that embody zero noncompliance tolerance and full restitution as the ultimate sanction, and with a sense of personal responsibility, based upon honor, shame, guilt, and luck (Douglas and Isherwood 1979). This mode of governance demarcates only a minimal role for the state. Society would, thus, be best governed when there is a strong market, a weak state, and a weak civil society.[133]

So, the neoliberal individualist-libertarian worldview readily denies that society would be better off if it is governed by contending governance modes.

- *Hierarchical Governance*: Under this mode, the power of the

---

132 Kooiman and van Vliet (2001, 360) see this as subsumed under the broader rubric of self-governance: "the capacity of social entities to provide the necessary means to develop and maintain their identity, by and large, by themselves—and thus show a relatively high degree of social-political autonomy." They distinguish between:

  - an *actor-* (agency-) *oriented* perspective—*an actor constellation system*, which draws upon internal or Eigen dynamics, where positive and negative feedback are central, to argue that a social system governs itself by means of a process of mutual stimulation between identifiable actors who are searching for mutually reinforcing or curbing behavior patterns (see also Kooiman 2000; Kooiman and Associates 1997), akin to Hayek (1991) spontaneous, or grown, order; which stands in contradistinction to

  - a *systems-* (structure-) *oriented* perspective on self-governance—*an autopoietic system*, which draws upon the biological metaphor of a closed living system that is self-referencing, self-organizing and self-steering, governs itself through a labyrinth of interaction processes involving the constituent members that make up its identity (see, for example, Kickert 1993; also Brans and Rossbach 1997; Dunsire 1996; Teubner 1993; but see Ostrom, Walker, and Gardner 1992).

133 The alternative triad of terms are: self-governing, hierarchical governing, and cogoverning (or interactive governing) (Kooiman 1997); markets, solidarity, and politics (Mayntz 1993); markets, clans and bureaucracies (Ouchi 1980); price, trust and authority (Bradach and Eccles 1991); and market, community, and state (Streek and Schmitter 1991) speculatively adding a fourth governance mode—associations—in recognition of the "specific contribution of associations and organized concertations to social order" (see also Hollingsworth and Lindberg 1985).

state is exercised by the politico-administrative elite[134] who have a territorial mandate, achieved because they have been elected or appointed to do so, because they have the hereditary right to do so, or because they have taken for themselves the power to do so. They are empowered to design and implement a set of enforceable statutory rights and obligations on individuals, groups of individuals, or organizations.[135] This ensures a strong state, a weak civil society, and a weak market (the collectivist-hierarchical worldview).

- *Co-governance*: Under this network[136] or interactive governance[137] mode (Kooiman 2001; Kooiman and van Vliet 1995; Torfing and Sørensen 2007), state power is shared with a network of communities of special interest, embracing communities of interest (groups of people or organizations joining together to represent, defend, or advance particular sets of interests) and communities of place (groups of people living in the same place bound by historically and culturally contingent values, belief, attitudes seeking to advance common interests).[138] Only by reinforcing community bonds and community

134 The societal governing elites comprises those individuals who are engaged in directing (the political elite) or administering (the administrative elite) a national territorial political unit.

135 This is in accord with idea of Plato's guardian-style governance (Plato [c360 BCE] 1955), under which only a minority of people—the philosopher-guardians—are capable of ruling, as they are particularly well qualified to do so (Hendriks and Zouridis 1999), because they are intelligent; have superior insight, virtue, and, thus, integrity; and have a selfless concern for the welfare of the governed, for whom they know what is best.

136 A network may be defined as "a relatively stable set of mainly public and private corporate actors. The linkages between the actors serve as channels for communication and for the exchange of information, expertise, trust and other policy resources. The boundary of a network is not, in the first place, determined by formal institutions but results from a process of mutual recognition dependent on functional relevance and structural embeddedness" (Kenis and Schneider 1991, 41-42). To Parsons (1995, 185) "The metaphor of a network ... seeks to focus on the pattern of formal and informal contacts and relationships which shape policy agendas and decision-making. ... Network analysis is based on the idea that a policy is framed within the context of relationships and dependencies" (see also Klijn and Koppenjan 2000).

137 Streeck and Schmitter (1991, 228) talk of interest governance and democratic corporatist governance (see also Elder Thomas, and Arter 1982; Kickert, Klijn, and Koppenjan 1997; Klijn, Koppenjan, and Terrier 1995; Kooiman 1993).

138 Laumann and Knoke (1987) identify the following forms of networks: state directed, concertation, pressure pluralist, clientela pluralism, parantela pluralism,

identities in this way can a society's survival, stability, and well-being be attained and sustained. The co-governing networks would voluntarily cede some autonomy to government, in return for agreed common rights and acceptable common obligations.[139] This form of societal governance emphasizes pluralist negotiations in recognition that "... freedom can only be pursued effectively if individuals join with their fellows" (Hirst 1994, 4) and that "... volunteerism, community spirit and independent associational life as protections against the domination of society by the state, and indeed as a counterbalance which helped to keep the state accountable and effective" (de Tocqueville [1835/1840] 1899).[140] This ensures a weak state, a strong civil society, and a weak market (the collectivist-egalitarian worldview).

- *Anarchical governance*: Under this mode, governance can be on the basis of (Hurka 1993; Miller 1984; Siebers 1994; Woodcock 1986):

  - natural laws and in accordance with perfectionist ethics (in the classical or utopian socialist anarchist tradition);

  - natural rights and egoism (in the individualist anarchist tradition); or

  - permanent and irreducible pluralism (in the postmodernist anarchist tradition).

  These would be the least alienating forms of societal governance, premised on the simple principle they minimize the potential for intentional and coercive collective action by constraining the power of the societal governing elites (see Wolff 1970). However, skepticism would certainly prevail about whether any transition process to some kind of stateless so-

industry-dominant pressure pluralism.

139 The presumption is that network interactions are on the basis of loyalty, trust (see Vangen and Huxham 1998) and reciprocity (see Rhodes 1996).

140 De Tocqueville ([1835/1840]) 1899) also evidenced foresight when he judged:

It is easy to see the time coming in which men will be less and less able to produce, by each alone, the commonest bare necessities of life. The tasks of government must therefore perpetually increase, and its efforts to cope with them must spread its net ever wider. The more government takes the place of associations, the more will individuals lose the idea of forming associations and need the government to come to their help. That is a vicious cycle of cause and effect.

ciety could ever deliver the necessary social order. So, all people who expect to be "cut off from political maneuvering and influence" (Douglas and Ney 1998, 123) want is to be left to conduct their affairs in their own interests, on the premise that the ordinary people have no general obligation to obey the commands of the state. Indeed, sociopolitical alienation is inevitable. This ensures a weak state, a weak civil society, and a weak market (the individualist-existentialist worldview).

The Public Interest

As democratic governance is about protecting and promoting the public interest (Dixon 2003; Dixon, Sanderson, and Tripathi 2006, 2007) conceptualized by Lasswell (1930, 264) as "the displacement of private affects upon public objects. The affects which are organized in the family are redistributed upon various social objects such as the state." At issue is whether the state can know what is in the interest of its citizens and can take intentional and instrumental actions to protect and advance those interests. Indeed, determining what the public interest is and how it differs from private interests, involves a delicate balancing act: on one side is self-interest or individual autonomy (promoting positive freedom), on the other side is the public interest or societal control (constraining positive freedom to promote negative freedom) (Dahl 1982; Elster 1991; Sandel 1982; Walzer 1983). To determine this individual autonomy-social control balance political institutions engage in aggregative and integrative processes to derive the "will" of the people.[141]

Neoliberalism advances two public interest propositions. The first is that the public interest is only knowable as the summation of all private interests of those affected or likely to be affected by collective action—what people want (their personal preferences). Government, however, has no means of knowing what people want (Arrow 1954) and, thus, cannot protect or advance their interests. Following Smith ([1776] 1976), neoliberalism links private interests with the good of society. It rejects any suggestion that the marketplace does not know what individuals' want, and that anyone else can only know what they think is good for them. Thus, the

---

141 An aggregative process identifies the public interest by means of political campaigns and political bargaining. An integrative process involves deliberation between the politico-administrative governors and those they seek to govern. What, then, is in the public interest is a matter of politics; how it is promoted and protected is a matter of societal governance (Kooiman 1993, 1999; see also Peters 1995; Peters and Savoie 1998).

public interest can only be promoted and protected by permitting private ends to be peacefully pursued. The second proposition, in the utilitarianism tradition, is the proposition that the wellbeing of society should be the overriding goal of public policy, thus collective action is right if it maximizes social wellbeing by, in Benthamite terms, achieving the greatest happiness for the greatest number of people (Bentham [1789] 1970; Mill [1863] 1968).

So, the neoliberal individualist-libertarian worldview readily denies that society would be better off with a different conceptualization of the public interest.

- *As the indivisible common good:* This is what is for the good of society-as-a-whole rather than for the good of a particular groups within it (Gross 1964; Ley and Perry 1959), as an expression of the general will (Rousseau [1762] 1973). The expectation is that people would make contributions and sacrifices in the public interest for the wellbeing of others, as dutiful acts of social solidarity (Widegren 1997). Indeed, the primary concern is with constraining negative freedom, perhaps for the good of those whose liberty has been restricted—even against their will—in order to achieve collectively determined goals, which may well involve the promotion of others' positive freedom—providing them with a greater capacity for individual autonomy. Mill ([1863] 1968) argued that there is an ethical imperative for the state to protect its most vulnerable citizens, because of the positive social consequences that would follow (such as social harmony and social stability). This is the collectivist-hierarchical worldview.

- *As an inclusive set of categorical interests:* This is what is in the interest of the communities to which members of a society belong, reflecting the sectional interests of particular communities of place and special interest (Streeck and Schmitter 1991). Indeed, by capturing and articulating expressions of the will of the people as a set of categorical interests, community members can embrace them in the belief that they are for their good of their communities (Cutting and Kouzmin 2011). Co-governance networks may well be in dissent with government from time-to-time, but, nevertheless, they would willingly engage in governance processes in order to ensure that their values and beliefs are at least heard, if not made the basis of collective action in the public interest. This is the collectiv-ist-egalitarian worldview.

- *As what the unknowing powers-that-be judge the public interest to be*: This is what people need that is in the interest of the pow-ers-that-be to provide. It is a proposition premise on the public interest being unknowable because of capriciousness and un-certainty and, in any event, it cannot be intentionally and instru-mentally promoted and protected. As Thompson, Grendstate, and Selle (1999, 13-14) put it, the issue would always be:

  > Why bother! Every penny that is spent to do something about something about which nothing can be done is a penny wasted, and it is important that resources not be poured into that bottomless pit. If the cat is out of the bag ... it cannot be put back.

  Thus, the expectation is that the powers-that-be will inevita-bly exercise the necessary power to govern society as they see fit. Such use of state power can, however, never be legitimized. This is the individualist-existential worldview.

The Market Sphere

The neoliberal individualist-libertarian worldview considers that the marketplace is benign and exploitable, because it is presumed to be knowable, within an acceptable degree of probability, by those who are enterprising, provided they have the necessary skills. The market, of course, knows best, for only it can require people to reveal their prefer-ences (wants) and only it can produce the most wealth from the limited resources available in any society. It should, thus, only be subject to min-imal public intervention, for it cannot be improved by such intervention.

So, the neoliberal individualist-libertarian worldview readily denies the validity of the contending perspectives on the market sphere.

- *The market is strange and isomorphic realm*: One that is per-verse, but tolerant of, the public intervention needed for it to be monitored and managed by strategies designed to protect the common good. This, at least, involves ensuring that market behavior and outcomes remain within acceptable social limits, thereby avoiding unbridled risk-taking entrepreneurial behav-ior, because markets is too experimental and exuberant, which is not in the interest of maintaining social harmony (Cantor, Henry, and Raynor 1992, 21-24). This is the collectivist-hierarchical worldview.

- *The market is an inhospitable realm*: One that threatens equality of outcomes, thereby necessitating public intervention to constrain interpersonal competition. This intervention is intended to avoid status (income) distinctions that are not in the interest of an egalitarian society. The market must be strictly held accountable for its processes and outcomes. This is best achieved by means of full and effective public disclosure, so as to ensure that any external costs imposed are the subject of a group-norming and group-forming values discourse before being addressed by public intervention. This is the collectivist-egalitarian worldview.

- *The market is a capricious and inhospitable realm*: One that exploits ordinary people, because it is avaricious and indifferent to their needs. It must be made less capricious and less exploitative, but there are no expectations of any success in so doing. This is the individualist-existential worldview.

Business Opportunities and Risks

The neoliberal individualist-libertarian worldview advances the proposition that business opportunities create prospects for personal reward. Success is, of course, expected because both entrepreneurial talent and new technology are presumed capable of mitigating any unforeseen consequences of exploiting business opportunities. Any associated social risks can best be objectively defined, measured, and evaluated by profit-seeking risk-takers, and the moral acceptability of any such risks should be judged against the consequential net material benefits generated or likely to be generated.

So, the neoliberal individualist-libertarian worldview readily denies that business opportunities should be exploited only after the desirability of such exploitation has been favorably judged in terms of the best interests of others.

- *Society-as-a-whole*: As defined by the governing elite and determined by government experts (the collectivist-hierarchical worldview);

- *The affected communities of place and special interest*: As defined by the affected communities and determined by those likely to be affected (the collectivist-egalitarian worldview); or

- *Those individuals likely to be most affected*: As defined and determined by them, on the basis of their experiential knowledge (the individualist-existential worldview).

The Public Sphere

The neoliberal individualist-libertarian worldview considers that the public sphere, as a pedantic rent seeker (Krueger 1974; Rowley, Tollison, and Tullock 1988; Tilly 1990), is a threat to the private sphere (Downs 1967; Niskanen 1973, 1975, 1994; Tullock 1976). This means that any private costs incurred that can be attributable to government actions should be both minimized and justly compensated (Epstein 1985; Fischel 1995). Thus the public sphere should be made smaller wherever and whenever possible by transferring as many of its responsibilities as possible to the private sector.

So, the neoliberal individualist-libertarian worldview readily denies alternative perspectives of the public sphere.

- *It should be expanded wherever and whenever possible:* This is to ensure that government meets the unmet private and social needs, the satisfaction of which is in the common good, as defined by the governing elite and determined by government experts (the collectivist-hierarchical worldview).

- *It should be expanded judiciously when necessary:* This is to ensure that there are no unequal power relations within the private sphere. But the public sphere must be treated with constant vigilance in order to be made benevolent (the collectivist-egalitarian worldview).

- *It should be avoided at all costs:* This is because it is an unknowable, capricious, and fearful realm that is indifferent to the ordinary person's needs (the individualist-existential worldview).

Government

The neoliberal individualist-libertarian worldview rejects the possibility that there is any basis upon which government can claim legitimate authority, as it is always and ever a threat to individual liberty (Tanner 1996). Its political narrative is grounded in the minimalization of the role and size of government, thereby permitting and facilitating private ends to be peacefully pursued.

So, the neoliberal individualist-libertarian worldview readily denies that society would be better off with an alternative style of government:

- *The Platonian guardian-style*: This affirms the centrality of government being elitist, stable, and strong,[142] where loyalty and compliance are expected and technical rationality rewarded (Hendriks and Zouridis 1999, 125; Ney and Molenaers 1999) (the collectivist-hierarchical worldview);

- *The Aristotelian deliberative-style*: This affirms the centrality of government promoting the active participation of its citizens,[143] through the communities with which they have affiliated (Cohen 1989; Fiskin 1991) (the collectivist-egalitarian worldview).

- *An anarchist style*: This affirms the centrality of no one having the right to exercise the state's coercive power—"Cities and individuals alike, all are by nature predisposed to do wrong, and there is no law that will prevent it" (Diodorus, an Athenian, during the Mytilenian Debate of 427 BCE, cited I Thucydides [401 BCE] 1972, 3.45)—although skepticism would prevail over whether the anarchistic dream is ever achievable (the individualist-existential worldview).

The Polity

The neoliberal individualist-libertarian worldview advances the proposition that the public sector must be judged by its cost-effectiveness, because this maximizes not only people's satisfaction (Simon [1945] 1960), but also public confidence in government (Wholey 1993) and the quan-

---

142 This recalls the Hegelian idea of the state being a spiritual entity (Hegel [1807] 1977), one with, in Hennis' words (cited in Messner 1997, 80), the "power to create unity," and the ability to be "protector, guardian, promoter of morality ... guarantor of moral standards."

143 This would be one in accord with the principles of associative democracy (polyarchy) (Dahl 1971; Hirst 1994), communitarianism (Etzioni 1993, 1995, 1998), corporatism (Schmitter and Lehmbruch 1979), and neocorporatism (Panitch 1977, 1980), and collaborative governance (Ansell and Gash 2008; Williams 2012).

tum of resources available to the private sector (Horton 1987). So, the polity must be able to ensure that government responds to the claims made by its various constituencies as cost-effectively as possible. It supports, therefore, the idea of a polity should:

- deter government from taking any intentionally instrumental actions, because it cannot know its citizens' preferences;

- treat government with constant vigilance, because the societal governing elite is inherently coercive, and intrusive; and

- hold government strictly accountable for its inputs and outcomes by means of effective public scrutiny, because it is both intrusive in intent and malevolent in outcome.

The polity should have a written constitution that:

- guarantees negative freedoms;

- creates a complex web of checks and balances to constrain the power of government, by ensuring a strict separation of the powers; and

- empowers local government within a decentralized, multi-tire political structure.

It should also have:

- a bicameral legislature, as part of its system of checks and balances;

- an electoral system that has first-past-the-post voluntary voting in single-member constituencies, with universal suffrage, so ensuring that everyone adult can vote and nobody can be excluded if they see a net benefit in so doing, but they can abstain if they do not, thereby implying their tacit consent;

- a judicial system that seeks four goals:

    - to enforce, property rights and maintain law and order, so as to maintain confidence and stability in the marketplace;

    - to undertake judicial reviews of administrative discretion, so that any uninformed and capricious government decisions can be identified and compensated sought;

    - to enforce freedom of access to most information on the

public sector, so that its inefficiencies can be identified and it can be culled for exploitable commercial opportunities; and

- to limit the power of the judiciary over the private sphere, by minimalizing judicial policymaking that impact adversely on the private sphere, by inhibiting the judicial review of management discretion, and by restricting freedom of access to any corporate information, which must remain secret because of its commercial sensitivity.

So, the neoliberal individualist-libertarian worldview readily denies that society would be better off with a different style of polity.

- *A polity that enables government to be elitist, stable, reactive, and, if necessary, even coercive*: One that advances a hierarchical political meta-narrative that speaks to legitimizing the hierarchical bonding of individuals, to reinforcing the supremacy of society over the individual in all spheres of life, and to preserving authority structures, reinforced by regulating the private sphere, and engaging in some form of economic planning. The ideal polity would have:
  - an unwritten constitution;
  - a unitary political structure with a strong center and unfettered executive dominance;
  - an electoral system with limited suffrage, based on the demarcation of status (age, educational attainment, or professional rank), voluntary voting, and a first-past-the-post voting system (to ensure political stability); and
  - a judicial system that:
    - upholds, most rigorously, law and order and the protection of (in accordance with the governing elite's determination of what will advance the common good;
    - limits the power of the judiciary over the other branches of government,
    - restricts freedom of access to any public sector information (in the national interest), and

- inhibits judicial policymaking that affects the public sphere).

This is the collectivist-hierarchical worldview.

- *A polity that enables government to be inclusive, participatory, collaborative, and deliberative*: One that emphasizes "the importance to effective democracy of fair and open community deliberation about the merits of competing political argument" (Uhr 1998, 4), and advances a political meta-narrative that speaks to reinforcing the collective's responsibility for the promotion of equality, human dignity and respect, and human rights, best achieved by bonding co-governance networks together against outsiders, so giving rise to a sense of bonding fellowship and community (Held 1984; Wildavsky and Chai 1994). The ideal polity would have:

  - a written constitution that assigns citizens' rights and obligation;

  - a devolved political structure (subsidiarity[144]) that permits and facilitates deliberative decision-making;

  - an electoral system with proportional representation, multiple-member constituencies, universal suffrage and, very definitely, compulsory voting (to deter abstentions due to irresponsible apathy); and

  - a judicial system that:

    - enforces, most vigorously, all human rights, and law and order in accordance with shared societal values;

    - undertakes judicial reviews of administrative discretions (to protect human rights) and exercises considerable discretion in judicial policymaking (to fill any policy vacuums); and

    - enforces statutory freedom of access to most information in the public and market spheres (to facilitate public scrutiny).

This is the collectivist-egalitarian worldview.

---

144 This is the location of authority at the lowest possible level of a hierarchy (Wincott 1996, 482).

- *A polity that requires government to be as remote and as minimally coercive and intrusive as possible*: One that advances a political meta-narrative that speaks to reinforcing the importance of understanding the existential human condition, the limitations of human reasoning, and the irreducibility of a person's first-person experience, and of addressing the needs of ordinary people. The ideal polity would have:

  - a written constitution embodying a strict separation of powers;

  - a unitary political structure with weak decentralized administration (so maximizing the distance between the governed and the politico-administrative institutions);

  - an electoral system that has first-past-the-post voluntary voting in single-member constituencies, because they value political stability and certainty but consider apathy (abstention) quite justifiable; and

  - a judicial system that limits citizen exploitation by the state and the marketplace by enforcing law and order, protecting human and property rights, undertaking judicial reviews of administrative discretion, enforcing statutory market regulations, and exercising making judicial policies (to fill any policy vacuums).

This is the individualist-existential worldview.

Citizenship Rights and Obligations

The neoliberal individualist-libertarian worldview supports the idea of giving citizens' rights and obligations (Dixon and Hyde 2009). These would aim to maximizing their negative freedoms, so as to maximize their personal liberty, and to minimize their positive freedoms, which permits them to deflect the acceptance of personal responsibility for their past life-choice decisions. This gives rise to the following rights and obligations:

- The right to engage in any voluntary market transactions.
- The right to make choice decisions in one's own interest.
- The right to own and benefit from private property.

- The right to be able to enforce contractual obligations with zero noncompliance tolerance and full restitution as the ultimate sanction.

- The right to self-ownership.

- The right to be free from the coercion and intrusiveness of others.

- The right to have equality of opportunity.

- The right to live a secure and safe life.

- The right to engage in political affairs.

- The right to engage in free speech critical of the conditions of political and civic life.

- The right to engage in or contribute or to collective action on a voluntary basis.

- The obligation to take control of one's life and to be personal responsibility for one's decisions and actions

- The obligation to meet contractual responsibilities.

- The obligation to ensure that one's decisions and actions do not cause harm to others.

So, the neoliberal individualist-libertarian worldview readily denies that citizens would be better off with a different basis for determining citizens' rights and obligations:

- *The assignment of citizenship rights and obligations were aimed at achieving social stability and social harmony.* They would, thus, include:

  - The right to live a secure and safe life in a society that has social order and harmony.

  - The right, where necessary, to access, through government, the resource of others to sustain a socially acceptable standard of living.

  - The right to engage in socially acceptable voluntary market transactions.

  - The right to criticize the conditions of civil and economic life.

- The obligation to be a law-abiding citizen.

- The obligation to be loyal and obedient to those in authority.

- The obligation to make sacrifices for others.

- The obligation to make a contribution towards the cost of collective action.

- The obligation to conduct one's life in a socially acceptable way.

- The obligation to make socially acceptable decisions.

- The obligation to exercise personal freedom in a socially acceptable way.

- The obligation to engage in political affairs in a socially acceptable way.

- The obligation to exercise freedom of speech in socially acceptable way.

This is the collectivist-hierarchical worldview.

- *The assignment of citizenship rights and obligations were aimed at achieving social inclusion, social participation, and equality of outcome. They would, thus, include:*

  - The right to join with others in communities of place or special interest to advance common interests.

  - The right to be treated with dignity and respect.

  - The right to be treated equality before law.

  - The right to be able to take control of one's life to achieve socially responsible life goals.

  - The right to have access, through government, to the resource of others needed to live independently with dignity and to take control of one's life.

  - The right to engage in socially responsible voluntary market transactions.

  - The right to criticize the conditions of political and economic life.

- The obligation not to be discriminatory in the treatment others.

- The obligation to treat others with dignity, respecting their norms, cultural and social practices, and language.

- The obligation to foster in others close communal and social bonds.

- The obligation to give others an equal opportunity to achieve socially responsible life goals.

- The obligation to contribute to any collective action decided upon one's communities of special interest or place.

- The obligation to engage in political affairs.

- The obligation to exercise freedom of speech in a socially responsible way.

- The obligation to make socially responsible choice decisions.

This is the collectivist-egalitarian worldview.

- *No citizenship rights and obligations were articulated.* This is on the premise that ordinary citizens may have rights but they are not enforceable, only obligations imposed upon them at the whim of the unknowing and untrustworthy powers-that-be that are enforceable. The powerless ordinary people can only expect to suffer when unknowing government decides to interfere in their lives. Indeed, whatever negative freedoms they may be granted may not be retainable, and any positive freedom granted would, in fate's hands, inevitably frustrating any steps they might take toward greater autonomy and self-determination. This is the individualist-existentialism worldview.

Public Policy

The neoliberal individualist-libertarian worldview supports the idea of a public policy process that makes policymaking the product of synoptic and instrumentally rational analysis, premised on the self-interest motivation of all policy actors, so as to facilitate optimal decision-making (Quade 1976; see also Stokey and Zeckhauser 1978; Weimer and Vining 1992; but compare Elster 1991). It is predisposed only to policy instruments that advance self-interest:

- Distributive policies appeal for the provision of public goods, but otherwise only if they do not create more competition in the marketplace or if they create exploitable business opportunities.

- Constituency (informational) policies would appeal only if they do not seek to constrain negative freedom or to limit business opportunities.

- Redistributive policies would have no appeal, as they would not only suppress the ambition of those who win from any redistribution, but also demotivate those who lose by reducing their meritorious rewards, thus stifling effort and risk-taking initiatives.

- Regulatory policies would appeal only if they help to maintain people's confidence in the marketplace, by defining and enforcing behaviors that are acceptable in the marketplace.

The preferred regulatory mode is self-regulation, achieved by means of enforceable contracts embodying a zero tolerance of noncompliance and full restitution as the ultimate sanction. With respect to the imposition of regulatory instruments:

- Economic instruments would be least objectionable, because they are, at least, indirect controls, operating through the creation of incentives that reward desired behaviors and disincentives that punish undesirable behaviors.

- Command-and-control instruments would appeal only if they maintain public confidence in the marketplace.

- Information instruments would appeal only if they closed down opportunities for competitors or created new opportunities for entrepreneurial exploitation.

In all cases, such regulatory instruments must be designed by those who understand how the marketplace works, for only they can anticipate what the market response is likely to be, and thus that the likely market outcomes will be.

So, the neoliberal individualist-libertarian worldview readily denies that better public policies would be made with a different policy process:

- *If the policy process is dominated by the governing elite in the executive branch of government.* This would involve institutional activity using functional-analytic analysis to facilitate satisficing decision-making by means of a hierarchical decision-making process. The governing elite would be predisposed only to policy instruments that enhance the collective's superiority over the individual:

  - Distributive policies would have a strong appeal, as they enable the governing elite to reinforce institutionalized inequalities.

  - Regulatory policies would also have a strong appeal, as they empower the governing elite to enforce, by sanction, desired individual, interpersonal, group, or corporate behaviors.

  - Constituent policies would have an appeal, as they give the governing elite influence, at least, over individual, interpersonal, group, or corporate behavior.

  - Redistributive policies would have limited appeal, as their outcomes would jeopardize institutionalized inequalities, thereby threatening the governing elite, although a degree of redistribution may be an acceptable cost to pay for social harmony and social stability.

  The preferred regulatory mode is hierarchical, whereby regulations are designed, authorized, and implemented by government experts accountable to the governing elite. They would, however, only be favorable disposed towards regulatory command-and-control instruments. These explicit controls permit the regulators to determine, and implement, with sanctions, what are acceptable (desirable) or unacceptable (undesirable) behaviors in terms of the desired governance outcomes, whether within the public or private spheres. This is the collectivist-hierarchical worldview.

- *If the policy process is dominated by a plurality of interest groups.* This would involve the use communicative-value policy analysis, so as to facilitate "consistent, congruent, and cogent" collective decision-making (Fischer and Forester 1993, 5-7), premised on the agreed need to achieve consensus decisions on what constitutes the practicable good, which is the product of the inclusive engagement of all the policy stakeholders. The communities of special interest or place engaged would be disposed only to policy instruments that promote their negotiated and agreed categorical interests in the public interest:

- Distributive policies would have little appeal, as they reinforce existing inequalities.

- Constituency policies would appeal only if they do not impose controls over individual, interpersonal, group, and organizational behavior.

- Redistributive policies would have a strong appeal, as they not only require engagement in a values-laden discourse to determine who should be the policy winners or losers (by how much, how and when), but also facilitate the removal of what is considered to be illegitimate distinctions between people.

- Regulatory policies would appeal only if they stimulate and facilitate voluntary behavior change.

The preferred regulatory mode is voluntary network regulation, whereby regulations are designed, authorized, and implemented by co-governing networks. They would, however, only be favorably disposed toward information instruments, which stimulate and facilitate voluntary, values-driven, goodness-of-heart changes (Douglas 1982), because such changes reveal and evidence a commitment to the desired regulatory outcomes, whether in the public or market spheres, provided there is partnership (joint) provision. This is the collectivist-egalitarian worldview.

- *If the policy process produces timely, sensible, and credible decision*: This would involve the use of meta-rational analysis (Weick 1995), on the premise that policy problems and issues have to be recognized as being situated in risky, unstable, and unknowable environments, given the unknowability of the future, the unpredictability of human behavior, and the limits of human cognition. So, the principles of garbage-can decision-making (March and Olsen 1976) would have to be tolerated. Policy instruments would have to enhance the opportunities for people to improve their life chances (Weber [1914/1922] 1968):

- Distributive policies would have a strong appeal because ordinary people would, at least, have a chance of being included as beneficiaries.

- Constituency policies would appeal only if they did not impose controls that permit or facilitate their abuse and exploitation, whether by the public or market spheres.

- Redistributive policies would not appeal, as the untrustworthy and unknowing powers-that-be, when determining who should win and lose, by how much, how and when, would inevitably cast ordinary people among the losers.

- Regulatory policies would appeal only if they offered ordinary people some protection against state or market abuse and exploitation, although they would expect the powers-that-be to get it all wrong.

No particular regulatory mode would have any great appeal. Of some appeal would be hierarchical command-and-control, if ordinary people gained some protection against the abuse and exploitation; and economic instruments, if ordinary people gained some reward should they choose to comply with them. This is the individualist-existential worldview.

Public Services Provision

The neoliberal individualist-libertarian worldview considers that the state should only provide the minimally necessary public services. These should, moreover, be designed, wherever possible, in accordance with the end-users' preferences. Only the provision of the necessary public goods should remain a public sector responsibility, otherwise the sectorial allocation should be determined by the relative cost-effectiveness of public, private, or joint provision. The cost of any public-interest service obligations imposed on nongovernmental providers must be offset by appropriate public subsidies (public interest expenditures).

So, the neoliberal individualist-libertarian worldview readily denies that society would be better off with a different way of determining public service provision:

- *Politicians determine the provision of public services.* This would be on the basis of government expert assessments of the social and individual needs that should be satisfied in the public interest at public expense, while also meeting all the public-interest service obligations imposed by government, such as to abide by particular meritorious administrative processes (such as freedom of information, occupational health and safety, equal employment opportunity, and judicial and merit review processes), and particular requirements with respect to both service characteristic (such as health and safety, environmental protection, and energy conservation) and service recipients (such as access for the disabled, or preferential treatment of designated recipient categories). This is the collectivist-hierarchical worldview.

- *The relevant communities of special interest or place jointly with government determine the provision of public services.* This would be on the basis of the collaborative planning, delivering, and over-sighting of the public services that those communities believe are needed (Considine 2003) on the basis of their assessments of the social and individual needs that should be satisfied in the public interest at public expense. This provision would have to meet all agreed public-interest service obligations, particularly requirements with respect to service characteristic (especially environmental protection and energy conservation), and to service recipients (such as preferential treatment of designated disadvantaged and marginalized recipient categories, as determined by the communities involved). This is the collectivist-egalitarian worldview.

- *Independent professionals, whether drawn from the public, private, or community sectors, should advise government on the provision of public services.* This would be on the basis of abandoning any attempts at meaningful instrumental planning of public provision, and engaging in Weickian-like sense making, processes (Weick 1995). This would involve learning by trial and error what public services can best be provided by the public and other sectors. This is on the premise that so-called experts will do what the powers-that-be decide has to be done, regardless of real needs of ordinary people. Otherwise, how public services are delivered is of no importance, as the needs of ordinary people are of no interest or relevance to anyone except themselves. This is the individualist-existential worldview.

The Public Sector Reform Agenda

The neoliberal individualist-libertarian worldview envisages a public sector reform blueprint, one that seeks to inculcate market forces into the public sector (Barzelay 2000, 2005; Kettl 2000; Lane 2000) so as to achieve public ends by private means (Donahue 1989). Its rallying point is downsizing the state, so creating an enabling state (Gilbert and Gilbert 1989), one willing to devolve the provision of public services. This privileges a transition towards market self-governance by reducing the size, intrusiveness, and cost of the public sector. The outcome of such public sector reforms, if and when they are successfully implemented, can be typified as the creation of the hollow or hollowed-out state (Rhodes 1994; Weller, Bakvis, and Rhodes 1997; see also Kouzmin, Leivesley, and Korac-Kakabadse 1997; Kouzmin, Dixon, and Korac-Kakabadse 2001; Milward, Provan, and Else 1993) or the managerial state (Clarke and Newman 1997). This can be achieved in a variety of ways.

- *State withdrawal from the provision of public services*: This could, perhaps, be initiated by the adoption of fiscal austerity measures to reduce public expenditures in order to reduce budget deficits, so as to finance public debt repayment or to reduce the tax burden. It necessitates substitute provision by families (familialization) or by individuals (individualization).

- *Privatization*: This can be achieved by corporatizing a state organization and selling shares on the stock market (share issue privatization), or selling an entire public organization, or part thereof, to a strategic private investor, typically by auction (asset sale privatization).

- *Public–private partnerships*: Under a contract with government, a private investor constructs an asset to be used for the provision of a public service, with the private partner assuming some of the financial, technical, and/or operational risk, and with the cost borne by the future revenue stream generated by service provision, with government providing a capital subsidy (perhaps a one-time grant), revenue subsidies (including taxation advantages), revenue (even profit) guarantees for a fixed period, or availability payments (compensation irrespective of actual usage, thereby ensuring that the service is made available). Such partnerships can take a variety of forms, including:

- *Long-Term Lease Agreement*: Under which in exchange for an upfront fee to government, a private entity receives, for a fixed period of time, the right to collect revenues associated with an existing public asset.

- *Sale/Leaseback*: Whereby a government entity sells a public asset and then leases it back from the private buyer.

- *Design-Build-Finance-Operate-Maintain*: Whereby a private entity that is involved in some aspects of the financing, designing, building, operating, and maintaining a public asset is compensated by receiving the right to collect future revenues associated with that asset (such as user fees) for a fixed period of time.

- *Subsidization of substitute private services*: Whereby the state subsidizes the private provision of services that are a substitute for public provision.

- *Contracting-out*: Whereby the state contracts the provision of a public service to private providers when it is cheaper than public provision.

- *Marketization*: Whereby the state creates a statutory market by making mandatory the purchase of a private commodity as a substitute for, or to augment, public provision.

- *Outsourcing*: Whereby the state purchases private intermediate good or service when it is cheaper that public provision.

- *Sub-contracting*: Whereby the state contracts a private provider to perform a designated task related to the provision of a public service when it is cheaper that public employment.

- *Corporatization*: Whereby the state assigns responsibility for the commercial or quasi-commercial provision of public services to a separate government-owned legal entity, whether for-profit or not-for-profit in orientation.

- *Commercialization*: Whereby the state enables a public organization to sell its public services to end-users on a full or partial cost-recovery or profit basis.

So, the neoliberal individualist-libertarian worldview readily denies the appropriateness of other public sector reform visions:

- *Civil service reform*: This is on the premise that hierarchical governance and its style of public administration do not need fundamental reform. Such reform, then, must not threaten the governing elite and should be implemented within the relevant laws enacted and the rules, regulations, and instructions promulgated. Its rallying point is that efficiencies and economies can be achieved by administrative reform that focus on:

  - *The restructuring of the machinery of government*: Focusing on creating public organizations to deliver new government functions and responsibilities, and on moving existing functions and responsibilities between public organizations.

  - *The enhancing of procedural efficiency and justice*: Focusing on making systems and procedures simpler for end-users to follow and quicker for public officials to complete and on the fairness and the transparency of decision-making processes, particularly with respect to dispute resolution and resource allocation.

  - *The improving of the quality of human resources*: Focusing on improving staff recruitment, selection, assignment, appraisal, remuneration, training and development, and promotion.

  - *The improving of the processes for forecasting, planning, organizing, coordinating, controlling, and commanding work processes*: Focusing on improving work planning, work methods, and work surveillance.

  - *The enhancing of the probity of governance and public administration*: Focusing on reducing the incidents of the use of state power (public office) or public resources for personal gain, particularly when it is made possible because of organization values or administrative process.

  This is the collectivist-hierarchical worldview.

- *Collaborative public administration reform*: This requires the embedding of inclusive, participative, deliberative, and collaborative processes into the practices of public administration—"networking in the shadow of hierarchy" (Scharpf 1994, 41; see also Jessop 1997, 575)—the outcome of which can be typified as government by proxy (Kettl 1988, 1993), third-party government (Salamon 1981, 1987, 1995), and even the shadow state (Wolch 1990). The rallying points of such reforms are (Dugan 2003; Huxham and Vangen 2005; Vigoda-Gadot 2002; Wilkinson 1998):

- To facilitate the active participation of communities of special interest or place in the processes of policy design, implementation, evaluation, and termination, on the basis of empowering communities that voluntarily cede some autonomy to the society to which they belong, in return for agreed common rights and acceptable common obligations.

- To work with communities of special interest or place, to provide desirable public policy outcomes, on the basis of consensus-seeking group-norming values discourses grounded in their shared values and language.

- To conduct public administration according to the principles of inclusiveness, participation, and collaboration, as determined through constrained, consensus seeking values discourses with internal and external stakeholders, so as to ensure that potentially conflicting stakeholder interests are negotiated.

- To build organizational capacity through stakeholder collaboration—working together toward results that are grounded in a share values and a common vision; and through inclusive stakeholder empowerment—engaging in discourse in an open environment—facilitated by decentralizing authority, and emphasizing teamwork and continuous improvement to increase participation—with management control determined by how participation is implemented.

- To inculcate a commitment to a coaching style of leadership, within a participative-group type of management system, one attribute of which is the empowering individuals by the sharing ideas and the facilitating consensus decision-making.

This is the collectivist-egalitarian worldview.

- *Cognitive reform of public administration*: This involves enabling public officials to challenge convention[145] by constructing a sensible interpretation (Weick 1995) of the public sector reality and the needed reform agenda. This can provide the means of thinking outside imprisoning bureaucratic mindsets[146]—Weber's ([1905/1930] 1992) bureaucratic "iron cage"—*Stahlhartes Gehäuse*—that underpin the alienating human encounters that bedevils rule-driven administrative processes. This prioritizes the embracing of new creative and imaginative ways of thinking about bureaucratic ways and means, the achievement of which would be facilitated by "deterritorialization as removal of the grid that is imposed on the study of issues and situations by the way that thinking is conducted and by the way that the business of thinking is structured: The principal culprits were rigid disciplinary boundaries" (Farmer 2007, 287) that inhibit epistemic plurality (Farmer 2007, 2010). The expectation is that new ways of thinking can identified new ways to make better sense of the conundrums, paradoxes, and absurdities that plague bureaucratic human encounters— as satirized by Heller's (1961) *Catch-22s*. This is the individualist-existential worldview.

Privatization

The neoliberal individualist-libertarian worldview posits that society would be better off if business is left to determine the characteristics of privatized public provision, on the basis of revealed preferences (Dixon, Dogan, and Kouzmin 2004, but see Kouzmin and Dixon 2003, 2005, 2010). Thus, any public-sector business opportunities created by privatization should be led by private entrepreneurs who have the necessary

145 This is achieved by accepting Heidegger's proposition that, "thinking only begins at the point where we have come to know that Reason, glorified for centuries, is the most obstinate adversary of thinking" (cited in Barrett 1958, 184), thereby permitting reasoning—in the process of searching for the elusive truth—to transcend drawing conclusions using inductive or deductive reasoning, whether within a framework of bounded rationality or synoptic rationality, in recognition of importance the alternative ways of learning—learning-by-doing, learning-from-experience and, most importantly, learning-from-reflection.

146 This can be the essential counterfoil to Nietzsche's much dreaded the will-to-truth, which drives the pursuit of objective truth as a tool for domination and control to be used by those who believe "the world as it should be really exists" and "who do not wish to create the world as it should be" (Nietzsche [1883–1888/1895] 1967, 56, see also [1878] 1994).

skills, and should be subject only to minimal public regulation. The imposition of any residual public-interest community service obligations should have clearly articulated measurable standards of performance that can be fully costed, so that any negative impact on profits can be offset by public interest subsidies. In this setting, the privatization of public services would be delivered with more production efficiency (by reducing inputs or increasing productivity) and with more allocative efficiency (by selling them at the highest possible price, so maximizing the utility derived from those services), achieved by altering consumer (service recipient) behavior through education, regulation, and economic incentives. This would make government, more cost-efficient and more cost-effective in the use of its resources.

So, the neoliberal individualist-libertarian worldview readily denies that society would be better off with a different way of determining the nature of privatized public provision:

- *By government*: On the basis that privatized public provision must advance the common good, grounded in governing elite's assessments of the social and individual needs that must be satisfied in the public interest. Thus, any public-sector business opportunities created by privatization should be led by government experts, because they are able to judge and implement what is in the best interest of society-as-a-whole, and should be subject to whatever public regulation and community service obligations they consider necessary to protect and promote the public interest. This is the collectivist-hierarchical worldview.

- By *communities of special interest or place*: On the basis that that privatized public provision must advance their categorical interests, grounded in their assessments of the social and individual needs that must be satisfied in their sectional interest. Thus, any public-sector business opportunities created by privatization should be led by those communities, because they are able to judge what is in their best interests. They can be trusted to ensure that the various stakeholders and business engage in extensive mutual consultation to balance the inclusive set of interrelated categorical interests involved, and that business is subject to whatever public regulation and community service obligations they consider necessary to protect and promote their sectional interests so as to ensure society's stability and wellbeing. This is the collectivist-egalitarian worldview.

- *By independent professionals:* On the basis that privatized public provision must meet realistic social and individual needs. Thus, any public-sector business opportunities created by privatization should be led by those who have relevant practical past experience, from wherever they can be found, upon which to base their judgments on what is realistic. Moreover, privatized providers should be subject to whatever public regulation and community service obligations they consider necessary to ensure that privatized provision has minimal adverse consequences on service recipients and society-as-a-whole. This is the individualist-existential worldview.

CONCLUSION

The neoliberal individualist-libertarian worldview embodies a distinctive set of descriptive and normative propositions about how society should be governed. It has, of course, complete and enduring faith in the efficacy and ethicality of marketplace. Only it can maximize personal wealth—and so society's wealth—given limited resources, in order to as to satisfy better people's unlimited wants—at a price—provided there is minimal public intervention. This is even so in the face of entrepreneurial risk-taking, the benefits of which should be judged against the net material benefits generated. So it demarcates only a minimal role for a hollowed-out state. Thus, neoliberalism questions the governance legitimacy and efficacy and ethicality of sovereign national governments.

The contending answers to the following fundamental questions are at the heart of the discourse on societal governance.

- *Society,* would it be better off if its governance is left to the market marketplace, rather than being subject to a mode of governance that empowers the state (alone or in conjunction with communities of special interest or place) to promote the positive freedom in the common good, by constraining negative freedom as necessary? Or is it better to disempower all the powers-that-be?

- *Government,* should it be considered a threat to individual liberty, or is it rather a vehicle to promote its citizens' positive freedom on the basis of government expert, community, or independent professional assessments of the social and individual needs that should be satisfied in the public interest at public expense? Or, does it really make any difference who has the authority to exercise the state's coercive power, as, come what may, the powers-that-be judge what is in the public interest in the light of their own egocentricities?

- *Society*, is it governable only when there is:

  - *A strong market, weak state, and a weak civil society*: Because it is only by granting, enforcing, and protecting the fundamental right of people to use their private property to satisfy their own wants can a society's wellbeing be advanced?

  - *A strong state, a weak civil society, and a weak market*: Because it is only when the governing elite are empowered to use the coveted power of the state as they see fit can social order, stability and harmony be advanced?

  - *A strong civil society, weak state, and a weak market*: Because it is only when a broad array of community interests is advanced in the public interest can social cohesion and inclusion be sustained and advanced?

  - *A weak state, weak civil society, and a weak market*: Because it is only when people are able to live their lives—and behave—as they see fit—without the intrusiveness and coercion of the political, economic, and social powers-that-be—can any sense of social alienation[147] be reversed or even contained.

There are fundamentally and profoundly different answers to these questions, which gives rise to an either–or conflict of perspectives. Neoliberalism's particular configurations of governing principles—individual liberty, democracy, minimal state intervention, and meliorism— are self-evidently held to be universally applicable and superior—regardless of ethnicity, socio-cultural customs, traditions and values, and religiosity. To neoliberalism, then, the market (self-regulation) mode of governance is beyond reproach.

---

147 Social alienation is "a condition in social relationships reflected by a low degree of integration or common values and a high degree of distance or isolation between individuals, or between an individual and a group of people in a community or work environment" (Ankony 1999, 1).

5.

NEOLIBERALISM:
BUSINESS-LIKE PUBLIC ADMINISTRATION

The idea that government should be run like a business is a popular one. ... But this betrays a basic misunderstanding of the roles of the private and public sector. We should no more want the government to be run like a business than a business to be run like the government.

Those popularizing this notion feel this way because they see business as more efficient. This must be the case, so the logic goes, or the entity in question would lose market share and go bankrupt. Only the fit survive. Meanwhile, government agencies face no backlash.

Harvey (2012)

INTRODUCTION

Public choice theory considers that hierarchical public organizations are best conceptualized as an amorphous, instrumental, rational-legal form of hierarchical organizations presumed to be administered by rationally self-interested—immoral—officials (Kaufman 1976) considered to be consummate empire-building bureaucrats[185] perhaps with a Machiavellian flair. According to Tullock (1965, 29-30, emphasis added) they can normally be treated "*as if* [they] were behaving out of selfish motivation" (see also Downs 1967; Niskanen 1971, 1973, 1975, 1994; but see also Udehn 1996), intent to maximizing their variously constituted utility functions. This ultimately means maximizing the size of their agencies (Tullock 1976, 26-35) in terms of personnel (Noll and Fiorina 1979), budgets (Niskanen 1973, 22-23, 1994), or discretionary budgets (defined as the difference between the budget received and the minimum cost of producing the required outputs) (Niskanen 1975). The result is

---

185 In terms of Burns' (1966) three organizational social systems, bureaucrats, as politically competitive people promoting their self-interest, would choose to use the political system within an organization as the way they react to formal decisions made within a power structure.

their inherent tendency to be deceitful, or even dishonest by, among other things, distorting information communicated upwards (Downs 1967, 77-78). Such behavior creates a bureaucracy that is perpetually expanding. This requires a hierarchical authority structure (Hayek 1960; Mises 1944), one based on rational rules that is held to be legitimate by all its members, in order to achieve co-operation (Downs 1967, 162), even though the capacity for top-down control diminishes as bureaucratic size increases, to the point where a large organizations can never be fully controlled or even coordinated (Downs 1967, 143). Bureaucratic failure is, thus, inevitable; the bureaucratic solution to which, is typically, according to Perlman (1976, 76), "to create another bureau to oversee those who have lapsed into sin. Bureaux are piled on bureau and the bureaucracy grows on" (see also Downs 1967, 148). This process of ever expanding vertical and structural control is a response to the need for a governance mechanism that minimizes the cost of any mismatch between controls and tasks by making bureaucracies responsible for the tasks they perform. A situation is, thus, created where monitoring bureaux become increasingly involved with the minutiae of administration and, thus, have a growing demand for control-oriented information. Hence Downs' (1967, 150) observation that "[t]he quantity and detail of reporting required by monitoring bureau tends to rise steadily over time, regardless of the amount, or nature, of the activity being monitored." The neoliberal solution is to institute wide reaching organizational transformations to make them more business-like and, thus, more cost-efficient and cost-effective (Dixon and Dogan 2003, 2005; Dixon, Kouzmin, and Korac-Kakabadse 1997), which has come to be known as the New Public Management (Hood 1991).

The purpose of this chapter is to articulate neoliberalism's perspectives on the ideal public organization and its management; to explore the character of the managerialist public manager; and to enunciate its managerialist reform agenda, its associated reform paradoxes, and their accommodation. It concludes with a discussion on the challenges confronting neoliberal administrative reform.

THE NEOLIBERAL VISION OF A PUBLIC ORGANIZATION

The neoliberal individualist-libertarian worldview considers the ideal public organization to be a cost-effective service-delivery mechanism with an entrepreneurial orientation (Mintzberg 1989). This requires the de-coupling of the administration of public services, as far as possible, from political structures and processes, thereby leaving their management to cognitive, goal-oriented, problem-solving, decision-making and interventionist technocrats (Flam 1990, 225).[186] Employees would be expected to have an organizational commitment, in Morrow's (1983) terms, based on their careers, which would achieve Etzioni's (1961) remunerative-calculative organizational engagement. Instrumental compliance (Etzioni 1961) is expected to follow an economic calculation of the compliance costs and benefits.

The envisaged service-delivery mechanism is conceptualized as a production unit (an open system), within which measurable "inputs" are used in a "production process" (so generating "tasks") to produce measurable "outputs," which have an "impact" (generating material "costs" and "benefits", whether intended or not) that seeks to achieve measurable objective-related "outcomes," which allows "organizational performance" to be measured against given and known "organizational objectives" that are compatible with given and known "government policy objectives" (Dixon 2003, 2016a). This archetypal public organization can be characterized as follows:

- It is best pictured either as a living organism (preoccupied with adaptiveness rather than orderliness, and thus with an open and flexible system that gives full scope to human capacities), or as being in a state of flux and transformation (constantly changing) (Morgan 1986).

- It has an organic structure with a significant degree of horizontal and/or spatial subunit differentiation, a strategic apex with little or no technostructure.

- It has an organizational culture[187] that focused on tasks (Altman and Baruch 1998), thereby giving management the

---

186 In terms of Burns' three organizational social systems (1966), technocrats would prefer to promote their self-interest through the cooperative career systems.

187 "Like the culture of a tribe, a corporate culture is an amalgam of the heroes and villains, of the commandments, of the crimes and punishments, of all the oral mythology that permeates the tribe" (Foy 1980, 2; see also Schein 1991). Schein (1985) identifies three layers of organizational culture: basic assumptions—those learned, unconsciously held responses that determine group perceptions, which may generate less-than-satisfactory crisis agreements (Taras 1991); values and beliefs; and visible artifacts, such as dress codes and office layout (see also Domahidy and Gilsionan 1992).

role of solving a series of task-related problems involving the adjustment, redefinition, and renegotiation of individual employee's tasks (Handy [1976] 1993 9), and on supporting *quid pro quo* exchanges between employees (Douglas 1994). So, it exhibits Hofstede's (1980, 1991) organizational culture dimensions of low power distance[188] and uncertainty avoidance,[189] but high individualism[190] and masculinity.[191]

- It confronts an external environment that is considered to be "disturbed reactive" (Thompson and Taylor 1986, 12; see also Emery and Trist 1965), in terms of its rate of change and the predictability of its direction. The appropriate response is that of a prospector (Altman and Baruch 1998, 780), forever seeking out and exploiting new opportunities, even at the risk of over-extension (Miles and Snow 1978). So, it operates at the edge of its competence, which means that when it is dealing with what it does not yet know, it uses an integrative approach to problem solving that challenges established practices by going beyond received wisdom (Kanter 1984, 1989).

So, the neoliberal individualist-libertarian worldview readily denies the worth of any alternative conceptualization of a public organization.

- *A bureaucratic organization*: This organizational archetype has a rational-legal orientation (Weber [1914/1922] 1947) and overtly acknowledges the supremacy of the formal authority system (Burns 1966; Burns and Stalker 1961), unless relational dominance (Ho, Chan, and Zhang 2001; Ho and Chiu 1998) empowers the informal authority system (Dixon and Wong 2015; Ho 1998; Redding and Wong 1992). It has administrative

---

188 This is the distance or personal gap that is felt to exist between subordinate and superior.

189 This is the degree to which the members feel uncomfortable with uncertainty and ambiguity.

190 This is the degree to which individualism (which emphasizes the right of an individual to a private life and opinion and to take personal initiatives and seek achievement if desired) dominates collectivism (which emphasizes the protection of the individual by group membership in return for group loyalty).

191 This is the degree to which the masculine values of performance, money, material standards, speed and size dominate the feminine values of quality of life, the importance of people and environment, and the propositions that service *per se* motivates and that small is beautiful.

processes that are strictly controlled by rules and regulations.[192] Because it has standardized work processes, specialized work tasks, order and discipline, and a unity of direction (through a scalar chain[193]), minimal discretion is given to public officials.[194] This archetypal public organization can be characterized as follows:

- It is best pictured either as a machine (an orderly and benevolent set of arrangements about who does what and who controls whom) or as a brain (with intelligent people spread throughout it, which enables it to correct errors, deal with uncertainty, and accept self-criticism) (Morgan 1986).

- It has a mechanistic structure, with high complexity, high formalization, and high centralization (Burns and Stalker 1961; Hague 1978; Mintzberg 1978), and a centralized technostructure.

- It has a club organizational culture that emphasizes role (Altman and Baruch 1998) and reinforces leaders who have power and are able to use it (Handy [1976] 1993). So, it exhibits Hofstede's (1980, 1991) organizational culture dimensions of high power–distance, masculinity, and un-

---

192 Thus, it insists on hierarchical obedience (Milgram 1963, 1974) and organizational loyalty (Burns 1966; Burns and Stalker 1961; Fayol [1916] 1949; Radner 1992; Taylor [1911] 1947). This means it subordinates employees' interests to organizational interests, unless it is in management's interest to draw upon the power of dominant customary relationships to avoid interpersonal conflict and to gain organizational commitment and compliant behavior (Dixon and Wong 2015; Ho, Chan, and Zhang 2001; Ho and Chiu 1998). Any organizational bonding of individuals is through the fostering of an appropriate *esprit de corps*. It has, then, "the potential to provide the setting both for constructive human relationships and for individual creative expression and dissatisfaction" (Jaques 1976, 13; see also Beetham 1987; Colebatch and Lamour 1993; du Gay 2000; Goodsell 1983; Schofield 2001).

193 This is a chain of all supervisors from the top management to the person working in the lowest rank, which ensures the downward flow of unambiguous communication from management (Marcellino 2006).

194 This subordinates employees' interests to organizational interests, unless it is in management's interest to draws upon the power of customary relationship—relational dominance—to avoid interpersonal conflict and to gain organizational commitment and compliant behavior, by respecting, facilitating and managing those customary relationships. In any event, there would be an insistence on hierarchical obedience and organizational loyalty (Burns 1966; Burns and Stalker 1961; Fayol [1916] 1949; Radner 1992; Redding and Wong 1992; Taylor [1911] 1947).

certainty avoidance, but low individualism. There is little questioning permitted of the rules and instructions given by a legitimate authority (Bardach and Kagan 1982). This reinforces employee compliance.

- It confront an external environment that is consider to be "turbulent" (Thompson and Taylor 1986, 12; see also Emery and Trist 1965), the organizational response to which would be that of an analyzer (Altman and Baruch 1998, 780) seeking to balance risk and outcomes as a follower rather than an initiator of change (Miles and Snow 1978).

This is the collectivist-hierarchical worldview.

- *A post-bureaucratic organization*: This archetypal organization has a missionary orientation, with a primary concern with inclusive-participative processes (Mintzberg 1978)[195] It has an organizational form that is flexible, adaptable, and informal—an adhocracy (Dolan 2010)—one, more suitable for a postmodern world (Bogason 2004; Lyotard 1979). Its vision is to empower public officials so that they are able to collaborate with internal and external stakeholders in order to enhance organizational performance (Vigoda-Gadot 2004: see also Bingham, Nabatchi, and O'Leary 2005).[196] This archetypal public organization can be characterized as follows:

  - It is best pictured either as a political system (having many stakeholders with potentially conflicting interests that need to be negotiated) or as a configuration of cultures (people in each subculture sharing common values, ex-

---

195 This reflects the proposition that public organizations should be post-bureaucratic (Bud 2007; Heckscher and Donnellon 1994; Kernaghan 2000; but see Davies 2011), which means it is not staffed by disempowered cog-in-the-machine bureaucrats, who are headless, soulless, and able to display little humanity and no imaginative creativity (Farmer 2005), and who are disengaged from their stakeholders (Vigoda-Gadot 2004).

196 It has a primary concern with enabling public officials to take collective responsibility for their own work design and performance. It uses mutual control as its control mechanism, involving the group enforcement of mutually agreed behavior norms relating to inputs (as standards of recruitment to the group), processes (as work methods), outputs (as performance standards), and values (as ethical standards) (Hales 2001, 47). It solicits employee compliance on the basis of moral commitments (Etzioni 1961). Empowering employees, within a framework set by government policies, builds their commitment to those policies, and their willingness to take ownership of their desired outcomes.

pressed through language, symbols, and ceremonies, that enable them to interpret situations and events in similar ways) (Morgan 1986).

- It has an organic structure, so as to disperse power, with low complexity, low formalization, and low centralization (Burns and Stalker 1961; Hague 1978).

- It has an organizational culture that is person centered such that the organization would be perceived as existing in order to help employees achieve their personal goals (Altman and Baruch 1998; Argyris 1957, 1962, 1972, 1973; Handy [1976] 1993). So, it exhibits Hofstede's (1980, 1991) organizational culture dimensions of low power-distance, individualism, and masculinity, but high uncertainty avoidance.

- It confronts an external environment that is consider to be "placid clustered" (Thompson and Taylor 1986, 12; see also Emery and Trist 1965), the organizational response to which would be that of a defender (Altman and Baruch 1998, 780), seeking to ensure stability by doing what the organization knows how to do well (Miles and Snow 1978).

This is the collectivist-egalitarian worldview.

- *An autocratic public organization*: This archetypal organization has a primary concern with inputs and process. It has an obsession with control, which is a conceptualization grounded in the first-person experiences of those who consider its organizational reality to be inexplicable and unpredictable. So, the unknowing and the untrustworthy are seen to dominate its autocratic decision-making processes (Vroom and Yetton 1973). This means that it is considered to be unable to learn from its mistakes, because management buries them, after apportioning blame on the lesser organizational mortals, but management is ever willing to claim the discovery of new and meaningful organizational truths through pseudo-rational analysis.[197] This archetypal public organization can be characterized as follows:

---

197 Inevitably, conflicts are never resolved; uncertainties are always avoided; and solutions are habitually shortsighted and simplistic. Its organizational goals are ambiguous and contradictory, and its organizational processes predictably give rise to "low-cooperation, rule-bound approaches to organization" (March and Olsen 1989, 9)—organized

- It is best pictured either as a psychic prison (individuals become trapped in a particular cognitively and emotionally dominant organizational mind-set, as suppositions fuel perceptions and perceptions fuel emotions in a way that does not allow them to see organizational reality clearly from any other perspective); or as an instrument of domination (willingly glorifying the managing elite at the expense of sacrificing employees) (Morgan 1986);

- It has a mechanistic structure exhibiting high complexity, high formalization, and high centralization (Burns and Stalker 1961; Hague 1978; Mintzberg 1978).

- It has a club organizational culture that reinforces strong leadership by those who are willing and able to exercise power (Handy [1976] 1993), which supports the authority of superiors over subordinates. So, it exhibits Hofstede's (1980,1991) organizational culture dimensions of high power-distance, masculinity, and uncertainty avoidance, but low individualism; and

- It confronts an external environment that is considered to be "placid randomized" (Thompson and Taylor 1986, 12; see also Emery and Trist 1965), the organizational response to which would be that of a reactor (Altman and Baruch 1998, 780), characterized by a hesitancy born of the uncertainty and the confusion that inevitably follows (Miles and Snow 1978).

This is the individualist-existential worldview.

THE NEOLIBERAL VISION OF PUBLIC MANAGEMENT

The neoliberal individualist-libertarian worldview embraces the New Public Management (Hood 1991; see also Ferlie et al. 1996). This managerialist ideology has guided the charge of the neoliberal reform brigade over the last three or so decades (Peters and Savoie 1998). The New Public Management advocates managing for performance: "good government

---

anarchy (March 1988, 1994; see also Cyert and March [1963] 1992; Cohen and March [1974] 1983; March and Olsen 1976, 1989). Moreover, who is involved in what is ever changing—because people are capricious and unpredictable.

and good organization results from deliberate intentions, detailed plans and consistent decisions" (Prasser 1990, 194). This initiated a drive to modernize the management of public organization by the adoption of business-like performance-oriented management practices[198] (Rainey 2014; Rainey, Bckoff, and Levine 1976; Rainey and Bozeman 2000; Rainey and Chun 2005). This set of management propositions is grounded in Herzberg's Adam concept of human nature (people's "overriding goal is...to avoid pain") ([1966] 1974, 168) and Theory X human nature assumptions (essentially, people are work-shy) (1960, see also 1967). These behaviors may well follow public employees being trapped in Weber's ([1905/1930] 1992) bureaucratic "iron cage," the product of the technically ordered, rigid, and dehumanized bureaucracy that comes with its instrumental role that requires rational reckoning and strict controls.

This managerialist perspective is underpinned by the presumed superiority of "scientific knowledge and of progress over democratic process and outcome" (Finer [1941] 1966, 247; see also Friedrich [1940] 1966; Rosenthal 1990) and by an inclination towards technocracy—a situation where professional career public official more fully control the public policy than do politicians. This vision, indeed, calls for far-reaching bureaucratic transformation. There is, however, a missing link.

Private-sector decision-making, with its self-correcting dynamic feedback loops—the market's automatic disciplining mechanisms—is difficult to replicate in the public sector, where management cannot be de-coupled from government policies and political process. This coupling results, in the words of March and Olsen (1983, 292), in "incremental adaption to changing problems with available solutions within gradually evolving structures of meaning." As Prasser (1990, 194) remarks, "intentions are changed, plans become irrelevant and consistency becomes an impediment to the day-to-day management of issues, crises and problems." This reflects the process of governance—described by Waldo's (1984, 128) "seamless web of discretion and action"—that Marini (1993) considers is integrally bound to the evolution of civilization. Public management, then, requires not only the science of management, but also the art of statecraft (Borins 1992; Peters 1995) and a respect for what Goodsell (1989, 161) describes as "administrative ritual" (repetitive, staged, and time-specific rites, cyclically repetitious formalistic processes, and ex-

---

198 Including management by objectives, performance objectives, performance indicators and measurement, performance management, performance reporting, and performance-related employment contracts and remuneration, and performance-based budgeting.

pressive programs). This, he considers, "can foster the community spirit that is essential to holding together and governing a civilized society" (p. 161). Much of the legitimation of the New Public Management depends heavily upon the ideological proclivity to accept the primacy of the marketplace in the governance processes and the appropriateness of market metaphors in the public administration (Kouzmin, Leivesley, and Korac-Kakabadse 1997).

The modernized management of public organization focuses on management processes that improve organizational performance by decentralizing authority distribution, so as to expand the ways in which work is conducted, and by creating financial incentives to reward individual performance improvement. These managerialized public managers are expected to use their devolved authority to achieve organizational targets, with control being exercised *ex post facto* (Feldman and Khademain 2000, 150)—self-control (under the self-determined coercive influence of financial incentives embedded in remunerations). The intention is to encourage conformity with a set of internalized rules and norms of behavior relating to work processes (methods of work), outputs (standards), and internalized values (ethical work conduct) (Hales 2001, 47), achieved by modifying, repressing, or inhibiting unacceptable behaviors. This is, of course, in line with Barnard's proposition that "incentives represent the final residue of all conflicting forces in organization" and that people are reasoning agents who respond to inputs (such as instructions) in systematic ways and can best be motivated by financial incentives (1938, 159; see also Buschardt, Toso, and Schnake 1986; Clark and Wilson 1961; de Grazia 1960; Fayol [1916] 1949; Gellerman 1968; Taylor [1911] 1947; Whyte 1955).

The underlying motivation presumptions are four-fold. The first is that individuals value financial rewards as a means of satisfying their needs, the most important of which are Maslow's (1970) physiological, safety (security), and esteem needs, and Riesman and Packard's prestige needs (Packard 1959; Riesman 1950; see also Furnham 1984). The second is that these rewards justify the extra effort expected. The third is that organizational performance can be measurably attributed to an individual's work contribution. The fourth is that any increased individual performance does not become a new minimum standard (Handy [1976] 1993; see also Vroom 1964). Thus, an employee's psychological contracts—the unwritten sets of expectations (Schein 1980)—specify quite explicitly the financial rewards that follow the rendering of specified services. This gives rise to an organizational commitment, in Morrow's terms (1983), based on their careers, which achieves Etzioni's (1961) remunerative-calculative organizational engagement. Instrumental compliance (Etzioni 1961) thus follows an economic calculation of the compliance costs and benefits.

The archetypal managerialized public manager's leadership style is that of a developer (Altman and Baruch 1998, 780), within a consultative management system (Likert 1961, 1967). Hershey and Blanchard (1969, 1993) have characterized this leadership style as having the dimensions of a low-relationship[199] and a low-task[200] behavior pattern. This broadly corresponds with Stogdill and Coons' (1957) low consideration (relationship behaviors) and low initiating structures (task behaviors) leadership style, and with Blake and Mouton's (1982, 1984) low concern-for-production and low concern-for-people, or impoverished, leadership style, because it provides little structural or socio-emotional support when needed. This leadership style facilitates individual autonomy by appropriately delegating decision-making and implementation responsibility. In terms of Tannenbaum and Schmidt's (1958) leadership behavior continuum, this leadership style involves managers defining limits and followers making decisions.

So, the neoliberal individualist-libertarian worldview readily denies that public organizations would be better served with a different management oriented.

- *Managing for process*: This focuses public management on employee compliance (Dixon and Frolova 2013), which requires public mangers to

    - determine, monitor, and police what are acceptable (desirable) or unacceptable (undesirable) behaviors in terms of the desired organizational outcomes.

    - practice *ex ante* control (Feldman and Khademain 2000), achieved by direct management supervision (personal

---

199 This is the extent to which leaders are likely to maintain personal relationships between themselves and their followers by engaging in other facilitating behaviors (such as, providing socio-emotional support and giving psychological strokes) (Hershey and Blanchard 1993, 129).

200 This is the extent to which leaders are likely to organize and define the roles of their followers, by, for example, establishing well-defined organizational patterns, communication channels, and ways of accomplishing jobs (Hershey and Blanchard 1993, 129).

monitoring and work surveillance) (Hales 2001, 47–48).[201]

- achieve employee compliance by assisting them make a cognitive commitment to the organization (Etzioni 1961) based on a rational calculation.[202]

This management orientation is premised on public employees:

- being very largely indolent, unambitious, indifferent to organizational needs;[203]

- valuing the satisfaction personal needs[204] that result from the order, clarity, and authority provided by well-defined work system and practices; and

- needing psychological contracts that make quite explicit the organization's obligations in terms of the employee needs that would be met in return for services rendered (Handy [1976] 1993).

This is the collectivist-hierarchical worldview.

- *Managing for inclusion*: This focuses management on empowering;

  - an inclusive network of external stakeholders to build organizational capacity in order to achieve desired policy and organizational results (Heckscher and Donnellon 1994; Vigoda-Gadot 2002, 2004); and

---

201 This is in the context of administrative processes embedded in, and defined by, the established rules, procedures, and accepted practices in relation to inputs (about recruitment, qualifications, and experience), processes (as technical methods and procedures), outputs (as activity measures and standards), and organizational values (ethos or philosophy).

202 This is in the context of its prescribed rules and regulations or customary practices, supported by a deontological moral code that places a high value on organization loyalty (Morrow 1983), which achieve a weak form of Etzioni's (1961) organizational engagement.

203 Thus, they prefer to be directed (so as to avoid responsibilities), and gullible (reflecting Herzberg's (1966) Adam concept of human nature, and McGregor's (1960, see also 1967) Theory X human nature assumption).

204 These are prioritized as Maslow's (1970) physiological, safety (security), social (affiliation) and esteem needs; Ardrey's (1967) identity, security, and stimulation needs; Adler's ([1929] 1969) power needs; White's (1959) competence needs; and McClelland's (1961) achievement, power, and affiliation needs.

- employees to perform their tasks with a greater sense of commitment and responsibility, as members of work groups striving for the common good.[205]

This style of public management requires public managers to:

- enable all stakeholders to collaborate (Huxham and Vangen 2005) by engaging in discourse with management in an open environment characterized by broadly diffused transformations (Bakhtin [1934–1941] 1981; Foucault 1978);[206]

- increase employee participation in decision-making by decentralizing authority (Dugan 2003; Feldman and Khademain 2000; FRIDE 2006; Gergen and Thatchenkery 1998);

- communicate a value-driven performance philosophy that inculcates a sense of performance consciousness—in the form of a mutually agreed set of high-performance expectations;[207] and

- adopt an approach to employee compliance that involves mutual control, as empowerment is motivating.[208]

This management orientation is premised on public employees:

- valuing work the as an end in itself; [209]

---

205 This is achieved by encouraging cooperation (Whetten and Cameron 2002), and by developing in them a sense of meaning in relation to their work, self-efficacy, self-determination, personal responsibility, and trust in other people (Spreitzer 1995; Whetten and Cameron 2002).

206 By so doing, this builds their commitment to common policy goals on the basis of shared common values and a common vision, even if it means that the patterns of organizational activity are ever dynamic, and decision-making, at times, incremental and disjointed (Gergen and Thatchenkey 1998, 28).

207 This is achieved by stimulating and facilitating the necessary behavior changes that will enable employees to become innovators, accomplished by the practice of management-by-wandering-around (Peters 1994; Peters and Waterman 1982).

208 This is because it permits employee needs to be met, prioritized as Maslow's (1970) social (affiliation or acceptance), esteem and self-actualization (distinctive psychological potential) needs; Ardrey's (1967) identity, security, and stimulation needs; Alderfer's (1972) existence, relatedness, and growth needs, McClelland's (1961; see also McClelland et al. [1953] 1976) achievement, power, and affiliation needs; and Herzberg's (1966; see also Herzberg, Mausner, and Snyderman 1959) achievement, recognition, responsibility, and advancement needs.

209 This, thereby, ensures their absorption and involvement in their jobs, and their

- wanting empowerment;[210] and

- needing psychological contracts that identify which organizational goals are to be pursued collaboratively in return
  for just rewards, and how they are to be given more voice
  in their selection and more discretion in the choice of
  goal-achievement strategies (Handy [1976] 1993);

This is the collectivist-egalitarian worldview.

- *Managing for survival*: This focuses public management on
  surviving the inevitable and unexplainable organizational trials and tribulation, achievable only doing what is plausible,
  since learning can only be by trial and error and human behavior is unpredictable. This is because people are constrained
  by their subjective perceptions of organizational reality—what
  they believe to be real is, in fact, reality—so they engage in
  nonrational reasoning, because validity and truth are irrelevant, expecting only organizational alienation. This style of
  public management requires public mangers to:

  - exercise strict external management control (Hales 2001,
    47),[211] and

  - enforce strict employee compliance.[212]

---

commitment to the organizational interest (a willingness to direct their behavior towards organizational goals and to be creative organizational problem-solv-
ers) (reflecting Herzberg's ([1966] 1974) Abraham concept of human nature, and
McGregor's (1960; see also 1967) Theory Y human nature assumptions).

210 This is because they want to share responsibility for goal-setting and goal-achievement decisions, and because there is a congruence between individual and organizational goals, the attainment of which is justified by their achievement of Etzioni's
(1961) normative-moral organizational engagement, on the premise that this suggests that they would respond favorably to the creation of friendly workgroup environment, to the provision of employee support, to the availability of more and better
organizational information, and to open and frequent discussions with management
on the organization's objectives.

211 This is achieved by means of the "contrived randomness" with hierarchical accountability (Hood 1998, 64-68; see also Rose-Ackerman 1978). It involves, for example,
dual-key operations (that is, several people needed to commit funds or other resources, or the separation of payment and authorization processes), an unpredictable pattern of posting supervisors around the organization, and "random internal
audits" (Hood 1998, 65).

212 This is achieved only when employees are sufficiently fearful of the punishment
that follows noncompliance, because those threatening punishment have the power to punish, which results in Etzioni's (1961) coercive-alienative organizational

This management orientation is premised on public employees:

- having no work commitment;[213] and

- needing psychological contract that quite explicitly articulate the rules to be followed and the punishments in place for noncompliance (Handy [1976] 1993).

This is the individualist-existential worldview.

On the New Public Manager

The neoliberal individualist-libertarian worldview privileges the inculcation of business-like public management practices. This may be relevant in public organizations operating in a market or quasi-market environment, so necessitating a more business-like, more cost-efficient and cost-effective in the provision of public services. Such organizations include:

- Those that provide a service in a deregulated market in which there is private sector competition, or contestable markets in which there are a close but not perfect market substitute.

- Those that are being set up for future commercialization, corporatization, or privatization.

- Those that are engaged in public–private partnerships for the joint provision of capital infrastructure or public services.

- Those that provide services in a monopoly market in which there is a threat of new entrants.

- Those that provide a service in a regulated market that could be deregulated.

- Those that provide a service in a statutory monopoly market that could be deregulated.

The archetypal managerialized public manager has a distinctive set of salient attributes:

---

engagement, born of the fear of force, threat, and menace.

213 This is because they are very largely indolent and unambitious, without organizational commitment and indifferent to organizational needs; and prefer to be directed, so as to avoid responsibility (reflecting Herzberg's (1966) Adam concept of human nature, and McGregor's (1960, 1967) Theory X human nature assumption), which results in Etzioni's (1961) coercive-alienative organizational engagement.

- They accept the legitimate authority of the marketplace to steer public provision, because what the public wants—their private interests—can only be known from the preferences they reveal in a marketplace.

- They are willing to balance the individual rights (embracing property rights and consumer sovereignty) over the common good (embracing, for example, national interests, social justice, and social solidarity) in favor of individual rights.

- They accept the importance in determining the morality of their decisions and actions of reasoned enquiry into the resultant consequences, including whether or not to disobey a legitimate command if they decided that its overall effects would have net negative consequences.

- They would be held accountable of the outputs and outcomes they produce.

- They acknowledge the importance of public officials acting at all times to enhance the cost-effectiveness of public services and to reduce the cost of government.

- They accept, readily, their obligation to avoid becoming self-interested builders of perpetually expanding bureaucratic empires that at public expense.

- They place considerable emphasize on the need to ensure the state can be held accountable for the conduct of its financial and administrative affairs.

The archetypal managerialized public manager adopts a leadership style that facilitates individual target-oriented employee autonomy by appropriately delegating decision-making and implementation responsibility. This leadership style facilitates individual autonomy by appropriately delegating decision-making and implementation responsibility. In terms of Tannenbaum and Schmidt's (1958) leadership behavior continuum, this involves managers defining limits and followers making decisions.

So, the neoliberal individualist-libertarian worldview readily denies that public organizations would be better served if they champion a different ideal-type public manager.

- *Hierarchical public managers:* They can be characterized as conforming to Likert's (1961, 1967) benevolent-authoritative type, with a parent leadership style[214] (Altman and Baruch 1998). This involves presenting and explaining decisions, with background ideas and inviting questions, so providing opportunities for clarification; and monitoring performance, thereby ensuring leadership control (Tannenbaum and Schmidt 1958).[215]

This is the collectivist-hierarchical worldview.

• *Participative public managers*: They can be characterized as conforming to Likert's participative type (1961, 1967), with a coach leadership style[216] (Nichols 1986). Under this style of leadership, the production of outcomes is incidental to the lack of conflict and good fellowship. Such leaders permit followers to function within broad organizationally defined limits (Tannenbaum and Schmidt 1958). Their leadership focus is, thus, on sharing ideas and facilitating group decision-making, thereby empowering them as employees.

This is the collectivist-egalitarian worldview.

• *Authoritarian public managers*: They can be characterized as conforming to Likert's (1961, 1967) exploitative-authoritative type,[217]

---

214 Hershey and Blanchard (1969, 1993) have characterized this leadership style (Nichols 1986) as having the dimensions of high relationship and high task behavior pattern. This broadly corresponds with Stogdill and Coons' (1957) high consideration (relationship behaviors) and high initiating structures (task behaviors) leadership style, and with Blake and Mouton's (1982, 1984) high concern-for-production and high concern-for-people, or team, leadership style.

215 Whitehead (1936, 72-73) caught the essence of this style of leadership:
The leader shares with his group a profound loyalty to the technical procedures ... [He] is trusted as one who has unusual skill in these technical procedures ... [and] being a man [sic] of intelligence, obtains an unusual insight into the causal relations involved in his procedures ... [he] continues in his traditional procedures, because he sees the 'reasons why.' ... Sooner or later in his semi-irrational reveries and reflections, [he] stumbles on a technical improvement. He adopts this without misgivings because the group has accorded him the right to make decisions in technical matters. The group follows their leader and adopts the improved process without question.

216 Hersey and Blanchard (1969, 1993) have characterized this leadership style (Nichols (1986) as having the dimensions of high-relationship and low-task behavior pattern, which broadly corresponds with Blake and Mouton's (1982, 1984) country-club leadership style.

217 To Adorno et al. (1950), the authoritarian is characterized by a rigid adherence to conventional values; a readiness to punish others so as to achieve their conformity with social mores; an arrogance toward those considered to be inferior; a capacity

with a driver leadership style[218] (Altman and Baruch 1998). This involves leaders making decisions, providing specific instructions and closely supervising work performance thereby ensuring leadership domination (Tannenbaum and Schmidt 1958).[219]

This is the individualist-existential worldview.

Inculcating Business-like Managerial Reforms

As members of an administrative elite in whose hands the apparatus of government is placed, the ideal-type managerialist public managers expect to take a wider view of their management responsibilities. They are in favor of loosening the strictures of the hierarchical bureaucracy, so as to allow for more flexibility and adaptability to facilitate the achievement of greater efficiencies, enhanced effectiveness, better customer service, and lower public outlays. This requires them to be more flexibility, to make decisions using their judgment, to be more entrepreneurial, and to take risks, albeit within a risk management rather than a risk-averse environment. Managerialists are in favor of having greater public accountability (Behn 2001), achieved by measuring outputs and outcomes rather than just inputs and processes, which they would use to justify and encourage the downsizing of the public sector.

The challenge managerialists face in trying to inculcate business-like management practices into the public sector, relates to the reality that any extant public sector is the product of historically overriding forces associated with the nature of the host society: its political, ideological, economic, and socio-cultural values; its balancing of the governance roles of state, the marketplace, and civil society; and its assigned role for government—as protector, provider, controller, regulator, contractor, fa-

---

for prejudice; and an unwillingness to tolerate ambiguity; an extreme degree of conformity or over-deferentiality to authority; and a submissiveness both to positional authority figures and to the group's moral authority.

218 Hershey and Blanchard (1969, 1993) have characterized this leadership style (Nichols 1986) as having the dimensions of low relationship and high task behavior pattern. This broadly corresponds with Stogdill and Coons' low consideration (relationship behaviors) and high initiating structures (task behaviors) leadership style (1957), and with Blake and Mouton's high concern-for-production and low concern-for-people or task leadership style (1982, 1984).

219 In so doing they may be aware, from their interactions, that their alienated subordinates—judged to be no more than a small, marginally relevant, cog in a bureaucratic machine—probably have little or no confidence in them because they are unaware of what is, in practice, achievable, and so inevitably issue unrealistic work goals.

cilitator, and empowerer. This has given rise to a path dependency—the outcome of past decisions grounded in past circumstances (Liebowitz and Margolis 2000)—suggesting that the success of mangerialist reform depends upon not only present, but also the difficult-to-change past, decisions. As Liebowitz and Margolis (2000, 985) note, a strong dependency path is one that, however inefficient it may be, has to be followed because it cannot be reformed, which suggests historical determinism, albeit one tempered by institutional evolution (see also Thelen 2004; Page 2006).

The Managerialist Reform Paradoxes

Faced with the juxtaposition of managerialist reforms on extant hierarchical public administration structures, procedures and practices, public managers would confront a variety of paradoxes (Dixon 1996; Dixon and Kouzmin 1994a, 1994b; Tripathi and Dixon 2008; but see also Hood 2000; Thiel and Leeuw 2002).

Paradox 1:

That public managers are expected to manage efficiently and effectively, and so be accountable for their management of the inputs used to produce outputs (that may be difficult to even conceptualize let alone measure), which generate outcomes (that may be difficult to conceptualize and measure), which relate to program objectives (that may be difficult to articulate in mutually compatible and quantifiable terms), which must be compatible not only with policy objectives (that government may be unwilling or unable to articulate in quantifiable terms, and which may, themselves, be mutually incompatible) but also with customer objectives (that may difficult to ascertain (for public goods) and articulate and may be mutually incompatible).

Paradox 2:

That public managers are expected to be accountability for service efficiency and effectiveness, although they do not have complete control over service delivery design or implementation processes.

Paradox 3:

That public managers are expected to be results-oriented, although over-achievement is not adequately rewarded and under-achievement is not adequately punished.

Paradox 4:

That public managers are expected to be willing to take risks, in the context of better risk management, although politicians and public sector auditors are reluctant accept risk-taking behaviors that threaten administrative probity.

Paradox 5:

That public managers are expected to be accountable for performance outcomes they produce, although any judicial and merit review agencies are able to reverse administrative decisions.

Paradox 6:

That public managers are expected to not tolerate sub-optimal performances, although when sub-optimal performances are a product of behaviors that conform to cultural norms any challenging of those norms is likely to affect adversely their personal survival within the organization and/or to generate interpersonal conflicts.

Paradox 7:

That public managers are expected to increase both service quality and employee productivity, although, at the same time, they are expected to contain, if not decrease, costs.

Paradox 8:

That public managers are expected to meet market—customer or client—needs, although they must also ensure that those services provide value for money as perceived by legislative and other accountability mechanisms.

Paradox 9:

That public managers are expected to share a significant degree of decision-making power with their subordinates who are closer to the end-user (clients or customers), while being unable to devolve accountability for the consequences of their decisions.

The Challenge of Accommodating the Managerialist Paradoxes

Managerialist reformers face the challenge of enabling public managers to accommodate the reform paradoxes—as "a self referential, self contradictory vicious cycle" (Smith and Berg 1987, 199). This can be achieved either by their re-framing as puzzles, conundrums, or complexities; by placing them into a broader organizational or societal context, so as to diminish their apparent absurdity, contradiction or hypocrisy; or by addressing the emotional responses they stimulate. This would involve them in the getting of wisdom. Sagaciousness allows a more accurate apprehension of the true causality of organizational phenomena, and so avoiding the deceiving "naïve consciousness," which, according to Freire (1983, 281), "sees causality as an established static fact...[and]...considers itself superior to facts, in control of facts, and free to understand them as it pleases." It would, moreover, involve a learning process that improves understanding of the relationship between knowledge, decisions, and action (Harman 1989). And it would entail encouraging both management and organizational values and perspectives to be reframed or laterally re-conceptualized, in order to help make sense of the options available in relation to future courses of actions and the basis of their selection. This is comes under Beiner's (1983, 163) rubric of "instrumental judgment," as distinct from moral and political judgment (see also Anderson 1988).[220] Required, then, is for the public manager to be:

- a pragmatic strategic thinker;

- an effective persuader and communicator;

- willing and able to make decisions with incomplete information;

- a visionary with energy and resilience;

- a networker capable of solving problems;

- a consummate resource and contract administrator;

- an effective developer of subordinates and able to resolve contractual conflicts;

- a committed life-long learner able to integrate new ideas readily; and even,

- a successful social (quasi-commercial) entrepreneur.

Those suffering any resultant cognitive dissonance[221] as a result of these expectations may well be inclined to voice to the criticisms of the re-

---

220 Judgment, as an irreducible part of public administration, requires a capacity to place information into an appropriate, even if a somewhat paradoxical, value framework to determine how best to blend and manage contradictory demands and pressures. Thus, axiomatically, places stress on an individual's capacity to make judgments (Macadam and Bawden 1986). Soberingly, Banfield (1958, 27) warned, long ago, that in the art of judgment there is "...no science at all, either of organization or of anything else, which will help the executive much in performing his most essential and characteristic functions."

221 This is an agonizing motivational state caused when "two opinions, or beliefs, or

forms, or if the believe that their cognitive dissonance cannot be diminish by anyone, they may well disengage from the reform process and join the ranks of the alienated public officials. So, for managerialist reformers, not enabling public managers to accommodate these paradoxes would build opposition to their reforms (Dixon 2016).

The responses of those not committed to the managerialist style of public administration can be anticipated.

- *Hierarchical public managers*: As advocates of the collectivist-hierarchical worldview, they believe that they have no real capacity to shape their working lives, because they have chosen to give important others the authority to do so. Thus, they believe developing loyal and dutiful relationships with them can best advance their interests. Their predisposition is toward traditional bureaucratic (Weberian) public administration, and so to resist any form of administrative reform. They would be appalled and would, in all likelihood, seek to sabotage any managerialist reforms at all opportunities. They would not relish the prospect of having to engage with business-like people (imbued with a commitment to personal freedom and independence), who have no respect for hierarchical authority, but they would do so only out of sense of obligation to the organizational powers-that-be. Above all, they would not want their decisions and actions to compromise their own sense of obligation to be loyal and obedient to their superiors or to make hierarchically acceptable decisions. For them, only the rulebook has changed. Meeting client—let alone customer—needs, taking risks, and becoming quasi-commercial entrepreneurs are all anathema to them.

- *Collaborative public managers*: As advocates of the collectivist-egalitarian worldview, they believe that they have the capacity to influence how they conduct their working lives by engaging in discourse with others. Thus, they believe that

---

items of knowledge are dissonant with each other if they do not fit together; that is, if they are inconsistent, or if, considering only the particular two items, one does not follow from the other" (Festinger 1957, 25). The magnitude of the dissonance experienced depends on the relative importance of the cognitions involved. Aronson (1969) challenged cognitive dissonance theory on the grounds that dissonance arises not when a person finds his or her cognitions to be in conflict with factual evidence, but when they are in conflict with his or her self-concept.

building collaborative relationships can best advance their interests. Their predisposition is to fight for administrative reform that inculcates inclusive, participative, deliberative, and collaborative processes into public administration. They would be apprehensive but unlikely to sabotage the managerialist reform as it opens up the possibility of inculcating a reform twist towards processes they consider to be more appropriate. They would not relish the prospect of having to engage with business-like people who place too much emphasis on costs and performance without reference to values and ideals, but they would do so in expectation of engaging in robust values discourses with them. For them, the door to desirable change is ajar. Meeting client-determined needs, taking risks, and becoming quasi-commercial entrepreneurs are, however, all anathema to them.

- *Alienated public managers*: As advocates of the individualist-existential worldview, they are alienated and so disillusioned, perhaps even dissatisfied and disgruntled, in their work. This makes them disinclined to sabotage what they consider to be futile managerialist reforms that will inevitably fail anyway, unless they perceive, on the basis of own experience, that one of its outcomes is their further exploitation.

At issue, then, whether managerialized style of public management can—even should—be fostered in public organizations (Dixon 2016; Dixon, Davis, and Kouzmin 2004). This is a fundamentally and profoundly important in any public organization.

CONCLUSION

The neoliberal individualist-libertarian worldview considers the ideal public organization to be a cost-effective service-delivery mechanism, one that is de-coupled, as far as possible, from political structures and processes, and managed by goal-oriented and problem-solving technocrats, committed to implementing an array of performance-oriented management practices. The ideal public manager is, thus, one who places paramount importance on being more business-like in his or her management style, so as to achieve a more cost-efficient and cost-effective provision of public services, as this both enhances customer satisfaction and lowers public outlays.

The success of mangerialist reform depends on not only the contemporary decisions that reflect contemporary organizational and political realities, but also the difficult-to-change past decisions, grounded in past political, ideological, economic, and socio-cultural realities—the path dependency challenge. Indeed, a strong dependency path is one that, however inefficient it may be, has to be followed because it cannot be reformed. At the organizational level, the juxtaposition of managerialist reforms on extant hierarchical public administration structures, procedures, and practices, creates for public managers a variety of paradoxes, which managerialist reformers need to address in order to curb reform criticisms.

Neoliberalism arrogantly posits that its managerialist style of public organization and management should prevail. This is because the ideal public organization can only take the form of a business-like, cost-effective service-delivery mechanism, as this is required under its particular configuration of governing principles—individual liberty, democracy, minimal state intervention, and meliorism—all which are self-evidently held to be universally applicable and, of course, superior, regardless of ethnicity, socio-cultural customs, traditions and values, and religiosity. To neoliberalism, the managerialist reform agenda is beyond reproach.

6.

NEOLIBERALISM:
GETTING WHAT YOU DESERVE AND
DESERVING WHAT YOU GET

The market ensures that everyone gets what they deserve.

Monbiot (2016)

INTRODUCTION

Neoliberalism offers distinctive ethical guidance for the distribution of economic wellbeing—consumption, income, and wealth (OECD 2011, 2013)—across members of a society. It postulates that a just society is one in which

- everyone is entitled to the natural or man-made resources or the cash assets they possess, provided any actions taken in the procurement process were just; and

- any inequalities in the distribution of economic wellbeing are only the product of some individuals being better equipped to acquire the benefits of market engagement, because of:

  - their initial human capital endowments (physiological attributes, psychological traits, knowledge, and skills);

  - the actions they have taken to enhance that endowment; and

  - their past decisions made about how they exploit their human capacities, or latent qualities.

The purpose of this chapter is to examine what it means to be entitled to own resources (to acquire property rights justly), to get what you deserve (to gain a just meritorious desert), and to deserve whatever you get (to be justly held personally responsible for past decisions and actions).

Owning That To Which You Are Justly Entitled

The neoliberal individualist-libertarian worldview privileges the libertarian distributive justice principle—entitlement theory (Nozick 1974; Otsuka 2003; but see Kavka 1982; Pare 1984). This argues that a just distribution of resources depends on the justness of the actions of the acquiring individuals in the resource acquisition process. Thus, everyone is entitled to take ownership of—acquire property rights over—resources, whether natural or man-made or financial assets, provided their actions in so doing are in accordance with three justice principles (Nozick 1974, 1):

- *Justice in acquisition*: A just initial acquisition of a property right over previously un-owned natural resources is achieved when it does not involve making anyone "worse off than they would have been if the resource had not been appropriated" (Olsaretti 2004, 72) because they are no longer able to use (acquire?) those resources (but see also Locke [1688] 1960) (the compensation principle).

- *Justice in transfer*: A just transfer of property rights is achieved when the transferring process is voluntary and consensual, which imposes an obligation of non-interference on both parties, and when, in the case of natural resources, no one is made worse off by the transfer of property rights because they no longer able to use (acquire?) those resources.

- *Justice in rectification*: A just acquisition process is one that has provided compensation for any previous economic injustices in the natural resource acquisition process, whether instigated or merely tolerated by society, on the premise that the "world is not wholly just, and people sometimes acquire goods by force or fraud ... [so] a principle of rectification is also needed, to repair the effects of past injustices" (Wolff 1991, 78). This means that a public authority must legitimately maintain a legal apparatus that reliably convicts and punishes those who violate individual rights in the process of resource acquisition and compensates those suffering any economic injustices (Kavka 1982).

Once property rights have been justly acquired, any breach of that right constitutes an act of theft. This is taken to include the imposition of any tax obligation flowing from a just resource acquisition or the benefits earned from exploiting those rights. The question begged, of course, is how is it possible to ensure that these normative requirements are fully reflected in the design of the institutions that are responsible for assigning and protecting property rights?

GETTING WHAT YOU JUSTLY DESERVE

Neoliberalism take as axiomatic that individuals have personal autonomy and so they have individual authenticity and are capable of self-rule, including the capacity to reflect critically on their intentions. This gives them compelling free will, the capacity to decide, knowingly and responsibly, on the courses of action they need to follow to advance their self-interest, unconstrained by any punitive, oppressive, coercive, compulsive, or manipulative conditioning that could limit their freedom of choice and action. So, a morally acceptable (meritorious) distribution of income is one that reflects individuals' freedom of choice and action, and that requires them to be responsible for their actions and for their economic wellbeing. Under these conditions, the income they deserve can be judged on merit. This makes distributive justice a matter of each person getting what they deserve (merit-based desert) (Feinberg 1970; Lamont 1994; Pojman and McLeod 1999; Sher 1987) in the light of their actions (Feldman 1992, 1995a, 1995c), judged in accordance with a set of rules that are just and justly applied (procedural justice) (Maiese 2003).

Merit-based Desert

Neoliberalism's privileging of merit-based desert is in recognition that people are not homogeneous, because they are differentially purposeful, responsible, and creative. This is premised on all individuals having the same natural and civil rights, which means they are freely, willing, and able to apply their abilities and talents, in varying degrees, to productive work; and being rewarded by the market in accordance with their input[185] into the creation of the socially valued collective standard of living—the social product[186] (Miller 1976; Riley 1989)). In these circumstances, they deserve to be deserved (Zaitchik 1977), so making just getting what they

---

185 Rawls (1971) pointed out that a person born with greater natural endowments (genetic inheritance) does not morally deserve the benefits derived from those endowments, but he or she can have legitimate expectations (but see Nozick 1974, 214 and 228).

186 This has become the primary value relevant to desert-based distributions, as the application of the desert-based principle requires the specification of the activities that count as being socially productive, and hence deserving of reward (Lamont 1994).

deserve. The questions begged, of course, are twofold.

- What about people who are not able to freely choice what to make of themselves because they are not *causa sui,* and so are unable to determine their own fate and, thus, cannot be expected to accept responsibility for what they make of themselves? This can be the result of life-choices being:

  - limited, because of their intrinsic physiological attributes (related to age, gender, physical completeness, or ethnicity);

  - restricted, because they had impaired initial natural human endowments (physiological or neurological) as a result of genetic inheritance (the product of the natural lottery);

  - constrained, because they are chronically experiencing cognitive biases that function entirely at an unconscious level;

  - tainted, by irresistible influences of important others able to affect their choices or actions by means of argument, example, or force of personality; or

  - bounded, by the prescriptions of oppressively controlling others.

- How is it possible to ensure the normative requirements of desert justice are fully reflected in the design of the institutions that are responsible for allocating differential rewards?

Given the purpose of the market economy is to "give people the reason and the opportunity to race for the finish line" (Schmidtz and Goodin 1998, 85), the meritorious just desert principle (Eckhoff 1974) becomes integral to the promotion of economic efficiency, by providing the financial incentives that maximize aggregate production (production efficiency) and the capacity to pay for commodities that maximizes aggregate utility (exchange efficiency). The moral propriety of this distributive justice principle rests, then, on the claim that each individual is "a free agent with a set of skills and talents that he [sic] deploys to advance his goals. Justice is done when he receives back by way of reward an equivalent to the contribution he makes" (Miller 2000, 28).

Desert involves a tripartite relationship (Kleinig 1971; Lamont 1994; McLeod 2013; Olsaretti 2003) between:

- an agent (the deserving or entitled person),

- the grounds upon which the agent may be regarded as deserving (the basis of his or her claim[187]), be it:

  - *contribution*:[188] so being rewarded for his or her activities according to the contribution they made to increasing the social product (Miller 1976; Riley 1989);

  - *effort*: so being rewarded for the efforts he or she has put into the raising of the social product (Sadurski 1985; Milne 1986); or

  - *compensation*: so being rewarded for the cost he or she has incurred in relation to the raising of the social product (Dick 1975; Lamont 1997); and

- the treatment deserved: the object of the deserving claim or the deserved good.

Justice, then, requires that the deserving person proved not only the basis for their desert claims (Feinberg 1970), but also the claim that he or she was responsible for the desert basis—the contribution, effort, or costs incurred—that justifies the deserved treatment (Cupit 1996; Feldman 1995b, 1996). Any resultant distributional inequalities generated can then be judged to be fair, provide the same merit-basis desert standards and procedures are fairly applied to all individuals, regardless of their human capital endowment (procedural justice).

So, the neoliberal individualist-libertarian worldview readily denies contending understandings of distributive justice.

- *Needs-based distributive justice*: This is achieved only when those in society who are most in need are made better off than they had previously been—the Rawlsian Difference Principle (Rawls 1971).[189] Thus, those who unable to pay the costs of being a member a society who can avoid serious harm and can

---

187 Aristotle ([350 BCE] 2004) proposed virtue, or moral character, to be the best desert-basis for economic distribution.

188 The specification and implementation challenges for desert-based distribution principles relate to the difficulty in identify and measuring what constitutes a contribution, particularly if it is the product of factors over which the contributor has little or no control.

189 Luck Egalitarianism (Dworkin 1981a, 1981b; Sher 2010), however, argue for an

engage in social participation (Doyal and Gough 1991) have a right to have those costs paid by society, regardless of their social contribution (Titmuss 1958). Any distributive injustices ensure the continuance of the risks to the social order or harmony associated with people living in a state material and psychological deprivation relative to other members of society. This is the collectivist-hierarchical worldview.

- *Strict egalitarianism distributive justice*: This imposes a moral imperative on a society to reverse any and all inequalities in economic wellbeing on the premise of fairness grounded in the moral equality of all members of that society (Lamont and Favor 2016). Thus, every individual should have the same level of material goods and services, regardless of their contribution to society. Thus, those unable to pay for that level of consumption have a right to have those costs paid by society. Any distributive injustices ensure the continuance of the risks to the social order or harmony associated with those who have been socially excluded because they have been relegated to the fringe of society as a result of being socially disadvantaged relative to other members of society. This is the collectivist-egalitarian worldview.

- *Moral skepticism about distributive justice*: This is the belief that what constitutes a just distribution can only be considered a personal attitude, opinion, or feeling (moral skepticism) (Bambrough 1979), because it only has truth-value to the believer (individualist ethical subjectivism).[190] There are, then, as many distinct beliefs about a just distribution as there are peo-

---

extension of the Difference Principle in recognition that inequalities in natural human endowments are not necessarily distributed according to individual choices or to some morally relevant fact about an individual, for they can be the results of brute luck in the social lottery (the economic, social and political circumstances into which a person is born), the natural lottery (the genetic potentials with which a person is born), or even unforeseeable bad luck (Rawls 1971; see also Knight and Stemplowska 2011). Those so affected should be explicitly compensated so as not to be disadvantaged (by not having equality of opportunity) in their economic prospects (by not having equality of initial access to resources), which will give rise to the most just distribution.

190 Ethical "[s]ubjectivism holds that any moral judgment is but an expression of one's own personal opinion on the matter. ... These beliefs or reports are an expression of one's personal subjective state of mind—and as such they can be true or false in correspondence to that subjective state of mind. Hence, a moral judgment is true if and only if it is an accurate report of one's subjective state of mind. ... This means that

ple in society. Thus, distributive justice can never be served to everyone's satisfaction. Any distributive injustices ensure the continuance of the risks to social order or harmony associated with those experiencing a sense of being unjustly treated by their society, and so set apart from others (social alienation). This is the individualist-existential worldview.

Procedural Justice

The neoliberalism recognizes the importance of procedural justice in order to ensure that the making and implementing decisions and resolving disputes are in accordance with fair processes. Natural rights libertarianism (Nozick 1974) advances the proposition that "there is only a correct or fair procedure such that the outcome is likewise correct or fair, whatever it is, provided that the procedure has been properly followed" (Olsaretti 2004, 87).

Following Greenberg (1993), procedural justice can also be conceptualized along four dimensions:

- *Systemic justice*: This focuses on the structuring of the rules that assure a sense of fairness with respect to a procedural justice process.

- *Informational justice*: This acknowledges importance accuracy and the genuineness of any information provided in a procedural justice process.

- *Configural justice*: This is concerned with the structural and distributive implications of a procedural justice process.

- *Interpersonal justice*: This deals with the socially sensitive aspects of interaction within a procedural justice process.

Procedural justice, therefore, embraces consistency of treatment—whether the obligations on decision-making are universally enforced. Any distinctions between individuals made "should reflect genuine aspects of personal identity rather than extraneous features of the differentiating mechanism itself" (Maiese [2003] 2013). To achieve this requires:

- *Procedural impartiality and neutrality:* This is to ensure that

---

there exist moral facts, however, in contrast to realist/objectivist views, such moral facts are mind-dependent, i.e. they are only moral facts in relation to a particular subjective state of mind" (von Sophilos 2012).

decision makers carry out the designated procedures to reach a fair and accurate conclusion.

- *Transparency*: This is to ensure that there are mechanisms and procedures to ensure open and transparent decision-making, without secrecy or deception.

- *Protection of property rights*: This is to ensure that justly acquired property rights are respected and advanced.

- *Redress*: This is to ensure that those whose human and civil rights have been violated have the right of redress.

- *Stakeholder representation*: To ensure that those directly affected by a decision have capacity to exercise voice in the decision-making processes.

As achieving procedural justice is not a costless endeavor, the outcome sought is a fair balance between the costs of the necessary procedures and the benefits they produce.

So, the neoliberal individualist-libertarian worldview readily denies contending perspectives on procedural justice.

- Procedural justice should seek correct outcomes without undue regard to the costs involved (the collectivist-hierarchical worldview).

- Procedural justice should afford those claiming an injustice an opportunity to participate in the procedural decision-making process without undue regard to the costs involved (the collectivist-egalitarian worldview).

- Procedural justice can never be served to everyone's satisfaction, for whatever constitutes a fair procedure that will produce a fair outcome is a self-referential moral opinion (moral skepticism (Bambrough 1979)), which means procedural justice unachievable (the individualist-existential worldview).

DESERVING WHAT YOU GET

Neoliberalism holds that individuals are fully responsible for their life-outcomes. This is on the premises that character is "... a result of how persons act in the world and what they thus freely choose to make of themselves" (Machan 2006, 5; but see Cameron 2002). Because individuals are presumed to be *causa sui*, differential natural initial human endowments does not constitute an absolute set on constraints on the possibility of a person taking control of their life-choices, since human endowments can always be purposively developed and deployed. Thus, living in poverty is considered to be the fault of the poor.

On Poverty

In the objectivist tradition, poverty can only be conceptualized materialistically and measured empirically as the number of income units (individuals or families, however defined) who are living in a state of material deprivation, with their income persistently or episodically falling below a designated poverty line (MacPherson and Silburn 1998). This means that the extent, nature, and consequences of poverty can be empirically investigated, by reference to census and survey data. But any causal explanation of poverty by reference to the intentional mental states of those living in poverty can only be theorized. This raises a serious epistemological challenge. This causal theorizing is the result of a process of deductive reasoning based on drawing inferences about intentional mental states from observed present or past behaviors. Its validity depends, of course, on the veracity of neoliberalism's libertarian-utilitarian rational self-interest human nature premise. Thus, its truth-value can only be grounded in the assertion that it is an obviously self-justifying knowledge claim that does not need any further justification.

Neoliberalism's predisposition toward the naturalist-agency social reality standpoint means that it is blind to poverty's structural and metaphysical dimensions. Thus, it is unable to speak with any certainty about the extent, nature, causes, and consequences of poverty and its solution. The neoliberal poverty discourse is, essentially, a discourse on human nature. It asserts that the poor can choose not to be poor. This gives rise to an ideologically informed, assumption-based approach to the analysis of poverty and the poor.

Neoliberalism, logically, has no choice but to recognize that there are physiological attributes—that cannot change by acts-of-will—that can cause individuals to fall into poverty. Its solution is to draw a crucial distinction being drawn between the deserving and the undeserving poor. The deserving poor are those living in poverty for reasons outside their control, because they have personal qualities and attributes that make labor market engagement impossible or inappropriate (such as, old age or physical incapacity). In obvious contradistinction are the undeserving poor—the "underclass" [191] (Dixon and Dogan 2004; Dixon, Dogan, and Carrier 2005; Katz 2013)—who are responsible for their own poverty because they choose not to lift themselves out of poverty. Being rational and self-interested, they naturally prefer to live in "leisure" in a state of (near?) poverty receiving public welfare support rather than to earn income by being in (low?) paid employment.[192] Indeed, this has enabled them to refuse to change their hopes, aspirations, and goals, in order to correct for past poor life choices that have given rise to their unacceptable personal qualities.

Thus, those living in poverty can and must be identified for the purpose of designing an efficient and effective public policy response, so that, were at all appropriate, government can take the necessary steps—for their own good, of course—to ensure that those that can participate in the labor market do so. Once so engaged, neoliberalism argues that they will be better able to participate in the commodity and capital markets, so being better placed to enhance their material wellbeing.

Being Poor by Choice

The neoliberalism proposition is that those who end up at the bottom of society—stereotyped and labeled as the work-shy, idle, and non-autonomous—do so because of their own past decisions and actions. So, if they end up poor, it is because of poorly thought-out risk decisions. And, of course, their idleness and feckless—due to their lack of foresight and self-discipline—should not be rewarded by the collective redistributing income to their advantage, as this would be unfair on the deserving, however wealthy they may be. As Arneson (1997, 330-331, emphasis in original) points out "helping the undeserving and failing to help the deserving is deemed *intrinsically* unfair regardless of further consequences" (see also Husak 1992; Kekes 1997). It moralizes that the undeserving

---

191 This is the lowest possible category in a class hierarchy—Marx's (1852) lumpenproletariat—defined by Myrdal (1963, 10) as a "class of unemployed, unemployables, and underemployed who are more and more hopelessly set apart from the nation at large and do not share in its life, its ambitions and its achievements" (see also Devine and Wright 1993).

192 The framework that economists use to analyze labor supply behavior is the neoclassical model of labor-leisure choice (see Becker 1965).

poor have an obligation to assess critically the consequences for themselves and others of them not working when employment is available, and that they should be held responsible for not so doing (but see Iversen and Armstrong 2006). It concludes that the underserving poor-by-choice (Dixon 2012) cannot be trusted not to abuse tax-finance state welfare support.

The administration of tax-financed welfare supports must be governed by rules that induce instrumental compliance with the obligation to work or to seek work, so the cost to deserving taxpayers can be controlled and, with diligent administration, reduced. Thus, they deserve only rapid labor-force attachment. Employment—in any job, in any location, and at any wage—is the only means by which they can achieve the desirable end-state of being both self-determining and, with hard work, self-sufficient. Thus, they should have to do all that is possible to maximize their employment possibilities—even by commodifying their relationships with friends and partners—for all aspects of life should conform to market forces. Once achieved, employment will undoubtedly enhanced their self-esteem, which will give them greater life choices, will make them a better role model for any children they may have, and will enable them to learn the importance of authoring their own life. Once they are reasoning beings in full control of their destiny, they can identify, evaluate, and choose the best courses of action to maximize their material wellbeing. By so doing, they will also be addressing the dual threats of intergenerational poverty and welfare dependency.

A Critique of the Neoliberal Perspective on Poverty

The narrowness of the neoliberal construction of the reality of poverty can be highlighted by the contending alternative depictions of that reality that neoliberals deny, because they consider them to be grounded on flawed epistemological and ontological assumptions (see Dixon 2012). What, then, does it deny?

First, neoliberalism denies the validity of investigating poverty from a structuralist perspective—the poor are poor because of external structural factors. This would focus empirical search on the objective cultural, economic, gender, ethnicity, and class factors that could explain why people are living in poverty (the collectivist-hierarchical worldview). Neoliberalism can only dismiss such structuralist causal propositions as being inferior to its self-evidently true agency foundational belief that poverty is the product of agential factors, a knowledge claim they take—and expect others to take—on faith. This, then, gives neoliberalism no capacity to speak with any certainty on the causes of poverty.

Second, neoliberalism denies the validity of investigating poverty from a metaphysical perspective—knowable as a set of subjective first-person mental discernments of those living in poverty—because it is not an objective mode of investigation. The meaning of such mental discernments is subjectively contingent upon:

- how they are socially constructed and, thus, their truthfulness depends on convention, human understanding, and social experience grounded in the prevailing social, cultural, politico-economic, and linguistic milieu, which makes truth relative—true-for-us (the collectivist-egalitarian worldview); or

- what those who hold those mental discernments have a will-to-believe to be true about them—true-for-me (the agency-existential worldview).

Thus, neoliberalism can only reject the hermeneutic proposition that the truth about living in poverty transcends both the facts about its extent and its material characteristics and consequences, and the logic about its causation grounded in an unprovable human nature axiom. It sees no value in understanding the meaningfulness and significance of living in poverty from the perspectives of the poor—as a lived experience. It, thus, dismiss the proposition that poverty has an ideational dimension because the knowledge claims advanced are based on grounds short of certainty, and they cannot be taken on faith as self-evident knowledge claims that need no further justification. This gives neoliberalism no capacity to speak with any certainty on what poverty means to the poor or with any understanding of the potential effect that poverty has on the poor.

Third, neoliberalism denies that the intentional mental states of those living in poverty are subject to determining conditions internal to the individual (inherited genetic make-up and unconscious mental states) or external (shared values and beliefs). This means that the poor are presumed to be immune to:

- the pre-existing social norms, roles, and practices that are connected to any hierarchical groups to which they belong, which determine the courses of action judged by important others to be dutiful and obligatory (the collectivist-hierarchical worldview);

- the negotiated pre-existing social norms, roles, and practices that are connected to any egalitarian groups to which they belong, which determine the courses of action judged to be acceptable and expected by like-minded others with whom they share common values and beliefs (the collectivist-egalitarian worldview); or

- their own sense of unfolding identity during the course of living out their lives in a perpetual struggle to recognize their own unique consciousness and to gain supremacy over the forces of social constraint (the individualist-existential worldview).

Neoliberalism can only dismiss these explanations of the origins of the content of intentional mental states as beliefs that are inferior to their self-evidently true belief that the poor are free agents able to self-author their intentional mental states. This gives neoliberalism no capacity to speak with any certainty on the origins of the content of hopes, aspirations, and goals that give rise to social actions of those living in poverty.

Fourth, neoliberalism denies the validity of the proposition that those living in poverty can reject the idea of commodifying their social relationships in order to maximize their material wellbeing, simply because they prefer, instead to engage with other people:

- in hierarchical relationships with the expectation that they should be loyal and duty-bound to important others in order to gain or sustain their patronage (the collectivist-hierarchical worldview);

- with whom they share beliefs and values, with the expectation that they need to make and express common commitments in order to gain or sustain group connections and support (the collectivist-egalitarian worldview); or

- only when absolutely necessary, in expectation that they will otherwise be exposed to threats from unknowable and unpredictable people (the individualist-existential worldview).

Thus, they would deny the value of understanding why those living in poverty have the social relationships they have. Neoliberalism can only dismiss these alternative social-relationship beliefs as erroneous because they are contrary to their self-evident belief that individuals engage with others only to advance their material self-advancement. This gives neoliberalism no capacity to speak with any authority on why those living in poverty prefer not to lift themselves out of poverty by commodifying their social relationships.

Fifth, neoliberalism denies the validity of the proposition that decisions on appropriate courses of action to be taken by those living in poverty should be constrained by:

- any sense of duty to important others (the collectivist-hierarchical worldview);

- any common shared values established with like-minded others (the collectivist-egalitarian worldview); or

- past personal experience (the individualist-existential worldview).

Thus, neoliberalism rejects the proposition that those living in poverty can reasonably reject a course of action that would lift them out of poverty because it was unacceptable to important others; put them into values conflict with like-minded significant others; or was impractical on the basis of their past experience. Neoliberalism can, then, only dismiss such lines of reasoning as being irrational. This gives neoliberalism no capacity to speak with any authority on whether those living in poverty are irrational when they rejecting a course of action that will advance their materially wellbeing.

Sixth, neoliberalism denies the proposition that those living in poverty have the moral right to reject a course of action that would lift them out of poverty, if that course of action is contrary to:

- their moral obligations or duties to important others, because what makes an action morally right is judged by its intrinsic rightness established by standards set by important moral rule givers (the collectivist-hierarchical worldview);

- what a virtuous person would choose to do, because what makes an action morally right should be judged by the virtuousness of the decision maker or action-taker, on the premise that virtue, as a set of human qualities, precedes the choice of right decisions or right actions (the collectivist-egalitarian worldview); or

- their self-referential moral opinion on what constitutes a moral course of action (the individualist-existential worldview).

Neoliberalism can, then, only dismiss these moral positions as being subjective, the objective truth-value of which cannot be determined. This gives neoliberalism no capacity to speak with any authority on whether the poor are immoral if they decide to reject a course of action that would lift them out of poverty.

Seventh, neoliberalism denies the validity of the proposition that those living in poverty can be trusted not to calculatingly abuse tax-financed state welfare programs, because it denies the veracity of the propositions that the poor can be trusted not to behavior in such a way

- if they can be persuaded by important others that such behavior is wrong (the collectivist-hierarchical worldview);

- if they can be persuaded to make creditable commitment to like-minded significant others that would make engaging in such behavior shameful and unworthy (the collectivist-egalitarian worldview); or

- if their past actions justifies that they can be so trusted (the individualist-existential worldview).

Neoliberals can only dismiss these grounds for extending such trust to the poor as being subjective, the objective truth-value of which cannot be determined. This gives neoliberalism no capacity to speak with any authority on how to build and sustain a trust-inducing environment in relation to the delivery of tax-financed welfare programs.

Finally, neoliberalism denies the validity of the proposition that making those living in poverty comply with what they would not otherwise comply can best be achieved by use of

- legitimate, threat, expert or knowledge power, exercised by important others, involving directive rules that "ask, command, demand, permit [and] caution" (Onuf 1989, 86) (the collectivist-hierarchical worldview);

- normative, integrative, personal or referent power, exercised by like-minded significant others with whom values are shared, involving instructive rules that state beliefs that are expected to be accepted (Onuf 1989, 85, but see also 120) (the collectivist-egalitarian worldview); or

- destructive threat, physical or coercive power, exercised by those with such power, involving directive rules with severe sanctions (the individualist-existential worldview).

Neoliberalism can only dismiss these alternative compliance inducements as erroneous, because they are contrary to primacy of its self-evident premises of individual free will and self-interest. This gives neoliberals no capacity to speak with any authority on whether compliance, rather than avoidance strategies, will be induced by the connecting the right to material welfare assistance to particular obligations being discharged, such as mandatory work tests.

What this all means is that one of neoliberalism's many articles of faith is that the so-called undeserving poor are poor-by-choice, because they are work-shy—quite self-evidently, a life of leisure on public welfare is obviously preferable to a life of work in paid employment. Indeed, neoliberalism's preferred way of generating knowledge places limits on what can be known about those living in poverty. What is in their minds can only be assumed, but, of course, with a certainty that follows from a holding a self-justifying human nature belief that is beyond any doubt, and, thus, does not need any further justification. Thus, neoliberalism prognosticate and proselytize with false confidence on what is self-evidently true-to-them about the causes of poverty, the impact of poverty on the poor, and the intentional mental states that give rise to social actions of those living in poverty.

So, the neoliberal individualist-libertarian worldview readily denies alternative explanations for, the existence of an underclass of undeserving poor:

- These are people who have lost their sense of social identity and, therefore, their acceptance of social obligation and responsibilities, the solution to which is to end the normlessness and unpredictability of their relatively random world by initiating controlling forces (such as tougher laws and more diligent policing) to reinforce more orderly and conformist behavior (the collective-hierarchical world view).

- These are people who have engaged in alternative forms of life that prevent, to their disadvantage, their engagement with mainstream society or community discourses, the solution to which is to persuade them to engage with empowering structures seeking common ends (perhaps involving benevolence, a just and legitimate civil order, or communal cooperation), thereby enabling them to become socially re-connected (the collectivist-egalitarian worldview).

THE IDEA OF NEOLIBERALISM

- These are people who have over identified with life-disempowering experiences associated with a living a life in poverty, which manifests as a lack of will to take control of life, encouraged by welfare dependency, the solution to which is to help them to embrace their existential isolation, to accept life's vicissitudes that flow from it, and to proceed, regardless, toward the construction of their own futures, thereby fulfilling their unique potential (Dixon and Frolova 2011) (the individualist-existential worldview).

CONCLUSION

The neoliberal individualist-libertarian worldview considers that a just society is one in which individuals have a right to own and exploit private property and an obligation to look after themselves and their families. This is made possible by, among other things, everyone being entitled to the property they have acquired and being deservedly rewarded for their work activity in accordance with their contribution to the social product. Any observed distributable inequalities are, thus, presumed to be the product of some individuals being better able appropriates the benefits of engagement in market transactions. Thus, the rich are entitled to their wealth, and to become wealthier. Unfortunately, the marketplace has no mechanisms for ensuring the justness of the private property acquisition process or the deservedness of income distribution processes.

Indeed, under the foundation principles of neoliberalism, it is quite irrational for anyone not to want to maximize their material wellbeing by engaging in market transactions. However, those unable to do so, for reasons outside their control—because they have personal qualities and attributes that make such market engagements impossible or inappropriate—do not deserve to be poor, thus they deserve society's support, albeit preferably on a voluntary basis, although residual (minimalist) public welfare support can be provided to those with limited means, in order to keep the peace. Those, however, who choose to be poor get what they deserve—membership of the underclass. They prefer, by choice, to live on other people's income rather than to engage in paid employment, so do otherwise would mean changing their attitudes and motivations in order to correct the consequences of their poor past life choices and their unacceptable personal qualities. Even the socially excluded, marginalized, or disadvantaged—the underclass—are considered capable of taking control of their lives, if only they would recognize that it is good for them to participate in the labor market. Indeed, they have a moral duty to themselves and to others—particularly their families—to conduct their lives in a way that maximizes their labor market participation and advantage.

The neoliberal social justice discourse is, essentially, a moral discourse on human nature. After all, everyone has free will; anyone can choose to be rich or poor. To neoliberalism, it is beyond reproach that people get what they deserve and, assuredly, deserve what they get.

7.

NEOLIBERALISM:
THE PAST REVISITED AS THE FUTURE TO BE

"What is neoliberalism? A programme for destroying collective structures, which may impede the pure market logic."

Bourdieu (1998)

INTRODUCTION

Neoliberalism harks back to the halcyon days of eighteenth-century classical liberalism—a time when David Hume and Adam Smith stood tall in their advocacy of the natural right to life, liberty, and property, and of the free market, in the face the Tyrannical State dragon, with its oppressive power over body and mind. Its zealous fire, however, has been gradually abated in liberal democracies by democratization. Indeed, it has gradually been empowered to take on the avaricious and rapacious *Laissez-faire* Capitalist dragon that emerged from the "dark Satanic Mills" [193] (Blake [1808] 2004, 289) of the nineteenth Industrial Revolution. It eventually won. Its victory, however, was not a lasting one. For with victory, the Tyrannical State dragon soon became the Welfare State dragon, which, in turn, quickly became fat on the land of the welfare estate, exposing its vulnerable underbelly to mortal attack. The *Laissez-faire* Capitalist dragon, eventually, sought revenge. As its keeper, protector, and champion, neoliberalism—as classical liberalism has been re-branded with a vengeance—sought to tame (nay hollow-out) the burdensome Welfare (née Tyrannical) State dragon. This is a dragon that has become mythologized—demonized—in the minds-eye of those who to want to replaced it with a dragon of another hue—the Free Market (née *Laissez-faire*) Capitalist dragon, thereby replacing the costly tyranny of state power with the profitable tyranny of market power.

The neoliberal vision is to return to the days when it was quite enough if government sought only to enforce contractual obligations and to de-

---

193 To what, precisely Blake was referring in his reference to "dark Satanic Mills" has long been in dispute (see Lienhard 1999; Wright 2007).

fend against any threats to individual and property rights—thereby sanctioning Locke's ([1689/1690] 2004) protective democracy. Only a weak, unobtrusive, and small government would maximize negative freedom—the right to be free from the coercion and intrusion of others—and minimize its intrusion into the private sphere by restricting public regulatory and tax burdens, so permitting the market to do what it does best, namely enhancing a society's material wellbeing. This aspiration was made economically credible as a late twentieth-century politico-economic vision when in the 1960s and 1970s an ideologically attractive logical explanation became available for the very evident public loss of faith in government as means of enhancing human welfare—public choice theory. This has given rise to two axiomatic articles of neoliberal faith.

- That government is inherently coercive and intrusive—unknowing of what is in the public interest (defined as what citizens want), and an inefficient producer of even what it considers that they needed (in the so-called common good).

- That the market can do a better governance job, because it is obvious that people know what they want and the market mechanism forces them to reveal their preferences, and so, most importantly, it has the incentive to produce efficiently what they are willing to buy—at a price—to satisfy those wants.

This is the message of rational neoclassical economic theory, which resonates with neoliberalism, because both are grounded in the same epistemological and ontological assumptions. While these assumptions provide a consistent account of the world of persons, it is an incomplete one.

Neoliberalism's Ontological Blinkers

Neoliberalism ontologically privileges the individual over the social. This permits the presumption that societies, communities, groups, organizations, and families do not separately exist in the world of persons, and so they have no impact on individuals' intentional mental states and, thus, on their social actions and social relationship. Society is, thus, perceived as an aggregation of as-strangers, each with untrammeled free will. Thus, no shared socio-cultural values and ideas, religious beliefs, or expressed commitments to others can create any sense of obligation—out of any sense of love, loyalty, duty, or deference—to satisfy the needs, wants, or expectation of others (whether alive or dead), or to follow their instructions that gives rise to a moral imperative that demands an action to be undertaken (if it is a dutiful action) or not to be undertaken (if it is a forbidden action).

NEOLIBERALISM'S EPISTEMOLOGICAL BLINKERS

Neoliberalism's epistemologically privileges the material (objective) properties of the world of persons over its ideational (subjective) properties. This enables it to deny its proximity to the unknowable, by dismissing the metaphysical dimension of the world of persons. It also distances its proximity to the unknown, by dismissing the veracity of subjective knowledge claims that cannot be verified by objective evidence-based reasoning. This, in turn, justifies the knowledge of these metaphysical elements of the world of persons to be deemed irrelevant to any decision or action, so they are descriptively and analytically ignorable. What, then, is knowable about that world is limited to what is factually true about its material properties, established by reference to the existence of confirming evidence and the absence of disconfirming evidence. What is knowable about causation in the world of persons is what is knowable about its constituent individuals. What is knowable about them are their observed actions. What is knowable about their observed actions is what is presumed to be true about their unobservable intentional mental states:

- That they are entirely self determined, because individuals, being *causa sui*, have the capacity to consciously and voluntarily exercise their free will.

- That they are the product of the cognitions of an autonomous self with an immaterial mind that is immune to agential (physiological and neurobiological) and societal (structural and discursive) freedom-limiting punitive, oppressive, coercive, compulsive, or manipulative conditioning factors.

- That they represent what is in individuals' best (expected utility maximizing) interest.

- That they are able to bring about social actions, because they can affect neurobiological states and processes taking place in the brain.

Thus, knowledge claim is best be warranted by reason, so privileging the truth of logic, and social explanation is best grounded in free will, so privileging an transcendental axiom that is beyond empirical verification or falsification.

Neoliberalism's Blinkered Worldview

Neoliberalism's distinctive worldview provides a coherent philosophy of life—one that informs and justifies a way of living in the world of persons as it is envisaged to be. This is grounded in its distinctive explanation of what it means to be human. It privileged the proposition that individuals are free being—in full control of their destiny—with a strong commitment to their material self-interest. Thus, their primary life-goal is the pursuit of their material wellbeing. This primacy of self over others means that others (individually or collectively) play no role in the development of their social or personal identities. Thus, their social engagements are superficial, instrumental, and utilitarian, involving only limited interaction and minimal emotionality, for reason (beliefs and choices) is privileged over emotions (feelings and imagination). On these premises, neoliberalism embraces the following propositions:

- Individuals are consistently and immutably motivated by self-interest.

- Social engagements and relationships are predicated on others-as-strangers and everybody advancing their own interests.

- Determining the trustworthiness of others-as-strangers involves an assessment of the material costs and benefits of extending trust.

- Making others-as-strangers do what they would not otherwise have done requires the use of exchange, resource, reward, or economic power.

- That a good society is one that values individual liberty, and thus the free market capitalism; popular sovereignty, and thus democracy, and meliorism, and thus modernity.

Neoliberalism's Myth of the Market

Neoliberalism accepts, axiomatically, the supremacy of the market as the basis for steering the allocation of the resources (the market (self-regulation) mode of governance) in a world that is construed as a benevolent positive-sum game. So, risks create opportunities to be exploited for personal reward. This requires allocative reasoning to be synoptic and strategic in orientation, which means that it focuses on identifying the best means of achieving an unexceptionable end—advancing material wellbeing—so permitting decision makers to select the strategy that creates the best opportunity for material improvement.

The market is seen as benign. It, and only it, knows people's preferences and has the incentive produce the most wealth from the limited resources available. This proposition is reinforced in the impeccable logic of neoclassical economic theory. This explains economic reality in terms of the consequences of exchange transactions between rational (utility or profit maximizing) economic agents as anonymous individuals-as-strangers. This behavioral assumption is a perfectly adequate depiction of the behavior of a large number of anonymous buyers and sellers in the macroeconomic environment. It can, thus, permit the answering the hypothetical question: does there exist in an economy a positive price vector at which the aggregate quantities demanded and supplied of each commodity, item by item, are equal? This makes neoclassical economic theory an example of:

- an "effective [working] theory"—"a framework created to model certain observed phenomena without describing all the underlying processes" (Hawking and Mlodinow 2011, 46); and

- an "approximate theory"—a framework that is "useful in a limited context but which may not be correct in all contexts" (Ferguson [1994] 2004, 32).

However, it is naïve-to-the-extreme to presume that all exchange transactions are between individuals-as-strangers (Dixon 2017).

Thus, the rational economic behavior assumption comes into question when neoclassical economic theory is used to explain phenomena by reference to exchange transactions occurring in an organizational, group, or familial setting involving agents who are, as would happen between intimates, friends, colleagues, and even acquaintances. To depict them as if they are individuals-as-strangers is to deny that their desired exchange goals and preferred exchange processes may be shaped by external societal factors (socio-cultural, religious, linguistic, discursive, or interpersonal), or by internal agential factors (their genetic physiological and psychological make-up), both of which negate the free will presumption that underpins rational economic behavior premise.

Whether the neoclassical economic model can be taken as a trusted guide to economic reality requires the acceptance, as an article of faith, of its rational behavior premise. This point-of-view model considers the economy as it ought to be—a rational (deterministic) cause-and-effect system—one in which economic agents act as they *ought* to be acting—self-interestedly—so giving rise to an economic reality as it *ought* to be—one in which self-interest follows reason to the betterment of society as a whole as well as self. This can be elaborated as the following set of proposition.

- All economic agents make decisions that produce the best possible outcome for themselves, because they are presumed to be rational and self-interested, so *any* and *all* transactional decisions made are, axiomatically, presumed to be optimal, on the premise that all alternative possible courses of action must have been assessed and the best decision must have been made in accordance with a freely determined set of ordered preferences. Thus:

  - the prices buyers are willing to pay for a commodity represents the maximum utility or satisfaction they expect to derive from consuming it; and

  - the prices sellers are willing to accept for a good or service represents the maximum profit they expect to derive from selling it.

- An efficient marketplace is a competitive one, where there are enough utility-maximizing buyers and profit-maximizing sellers of every commodity who are well enough informed to ensure that the price settled upon is beyond the control of one or a few buyers or sellers.

- A society's welfare is maximized when the output it produces is maximized, given its scarce resources and available technology, and sold to the highest bidders.

- Economic agents are entitled to their wealth because they have acquired, by a just process, the necessary property rights to permit them to exploit their resources for their own benefit.

- Economic agents deserve the income that they receive because it has been judged in the marketplace to be commensurate with their contribution to the production, so giving rise to a just income distribution. Any income inequalities are, then, the product of some individuals being better able to exploit their human capacities or latent qualities and so are better able to appropriate the benefits of market engagement.

- Government current expenditure must be as small as possible and paid from current government revenue, so as to avoid public borrowing, which crowds-out private investment in the capital market, slows down economic growth, places an unreasonable repayment burden on future taxpayers, and increases the size of the public sector.

It is recognized, however, that there are situations where the market can fail to optimize the wellbeing of a society.

- When it cannot ensure that the ownership of wealth-creating resources has been justly acquired because it has mechanism that can identify and rectify (compensate) any current or past injustices with respect to the acquisition of the property-rights over those resources (wealth acquisition injustice).

- When it fails to maximize a society's wellbeing because of its inability to provide public goods, which are jointly and non-rivalrously consumed, or to internalize external costs and benefits; and in the absence of property rights, information symmetry (economic inefficiency). (According to the theory of the second best, these sources of market failures cannot be readily corrected by public intervention without the prospect of further deteriorations in the wellbeing of society as a whole.)

- When it has no incentive to not satisfy the demand for demerit goods or no capacity to increase the demand for merit goods (flawed consumer sovereignty).

- When it cannot achieve an equitable distribution of income, because it cannot ensure that:

  - those who justly deserve rewards receive what they deserve (desert-based distributive injustice).

  - those in greatest need have the income they needed to pay the costs of being a member of a society, one who can afford to avoid serious harm and who can attain and sustain acceptable social participation (needs-based distributive injustice); or

- every individual has the same level of economic wellbeing, regardless of their contribution, because all people are morally equal (strict egalitarian distributive injustice).

NEOLIBERALISM'S MYTH OF GOVERNMENT

To Neoliberalism, government threatens negative freedom because it is inherently coercive and intrusive. It is certainly not a means by which human wellbeing can be enhanced. So, governance efficacy, even legitimacy, is questioned, by asserting that the market is much more efficient at identifying and meeting citizens' revealed preferences. Delineated is only a minimal role for the state, one limited to granting, enforcing, and protecting the rule of law—the law of property, tort, and contract—within which buyers and sellers negotiate enforceable contracts. The most efficient way of running society is, then, by granting, enforcing, and protecting the fundamental natural right for individuals to use their private property as they see fit, so as to satisfy their wants. This supports the ideas of maximizing citizens' personal liberty and of minimizing their capacity to deflect the acceptance of personal responsibility for past life-choice decision. The neoliberal presumption is that private interests are intimately linked to the good of society.

What is, then, in the public interest is only knowable as the summation of all private interests—people's preferences (what they want). This is unknowable to government. All it can know is what it believes to be in the common good (what it believes they need). Thus, the public interest can only be promoted and protected by permitting private interests to be peacefully pursued. To this end, the state should be made smaller wherever and whenever possible by transferring as many of its responsibilities as possible to the marketplace. Society is governable only when there is a strong market, a weak state, a weak civil society.

The principal task of any polity is to ensure that government responds as cost-efficiently and cost-effectively as possible to the legitimate claims made by its various constituencies, as this will maximize citizens' satisfaction with government, improve public confidence in government, and, above all, maximize the quantum of resources available to the private sector. This requires the use of a rational-comprehensive model of policymaking, involving the development of de-politicized, goal-oriented strategies, chosen after comprehensive instrumental-rational (means-ends mode) analysis and routinely implemented by managerialized, de-centralized, and performance-accountable reformed bureaucracies. The state, however, should only provide minimally necessary public services, designed, wherever possible, in accordance with the end-users' preferences, and delivered by, or in conjunction with, the private sector, depending on relative cost-effectiveness.

NEOLIBERALISM'S MYTH OF THE PUBLIC ADMINISTRATION

Bureaucracies are the *bête noire* of neoliberalism. Rationally self-interested public officials—neoliberalism's devils incarnate—administer them. Since the neoliberal behavioral presumption is that any and all actors on the politic-administrative stage are maximizers of their self-determined and self-interested utility functions, they are portrayed as consummate empire builders, assigning them an inherent tendency to be deceitful, or even dishonest by, among other things, distorting information given to their principals—politicians. This is especially significant because politicians have no ownership incentive to monitoring effectively the performance and management of bureaucracies. Emerging from these conceptualizations is a concern about opportunism in public administration. This is product of the self-serving bureaucrats, politician, and the policy beneficiaries, all of whom are ever conspiring to find new justifications for extending the role of the state, ever expanding the public sector and its bureaucracies (at the expense of the private sector expansion), and for increasing public expenditure (at the expense of current or future taxpayers).

The neoliberal solution to this ever-expanding bureaucracy scenario is three-fold. Firstly, downsize the public sector, thereby hollowing-out the state. Secondly, de-coupled, as far as possible, the administration of public policy from political structures and processes. Thirdly, institute far reaching organizational transformations to make the public agencies more business-like. This calls for greater accountability to the public (as citizens and customers), achieved by measuring performance (outputs and outcomes) rather than just inputs and processes, which can then be used to justify and encourage the downsizing of the public sector. The neoliberal challenge, however, is grounded in the reality that all public sectors are the product of historically overriding forces associated with the nature of the host society:

- its political, ideological, economic, and socio-cultural values;

- its balancing of the governance roles of state, the marketplace, and civil society; and

- its historically evolved role for government—as controller, protector, provider, regulator, contractor, facilitator, or empowerer.

This centers the reform discourses on what beliefs (worldviews), values (ethics and justice), decisions frames (for future actions), and behaviors (social actions) should be fostered in public administration, all of which are fundamentally and profoundly important in any society. Neoliberalism arrogantly posits that its worldview, its values, its decision frames, and its style of public administration should prevail because its particular configuration of foundational principles—individual liberty, private property, the free market order, and the assignment of personal responsibility—are self-evidently held to be universally applicable and superior—regardless of ethnicity, socio-cultural and religious beliefs, traditions, values, and practices.

To neoliberal the ideal public organization is not a rule-driven hierarchy but one that is a cost-effective program-delivery mechanism managed by goal-oriented and problem-solving technocrats. So, it would be expected also to operate at the edge of its competence. Thus, the appropriate response to dealing with what it does not yet know is to use an integrative approach to problem solving that challenges established practices by going beyond received wisdom contained in the bureaucratic rule-book.

Neoliberalism's Myth of the Public Management

Neoliberalism axiomatically accepts that the performance of government is linked to ability, authority, and accountability of instrumently rational managers—managerialism or the New Public Management. This has cast a long, and growing, shadow over public sector management across the world. It has initiated a drive to modernize public management by the adoption of business-like performance-oriented management practices. Neoliberalism's advocacy of performance management, however, downplays the public sector's intimate relationship to government policies (what government believes its citizens need, want, or will tolerate). This creates a dilemma for public managers. They are expected to manage efficiently and effectively, and so be accountable for the efficient and effective management of inputs used to produce outputs (that may be difficult to even conceptualize let alone measure), which generate outcomes (that may be difficult to conceptualize and measure), which relate to program objectives (that may be difficult to articulate in mutually compatible and quantifiable terms), which must be compatible not only with policy objectives (that government may be unwilling or unable to articulate in quantifiable terms, and which may, themselves, be mutually incompatible) but also with customer objectives (that may difficult to ascertain (as it would be for public goods) and, in any event, difficult to articulate and may well be mutually incompatible).

Managerialized public manager are required to master the science and the art of business management—at the expense of ignoring the art of statecraft—so that the modernized management of public organization focuses on processes that improve organizational goal-oriented performance. This is achieved by decentralizing authority distribution (thereby weakening hierarchical control by the politico-administrative elite), so as to expand the ways in which work is conducted, and by creating financial incentives to reward individual performance improvement. Managerialized public managers are, then, expected to use this devolved authority to achieve targets related to organizational performance goals.

NEOLIBERALISM'S MYTH OF SOCIAL JUSTICE

The neoliberal just society is one in which everyone owns what they are entitled to own and receives for their labors what they deserve; and decision are made and disputes resolved in accordance with fair processes that protect the inalienable right to self-ownership and to property ownership. It asserts that social justice is achieved if individuals deserve what they get and get what they deserve. Those who are better able to appropriate the benefits of market engagement deserve what they get, which is only just. Those who choose not to develop and/or exploit their human capacities, or latent qualities, to better appropriate such benefits, deserve what they get, which is also just.

Individuals, under neoliberalism, have a moral obligation to look after themselves and their families. Indeed, it would irrational for anyone not to want to maximize his or her material wellbeing by market engagement. This is made possible by, among other things, everyone being justly entitled to own the property they have acquired, and everyone being justly rewarded for their contribution to the social product. So, the distribution of material wellbeing should be left to the marketplace. The justness of this social justice standard is contingent upon the following propositions.

- That everyone is justly entitled to the property (resources) they possess, although the marketplace has no mechanism by which it can compensate any injustices incurred in past resource acquisition or transfer.

- That everyone has consumer sovereignty, which means that it is morally acceptable for suppliers to make a profit by satisfying the demand for a demerit good the consumption of which is, in some way, considered by experts to be disadvantageous or harmful to them.

- That everyone is freely willing and able to apply their abilities and talents to productive work as they see fit, and able to receive the rewards they deserve for that contribution, although the marketplace has no mechanism for ensuring either.

- That everyone accepts personal responsibility, in perpetuity, for their actions and who they have become, regardless of:

  - their intrinsic physiological attributes (related to gender, physical incompleteness, or ethnicity);

  - their initial natural human endowments (physiological or neurological) that are the product of their genetic inheritance; or

  - their unconscious mental states—the source of deviant pathologies, self-deceptions and cognitive biases, and a driver of human behavior—over which they have little control because they defy any sort of introspection.

Under neoliberalism, social justice is achieved when the rich can get richer and the poorer are incentivized to become richer. Thus, is in the classical liberal tradition, improving the lot of working class involves making the poor richer, not the rich poorer (Bentham [1795] 1952, 1, 226n).

CONCLUSION

The human, social, economic, and political consequences produced by governments adopting and implementing neoliberal policies and practices are the product of neoliberalism's blinkered worldview:

- Its libertarian presumptions that self-interest is a universally applicable and dominant human motivation, and that individuals are (should be) free to pursue their own material happiness without any *obligation* to satisfy the needs or wants of others.

- Its methodological presumption that social institutions or social phenomena can best be investigated by drawing deductive inferences from the actions of hypothetical and undersocialized social actors whose actions are presumed to be the product of maximizing their material wellbeing in accordance with a comprehensive sets of entirely self-determined ordered preference set.

- Its conceptualization of an economy as a closed, law-abiding (deterministic) system that is isolated from, and independent of, any socio-cultural, religious, and political influences in the host society.

- Its economic efficiency presumption that the enhancing of human wellbeing is contingent on more commodities being produced at the lowest possible cost and sold to those who are able to pay the highest possible price.

- Its social justice presumption that it is morally acceptable to maximize a society's wellbeing by letting the rich become richer, even if it still has—or, indeed, has more—needs-based distributive injustice.

- Its assertion that markets can advance human wellbeing much better than can the state.

- Its assertion that those who govern society and administer its public agencies are inherently coercive, intrusive, and constantly at risk of being inefficient, so justifying radical surgery to the role and functions of the state by downsizing (privatization and marketization) and by radically reforming to its public agencies (by inculcating market forces and business-like managerial practices).

Neoliberalism arrogantly posits that its individualist-libertarian values, its instrumentally rational decision frames, and its style of market governance, its minimalist (hollowed-out) vision of government, and its managerialized public administration should prevail because its particular configuration of governing principles—individual liberty, democracy, minimal state intervention, and meliorism—are self-evidently held to be universally applicable, regardless of ethnicity, socio-cultural customs, traditions and values, and religiosity. The irony is that the fiscal austerity that inevitably follows a government's adoption of the neoliberal prescription for the public sector—measures to reduce public expenditures in an attempt to reduce budget deficits, so as to finance public debt repayment, or to reduce the current and/or future tax burden—can result in:

- the loss of public confidence, even trust, in the capacity of a (hollowed-out) state to protect, let alone advance, the common good (perhaps conceptualized as promoting social solidarity), to the point of prompting social unrest;

- the transferring of business costs (and the cost of any risks to profits posed by public policies) to the state in the process of privatization, marketization, or regulation, while related business profits are treated as commercial-in-confidence and thus not subject to public scrutiny; and

- advancing corporate welfare (so sustain a viable corporate sector) at the expense of social welfare (so sustaining—even increasing—poverty and inequality).

For Dardot and Laval (2013, 8):

> Neoliberalism is not merely destructive of rules, institutions and rights. ... This norm enjoins everyone to live in a world of generalized competition; ... it aligns social relations with the model of the market; it promotes the justification of ever greater inequalities; it even transforms the individual, now called on to conceive and conduct him- or herself as an enterprise. For more than a third of a century, this existential norm has presided over public policy, governed global economic relations, transformed society, and reshaped subjectivity.

Metaphorically (with apologies to Hans Christian Anderson), the emperor's clothes—no less his underwear (see Pollitt 2000)—all made in the bygone era of the eighteenth and nineteenth centuries—are threadbare for the twenty-first century.

REFERENCES

Abrams, M.H. 1971. *Natural Supernaturalism Tradition and Revolution in Romantic Literature*. New York: W.W. Norton.

Ackermann, R. 1976. *The Philosophy of Karl Popper*. Amherst, MA: University of Massachusetts Press.

Adler, A. [1922] 1924. *The Practice and Theory of Individual Psychology*, trans. P. Radin. London: Kegan Paul, Trench, Trubner.

Adler, A. [1929] 1969. *The Science of Living*, ed. H.L. Ansbacher. Garden City, NY: Doubleday Anchor.

Adler, A. [1933] 1973. "On the Origins of the Striving for Superiority and of Social Interest." In *Superiority and Social Interest: A Collection of Later Writings*, eds. H.L. Ansbacher, and R.R. Ansbacher. New York: Viking.

Adler, A. [1938] 1943. *Social Interest: A Challenge to Mankind*. London: Faber & Faber.

Adorno, T.W., E. Frenkel-Bruns, D.J. Levinson, and R.N. Sanford. 1950. *The Authoritarian Personality*. New York: Harper.

Adorno, T.W., and M. Horkheime. [1947] 1972. *Dialect of Enlightenment*, trans. J. Cumming. London: Allen Lane.

Alderfer, C.P. 1972. *Existence, Relatedness, and Growth*. New York: Free Press.

Alexander, R.D. 1987. *The Biology of Moral Systems*. New Brunswick, NJ: Transtaction Publishers, Foundations of Human Behavior.

Alexander, J. 2003. *The Meaning of Social Life: A Cultural Sociology*. Oxford: Oxford University Press.

Al-Khalili, J., and J. McFadden. [2014] 2015. *Life on the Edge: The Coming of Age of Quantum Biology*. London: Black Swan.

Allport, G.W. 1955. *Becoming: Basic Considerations for a Psychology of Personality*. New Haven, CT: Yale University Press.

Alchian, A. A. and Demsetz, H. 1972. "Production, Information Costs and Economic Organization." *American Economic Review* 62 (4): 777–795.

Alston, W.P. 1989. *Epistemic Justification: Essays in the Theory of Knowledge*. Ithaca, NY: Cornell University Press.

Althusser, L. 1962. "Contradiction and Overdetermination: Notes for an Investigation." In *For Marx*, trans. B. Brewster. New York: Penguin Press. http://www.marxists.org/reference/archive/althusser/1962/overdetermination.htm (retrieved April 30, 2009).

Altman, Y., and Y. Baruch. 1998. "Cultural Theory and Organizations: Analytical Methods and Cases." *Organizational Studies* 19 (5): 769-785.

Anderson, S.M., and S. Chen. 2002. "The Relational Self: An Interpersonal Social-Cognitive Theory." *Psychological Review* 109 (4): 619-645.

Anderson, S.M., and S.W. Cole. 1990. "'Do I Know You': the Role of Significant Others in General Social Perception." *Journal of Personal Social Psychology* 59 (3): 384-399.

Andrews, C. and A. Kouzmin. 1998. "Discourse on New Public Administration." *Lua Nova: A Review of Culture and Politics*, 45: 97-129.

Andrews, C. and A. Kouzmin. 1999. "Naming the Rose: New Public Management Discourse in Brazilian and Other Reforming Contexts." *International Review of Public Administration,* 4 (1): 11-20.

Ankony, R.C. 1999. "The Impact of Perceived Alienation on Police Officers' Sense of Mastery and Subsequent Motivation for Proactive Enforcement." *Policing: An International Journal of Police Strategies and Management* 22 (2): 120-132.

Ansell, C., and A. Gash. 2008. "Collaborative Governance in Theory and Practice." *Journal of Public Administration Research and Theory* 18 (4): 543-571.

Aquinas, St.T. [1259–1264] 1905. *Summa Contra Gentiles [On the Truth of the Catholic Faith Against the Unbelievers]*. Abridged Edition, trans. and ed. J. Rickaby. London: Burns and Oates. http://www2.nd.edu/Departments/Maritain/etext/gc.htm (retrieved February 4, 2007).

Aquinas, St.T. [1264] 1974. *Selected Political Writings*, ed. A.P. d'Entreves. Oxford: Blackwell.

Aquinas, St.T. [1266–1273] 1948. *The Summa Theologica*, trans. Fathers of the English Dominica Province. New York: Benziger.

Archer, M.S. 1995. *Realist Social Theory: A Morphogenetic Approach.* Cambridge: Cambridge University Press.

Archer, M.S. 2000. *Being Human: The Problem of Agency.* Cambridge: Cambridge University Press.

Ardrey, R. 1967. *The Territorial Imperative: The Social Contract: A Personal Inquiry into the Evolutionary Sources of Order and Disorder.* London: Collins.

Argyris, C. 1957. *Personality and Organization: The Conflict between System and the Individual.* New York: Harper.

Argyris, C. 1962. *Interpersonal Competence and Organizational Effectiveness.* Homewood, IL: Irwin.

Argyris, C. 1972. *The Applicability of Organizational Sociology.* Cambridge: Cambridge University Press.

Argyris, C. 1973. *On Organizations of the Future.* Beverly Hills, CA: Sage.

Argyris, C., and D. Schön. 1978. *Organizational Learning: A Theory of Action Perspective.* Reading, MA: Addison-Wesley.

Aristotle. [350 BCE] 2004. *Nicomachean Ethics,* trans. W.D. Ross. Adelaide, AU: eBooks@Adelaide. http://www.etext.library.adelaide.edu.au/mirror/classics.mit.edu/Aristotle/nicomachaen.html (retrieved June 8, 2006).

Aristotle. [350 BCE] 2015. *On the Soul [De Anima],* trans. J.A. Smith. Adelaide, AU: eBooks@Adelaide. https://ebooks.adelaide.edu.au/a/aristotle/a8so/ (retrieved August 15, 2016).

Armstrong, D.M. 1968. *A Materialist Theory of the Mind.* New York: Humanities Press.

Armstrong, D.M. 1978. *Universals and Scientific Realism.* Cambridge: Cambridge University Press.

Armstrong, D.M. 1989. *Universals: An Opinionated Introduction.* Boulder, CO: Westview Press.

Armstrong, D.M. 2000. "Universals as Attributes." In *Metaphysics: An Anthology,* eds. J. Kim, and E. Sosa. Oxford: Blackwell.

Arneson, R.J. 1991. "Autonomy and Preference Formation." In *Harm's Way: Essays in Honor of Joel Feinberg*, eds. J. Coleman, and A. Buchanan. Cambridge: Cambridge University Press.

Arneson, R.J. 1997. "Egalitarianism and the Undeserving Poor." *The Journal of Political Philosophy* 5 (4): 327-330.

Aronson, E. 1969. "The Theory of Cognitive Dissonance: A Current Perspective." In *Advances in Experimental Social Psychology*, vol. 4, ed., L. Berkowitz. New York: Academic Press.

Arrow, K.J. 1954. *Social Choice and Individual Values*. New York: Wiley.

Arrow, K.J. [1969] 1983. "The Organization of Economic Activity: Issues Pertinent to the Choice of Market Versus Non-market Allocations" (The Analysis and Evaluation of Public Expenditures: The PPB System). In A Compendium of Papers Submitted to the Subcommittee on Economy in Government of the Joint Economic Committee, Congress of the United States, 1. Washington, DC: Government Printing Office. http://econ.ucsb.edu/~tedb/Courses/UCSBpf/readings/ArrowNonMktActivity1969.pdf (retrieved June 5, 2007).

Arrow, K.J. 1994. "Methodological Individualism and Social Knowledge." *American Economic Review* 89 (2): 1-9.

Arrow, K.J., and G. Debreu. 1954. "Existence of an Equilibrium for a Competitive Economy." *Econometrica* 22: 265-290.

Atherton, M., ed. 1999. *The Empiricists: Critical Essays on Locke, Berkeley, and Hume*. Blue Ridge Summit, PA: Rowman & Littlefield.

Austin, J. [1832] 1995. *The Province of Jurisprudence Determined*. Cambridge: Cambridge University Press.

Autor, D. 2010. "International Trade and the Principle of Comparative Advantage." http://ocw.mit.edu/courses/economics/14-03-microeconomic-theory-and-public-policy-fall-2010/lecture-notes/MIT14_03F10_lec11.pdf (retrieved July, 2016).

Ayer, A.J. [1936] 1975. *Language, Truth and Logic*. Harmondsworth, Gt. Lon., UK: Penguin.

Ayer, A. J. 1953. *The Foundations of Empirical Knowledge*. London: Macmillan.

Ayer, A. J., ed., 1959. *Logical Positivism*. New York: Free Press.

Bacharach, M., and D. Gambetta. 1997. "Trust in Signs." In *Trust in Society*, ed. K.S. Cook. New York: Russell Sage Foundation.

Bacharach, M., and D. Gambetta. 2001. "Trust as Type Detection." In *Trust and Deception in Virtual Societies*, eds. C. Castelfranchi, and Y.-H. Tan. Dordrecht, NL and Boston, MA: Kluwer Academic Press.

Baehr, J.S. 2006. "*A Priori* and *A Posteriori*." *The Internet Encyclopedia of Philosophy*. http://www.iep.utm.edu/a/apriori.htm (retrieved November 15, 2010).

Baert, P. 1998. *Social Theory in the Twentieth Century*. Cambridge: Polity Press.

Baggini, J. 2002. *Making Sense: Philosophy Behind the Headlines*. Oxford: Oxford University Press.

Baghramian, M. 2004. *Relativism*. London: Routledge.

Bakhtin, M.M. [1934–1941] 1981. *The Dialogic Imagination: Four Essays*, ed. M. Holquist, trans. C. Emerson, and M. Holquist. Austin and London: University of Texas Press.

Bambrough, R. 1979. *Moral Scepticism and Moral Knowledge*. London: Routledge and Kegan Paul.

Bardach, E., and R.A. Kagan. 1982. *Going by the Book*. Philadelphia, PA: Temple University Press.

Barnard, C. 1938. *The Functions of the Executive*. Cambridge, MA: Harvard University Press.

Barnett, W.A (2007). "An Interview with Paul Samuelson." In *Inside the Economist's Mind: Conversations with Eminent Economists*, eds. P.A Samuelson, and W.A. Barnett. Oxford: Blackwell.

Barrett, W. 1958. *Irrational Man: A Study in Existential Philosophy*. Westport, CT: Greenwood.

Bartlett, S.J., and P. Suber, eds. 1987. *Self-Reference: Reflections on Reflexivity*. Dordrecht, NL: Martinus Nijhoff.

Barzelay, M. 2000. *The New Public Management: Improving Research and Policy Dialogue*. Berkeley, CA: University of California Press.

Barzelay, M. 2005. "Origins of the New Public Management: An International View from Public Administration/Political Science." In

New Public Management: Current Trends and Future Prospects, eds. K. McLaughlin, S.P. Osborne, and E. Ferlie. London and New York: Routledge.

Bates, R.H. 1989. *Beyond the Miracle of the Market: The Political Economy of Agrarian Development in Kenya*. New York: Cambridge University Press.

Baumeister, R. 1993. *Self-Esteem*. New York: Plenum Press.

Becker, G.S. 1965. "A Theory of Allocation of Time." *Economic Journal* 65 (3): 493-517.

Becker, G.S. 1976. *The Economic Approach to Human Behavior*. Chicago, IL: University of Chicago Press.

Beetham, D. 1987. *Bureaucracy*. Buckingham, Bucks, UK: Open University Press.

Behn, R.D. 2001. *Rethinking Democratic Accountability*. Washington: Brookings.

Beiner, R. 1983. *Political Judgment*. Chicago, IL: University of Chicago Press.

Bellah, R.N., R. Madsen, W.M. Sullivan, A. Swidler, and S.M. Tipton. [1985] 2007. *Habits of the Heart: Individualism and Commitment in American Life*. Second Edition. Berkeley, CA: University of California Press.

Benedict, R. [1934] 1959. "Anthropology and the Abnormal." In *An Anthropologist at Work: Writings of Ruth Benedict*, ed. M. Mead. Boston, MA: Haughton Miffin.

Benedict, R. [1934] 1989. *Patterns of Culture*. New York: Houghton Mifflin.

Benson, P. 1987. "Freedom and Value." *Journal of Philosophy* 84: 465-486.

Bentham, J. [1789] 1970. *An Introduction to the Principles of Morals and Legislation*, eds. J.H. Burns, and H.L.A. Hart. London: Athlone Press.

Bentham, J. [1795] 1952. *Supply Without Burthen; or Escheat Vice Taxation in Jeremy Bentham's Economic Writings*, vol. 1, ed. W. Stark. London: George Allen & Unwin.

Berenson, M. 1976. "Freedom." In *Philosopher and the Teacher*, ed. D.T. Lloyd. London and New York: Routledge.

Berger, P., and T. Luckmann. 1967. *The Social Construction of Reality: A Treatise in the Sociology of Knowledge.* New York: Doubleday.

Bergson, A. J. 2004. "Durkheim's Theory of Mental Categories: A Review of the Evidence." *Annual Review of Sociology* 30: 395–408.

Berkeley, G. [1710] 1962. *The Principles of Knowledge,* ed. G.J.Warnock. London: Fontana.

Berlin, I. 1969. *Four Essays on Liberty.* London: Oxford University Press.

Bermúdez, J.L., A. Marcel, and N. Eilan, eds. 1995. *The Body and the Self.* Cambridge, MA and London: MIT Press.

Bernstein, P.L. 1996. *Against the Gods: The Remarkable Story of Risk.* New York: John Wiley.

Bhaskar, R. [1979] 1998. *The Possibility of Naturalism: A Philosophical Critique of the Contemporary Human Sciences.* Third Edition. London and New York: Routledge.

Bilton, T., K. Bonnett, P. Jones, T. Lawson, D. Skinner., M. Stanworth, and A. Webster. 1996. *Introductory Sociology.* Third Edition. London: Macmillan.

Bingham, L.B., T. Nabatchi, and R. O'Leary. 2005. "The New Governance: Practices and Processes for Stakeholder and Citizen Participation in the Work of Government." *Public Administration Review* 65 (5): 547-548.

Blackburn, S. 1993. *Essays in Quasi-Realism.* Oxford: Oxford University Press.

Blackburn, S. 2005. *Truth: A Guide for the Perplexed.* New York: Oxford University Press.

Blackmore, S. 2003. "Consciousness in Meme Machines." *Journal of Consciousness Studies* 10 (4-5): 19-30.

Blake, W. [1808] 2004. "And did Those Feet in Ancient Times." In *The Concise Oxford Chronicle of English Literature,* ed. M. Cox. Oxford: Oxford University Press.

Blake, R.R., and J.S. Mouton. 1982. *The Versatile Manager: A Grid Profile.* Homewood, IL: Richard D. Irwin.

Blake, R.R., and J.S. Mouton. 1984. *The Managerial Grid III.* Third Edition. Houston, TX: Gulf Publishing.

Blaug, M. [1962] 1996. *Economic Theory in Retrospect*. Fifth Edition. Caambridge: Cambridge University Press.

Blaug, M. 1993. "Pieter Henniepman on Paretian Welfare Economics: A Comment." *Economist-Leiden* 141 (1): 127-129.

Block, N. 1980. "Introduction: What is Functionalism?" In *Readings in Philosophy of Psychology*, ed. N. Block. Cambridge, MA: Harvard University Press.

Block, F.L., and M.R. Somers. 2014. *The Power of Market Fundamentalism: Karl Polanyi's Critique*. Cambridge, MA: Harvard University Press.

Blumer, H. 1969. *Symbolism Interactionism: Perspective and Method*. Englewood Cliff, NJ: Prentice Hall.

Bogason, P. 2004. "Postmodern Public Administration." In *Handbook of Public Management*, eds. E.B. Ferlie, L. Lynn, and C. Pollitt. Oxford: Oxford University Press.

BonJour, L. 1985. *The Structure of Empirical Knowledge*. Cambridge, MA: Harvard University Press.

BonJour, L. 2002. *Epistemology: Classic Problems and Contemporary Responses*. Blue Ridge Summit, PA: Rowman & Littlefield.

Borins, S.F. 1992. "Statecraft: The Effective Use of Political Power." *Business Quarterly* 57 (2): 52-56.

Boulder, K. 1990. *Three Faces of Power*. Newbury Park, CA: Sage.

Bourdieu, P. 1990. *The Logic of Practice*, trans, R. Nice. Cambridge: Polity Press.

Bourdieu, P. 1998. *Acts of Resistance: Against the New Myths of our Time*. Cambridge: Polity Press.

Bourdieu, P., and L. Wacquant. 1992. *An Invitation to Reflexive Sociology*. Chicago, IL: University of Chicago Press.

Bradach, J.L., and R.G. Eccles. 1991. "Price, Authority and Trust: From Ideal Types to Plural Forms." In *Markets, Hierarchies and Networks: The Coordination of Social Life*, eds. G. Thompson, J. Frances, R. Levacic, and J. Mitchell. London: Sage and Open University Press.

Brand, M., and D. Walton, eds. 1976. *Action Theory*. Dordrecht, NL: Reidel.

Brans, M., and S. Rossbach. 1997. "The Autopoiesis of Administrative Systems: Niklas Luhmann on Public Administration and Public Policy." *Public Administration* 75: 417-439.

Brennan, J.F. 1969. "Autoeroticism or Social Feeling as Basic Human Development." *Journal of Individual Psychology* 25: 3-18.

Brentano, F. [1874] 1995. *Psychology from an Empirical Point of View*, ed. L.L. McAlister, trans. A.C. Rancurello, D.B. Terrell, and L.L. McAlister. London: Routledge.

Bromely, D.W. 1990. "The Ideology of Efficiency: Searching for a Theory of Policy Analysis." *Journal of Environmental Economics and Management* 19 (1): 86-107.

Bryant, C.G.A. 1985. *Positivism in Social Theory and Research*. Basingstoke Hamp., UK: Macmillan.

Bryson, J.M., and P.S. Ring. 1990. "A Transaction-based Approach to Policy Intervention." *Policy Sciences* 23 (3): 205-229.

Buchanan, J.M. 1990. "The Domain of Constitutional Economics." *Constitutional Political Economy* 1 (1): 1-18.

Buchanan, J.M., and G. Tullock. 1962. *The Calculus of Consent*. Ann Arbor, MI: University of Michigan Press.

Bud, L. 2007. "Post-Bureaucracy and Reanimating Public Governance." *International Journal of Public Sector Management* 20 (6): 531-547.

Bunge, M. 1996. *Finding Philosophy in Social Science*. New Haven, CT: Yale University.

Burke, T.E. 1983. *The Philosophy of Popper*. Manchester, UK: Manchester University Press.

Burns, T. 1966. "On the Plurality of Social Systems." In *Operational Research and the Social Sciences*, ed. J.R. Lawrence. London: Tavistock.

Burns, T., and G.M. Stalker. 1961. *The Management of Innovation*. London: Tavistock.

Buschardt, S.C., R. Toso, and M.E Schnake. 1986. "Can Money Motivate?" In *Motivation of Personnel*, ed. T.A. Dale. New York: KEND.

Bushman, B., and R. Baumeister. 1998. "Threatened Egoism, Narcissism, Self-esteem, and Direct and Displaced Aggression: Does Self-love and Self-hate Lead to Violence." *Journal of Personality and Social Psychology* 75: 219-229.

Buss, D.M. 1999. *Evolutionary Psychology: The New Science of the Mind.* Needham Heights, MA: Allyn and Bacon.

Butler-Bowden, T. 2007. *50 Psychology Classics.* London and Boston, MA: Nicholas Brealey.

Butterfield, J. 1998. "Determinism and Indeterminism." In *Routledge Encyclopedia of Philosophy*, ed. E. Craig. London: Routledge.

Byron, M., ed. 2004. *Satisficing and Maximising: Moral Theory's Practical Reason.* Cambridge: Cambridge University Press.

Callinicos, A. 1999. *Social Theory: A Historical Introduction.* Cambridge: Polity Press.

Cameron, S. 2002. *The Economics of Sin: Rational Choice or No Choice at All.* Cheltenham, Glos., UK: Edward Elgar.

Campbell, J.K., M. O'Rourke, and H.S. Silverstein, eds. 2007. *Causation and Explanation.* Cambridge, MA: MIT Press.

Camus, A. [1942] 2005. *The Myth of Sisyphus*, trans. J. O'Brien. Harmondworth, Gt. Lon., UK: Penguin.

Cantor, R., S. Henry, and S. Rayner. 1992. *Making Markets: An Interdisciplinary Perspective on Economic Exchange.* Westport, CT: Greenwood.

Caplan, B. 2007. "Externalities." In *The Concise Encyclopedia of Economics.* Second Edition, ed. D.R. Henderson. Indianapolis, IN: Liberty Fund, Economics and Liberty. http://www.econlib.org/library/Enc/ Externalities.html (retrieved March 15 2016).

Carnap, R. [1928] 1969. *The Logical Structure of the World and Pseudoproblems in Philosophy*, trans. R.A. George. Berkeley and Los Angeles, CA: University of California Press.

Cassam, Q. 1997. *Self and World.* Oxford: Oxford University Press.

Cattell, R.B. 1965. *The Scientific Analysis of Personality.* Baltimore, MD: Penguin.

Chalmers, D. 1996. *The Conscious Mind: In Search of a Theory of Conscious Experience.* New York: Oxford University Press.

Charles, D., and K. Lennon, eds. 1992. *Reduction, Explanation and Realism*. Oxford: Clarendon.

Chesterton, G.K. [1908] 2007. *Orthodoxy*. New York: Filiquarian. http://books.google.co.uk/books?id=W6j4Qx2UF2AC&pg=PA97&lp-g=PA97&dq=chesterton+%22the+real+trouble+with+this+world+of+ours+is%22&source=web&ots=yunxnJFil&sig=0zbAi2pTbtupc-Cvt9JjErodLw2Y&hl=en (retrieved June 24, 2015).

Chisholm, R. [1964] 2002. "Human Freedom and Self." In *Free Will*, ed. R. Kane. Malden, MA: Blackwell.

Chisholm, R.M. 1989. *Theory of Knowledge*. Third Edition. Englewood Cliffs, NJ: Prentice-Hall.

Christman, J., ed. 1989. *The Inner Citadel: Essays on Individual Autonomy*. Oxford and New York: Oxford University Press.

Christman, J. 1991. "Autonomy and Personal History." *Canadian Journal of Philosophy* 21 (1): 1-24.

Cicero. [44 BCE] 1971. *De Fato [On Fate]*, trans. R.W. Sharples. Warminister, Wilts., UK: Aris & Phillips.

Clarke, R. [2000] 2004. "Incompatibilist (Nondeterministic) Theories of Free Will." In *The Stanford Encyclopedia of Philosophy*, ed. E.N. Zelta. http://plato.stanford.edu/entries/incompatibilism-theories/ (retrieved June 23, 2007).

Clarke, J., and J. Newman. 1997. *The Managerial State*. London: Sage.

Clark, P., and J. Wilson. 1961. "Incentive Systems: A Theory of Organizations." *Administrative Science Quarterly* 6 (1): 129-166.

Coady, C.A.J. 1992. *Testimony: A Philosophical Study*. Oxford: Oxford University Press.

Coase, R.H. 1937. "The Nature of Firms." *Economica* (new series) 4 (3): 386-405.

Coase, R.H. 1994. *Essays on Economics and Economists*. Chicago and London: University of Chicago Press.

Cohen, J. 1989. "Deliberation and Democratic Legitimacy." In *The Good Polity*, eds. A.S. Hamlin, and P. Pettit. Oxford: Blackwell.

Cohen, M., and J. March. [1974] 1983. "Leadership in an Organized

Anarchy." In *The Dynamics of Organizational Change in Education*, eds. J.V. Baldridge, and T.E. Deal. Berkeley, CA: McCutchin.

Cohen, M., J. March, and J. Olsen. 1972. "A Garbage Can Model of Organizational Choice." *Administrative Science Quarterly* 17 (1): 1-23.

Colander, D. 2000. "The Death of Neoclassical Economics." *Journal of the History of Economic Thought* 22 (2): 127-143.

Colebatch, H., and P. Lamour. 1993. *Markets, Bureaucracy and Community*. London: Pluto.

Coleman, J.L. 1980. "Efficiency, Utility, and Wealth Maximization." Yale Law School, Faculty Scholarship Series. Paper 4202. http://digitalcommons. law.yale.edu/fss_papers/4202 (retrieved January 23, 2006).

Coleman, J.S. 1990. *Foundations of Social Theory*. Cambridge, MA: Harvard University Press.

Collard, D. 1975. "Edgeworth's Propositions on Altruism." *The Economic Journal* 85 (338): 355-360.

Commons, J.R. 1931. "Institutional Economics." *American Economic Review* 21: 648-657.

Considine, M. 2003. "Governance and Competition: The Role of Non-Profit Organisations in the Delivery of Public Services." *Australian Journal of Political Science* 38 (1): 63-77.

Cook, G.A. 1977. "G.H. Mead's Social Behaviorism." *Journal of the History of Behavioral Science* 13 (4): 307-316.

Cowen, T. 1993. "Public Goods and Externalities." In *The Concise Encyclopedia of Economics*. ed. D.R. Henderson. Indianapolis, IN: Liberty Fund, Economics and Liberty. http://econlib.org/library/Enc1/ PublicGoodsandExternalities.html (retrieved March 18, 2001).

Cresswell, M.J. 1985. *Structured Meanings. The Semantics of Propositional Attitudes*. Cambridge, MA and London: MIT Press.

Crisp, R., and M. Slote. 1997. *Virtue Ethics*. Oxford: Oxford University Press.

Crossley, N. 1996. *Intersubjectivity: The Fabric of Social Becoming*. London: Sage.

Crumbaugh, J.C. 1973. "The Validation of Logotheropy." In *Direct Psychotheropy*, ed. R.M. Jurjrvich. Coral Gables, FL: University of Miami Press.

Cudd, A. 2013. "Contractarianism." *The Stanford Encyclopedia of Philosophy*, Winter Edition, ed. E.N. Zalta. http://plato.stanford.edu/archives/win2013/entries/contractarianism/ (retrieved March 18, 2015).

Cupit, G. 1996. "Desert and Responsibility." *Canadian Journal of Philosophy* 26 (1): 83-99.

Cutting, B., and A. Kouzmin. 1997. "Towards an Ontological Understanding of Good Governance Based on a Synthesis of Weber's Concept of 'Ideal Types' and the Enneagram Typology." *Indian Journal of Public Administration* 2 (2): 85-112.

Cutting, B., and A. Kouzmin. 2011. *Refounding Political Governance: The Metaphysics of Public Administration*. Sharajah, UE: Bentham Books.

Cyert, R.M., and J.G. March. [1963] 1992. *A Behavioral Theory of the Firm*. Oxford: Blackwell.

Dahl, R.A. 1971. *Polyarchy: Participation and Opposition*. New Haven, CT: Yale University Press.

Dahl, R.A. 1982. *Dilemmas of Pluralist Democracy: Autonomy versus Control*. New Haven, CT: Yale University Press.

Dahrendorf, R. 1968. "Homo Sociologicus." In *Essays in the Theory of Society*, ed. R. Dahrendorf. Stanford, CA: Stanford University Press.

Dale, J. 2002. *Ontology*. Montreal and Kingston, Ont., CA: McGill-Queen's University Press.

D'Andrade, R.G. 1984. "Cultural Meaning Systems." In *Culture Theory: Essays on Mind, Self, and Emotion*, ed. R.A. Shweder, and R.A. LeVine. New York: Press.

Dardot, P., and C. Laval. 2013. *The New Way of the World: On Neoliberal Society*. London: Verso.

Darwall, S. 2003. *Consequentialism*. Oxford: Blackwell Publishing.

Davidson, D. 1980. "Mental Events." In *Essays on Actions and Events*, ed. D. Davidson. Oxford: Oxford University Press.

Davies, P. 1992. *The Mind of God: Science and the Search for Ultimate Meaning*. London: Penguin.

Davies, J.S. 2011. "The Limits of Post-Traditional Public Administration: Towards a Gramscian Perspective." *Critical Policy Studies* 5 (1): 47-62.

Davies, P and J. Gribbin.1992. *The Matter Myth: Dramatic Discoveries that Challenge Our Understanding of Physical Reality*. New York and London: Simon & Schuster Paperbacks.

Davis, M.H. 1994. *Empathy: A Social Psychological Approach*. Boulder, CO: Westview Press.

Davis, T. 1997. *Humanism: The New Critical Idiom*. London: Routledge.

Davis, J. 2003. *The Theory of the Individual in Economics: Identity and Value*. New York: Routledge.

Davis, J. 2008. "The Socially Embedded Individual Conception." In *Companion to Social Economics*, eds. J. Davis, and W. Dolfsma. Cheltenham, Glos., UK: Edward Elgar.

Davis, J.B. 2011. *Individuals and Identity in Economics*. Cambridge: Cambridge University Press.

De Alessi, L. 1983. "Property Rights, Transaction Costs, and X-efficiency: An Essay in Economic Theory." *American Economic Review* 73 (1): 347-364.

Debreu, G. 1959. *Theory of Value: An Axiomatic Analysis of Economic Equilibrium*. New Haven: Yale University Press.

de Grazia, A. 1960. "The Science and Values of Administration: 1." *Administrative Science Quarterly* 5: 421-447.

Delger, C.N. 1991. *In Search of Human Nature: The Decline and Revival of Darwinism in American Social Thought*. New York: Oxford University Press.

DePaul, M., ed. 2000. *Resurrecting Old-Fashioned Foundationalism*. Blue Ridge Summit, PA: Rowman & Littlefield.

Derrida, J. 1976. *Of Grammatology*, trans. G.C. Spivak. Baltimore, MD and London: John Hopkins University Press.

Derrida, J. 1978. *Writings and Differences*, trans. A. Bass. London and New York: Routledge.

Descartes, R. [1637] 1951. "A Discourse on Methods." In *Discourse on Methods and Selected Writings*, trans. J. Veitich. London: Dent & Sons.

Descartes, R. [1641] 1975. "Discourse on Method and Meditations on First Philosophy." In *The Philosophical Writings of Descartes*, vol. 2, eds. J. Cottingham, R. Stoothoff, and M. Dugald Murdoch. Cambridge: Cambridge University Press.

Descartes, R. [1644] 1983. *Principia Philosophiae [Principles of Philosophy]*, trans. V.R. Miller, and R.P. Miller. Dordrecht, NL: Reidel.

de Tocqueville, A. [1835/1840] 1899. *Democracy in America*, trans. H. Reeves. http://xroads.virginia.edu/~hyper/DETOC/ (retrieved May 16, 2002).

Devine, J., and J. Wright. 1993. *The Greatest of Evils: Urban Poverty and the Amrican Underclass*. Hawthorne, NY: Aldine De Gruyter.

Devitt, M. 1984. *Realism and Truth*. Princeton, NJ: Princeton University Press.

Devitt, M., and K. Sterelny. [1987] 1998. *Language and Reality: An Introduction to the Philosophy of Language*. Second Edition. Oxford: Blackwell.

Dewey, J. [1895–1898] 1972. *The Collected Works of John Dewey*, vol. 5, ed. J. A. Boydston. Carbondale, IL: Southern Illinois University Press.

Dick, J. C. 1975. "How to Justify a Distribution of Earnings." *Philosophy and Public Affairs* 4 (3): 248-272.

Dilthey, W. [1910] 2000. "The Formation of the Historical World in the Human Sciences." In *Wilhelm Dilthey: Selected Works*, vol. 3, eds. and trans. R.A. Makkreel, and F. Rodi. Princeton, NJ: Princeton University Press.

Dirac, P. 1963. "The Evolution of the Physicist's Picture of Nature." *Scientific American* 208 (5): 45. http://www-history.mcs.st-and.ac.uk/Quotations/Dirac.html (retrieved April 22, 2016).

Dixon, J. 1996. "Reinventing Civil Servants: Public Management Development and Education to Meet the Managerialist Challenge in Australia." *Journal of Management Development* 15 (7): 62-82.

Dixon, J. 2003. *Responses to Governance: The Governing of Corporations, Societies and the World*. Westport, CT: Praeger.

Dixon, J. 2010. "Naïve Economics and the Promised Land of Privatization: A Critical Analysis of the Rational Actor Model of Man." *Administrative Theory & Praxis* 32 (3): 348-372.

Dixon, J. 2016. *The Public Administrator: Contenders, Contentions, and Tensions*. Washington, DC: Westphalia Press.

Dixon, J. 2017. "Exchange Transactions Revisited: On the Universal Applicability of Homo Economicus." *International Journal of Social Economics* 44 (4).

Dixon, J., and R. Dogan. 2003. "A Philosophical Analysis of Management: Improving Praxis." *Journal of Management Development* 22 (6): 458-482.

Dixon, J., and R. Dogan (2004), "The Conduct of Policy Analysis: Philosophical Points of Reference." *Review of Policy Research* 21 (23): 559-80.

Dixon, J., and R. Dogan. 2005. "The Contending Perspectives on Public Management: A Philosophical Investigation." *International Public Management Journal* 8 (1): 1-22.

Dixon, J., and Frolova, Y. (2011). "Existential Poverty: Welfare Dependency, Learned Helplessness and Psychological Capital." *Poverty and Public Policy* 3 (2): Article 6.

Dixon, J., and Y. Frolova. 2013. "The Hierarchical Civil Servant: The Resurrection of an Administrative Archetype?" *Administrative Theory & Praxis* 35 (2): 199-219.

Dixon, J., and M. Hyde. 2009. "Citizenship, the Public Interest and Governance." In *Citizenship: A Reality Far from Ideal*, eds. N. Korac-Kakabadse, A. Kakabadse, and K.N. Kulu. Basingstoke, Hants, UK: Palgrave Macmillan.

Dixon, J., and A. Kouzmin. 1994a. "Management Innovations for Improving Governance: Changes and Trends in Australian Public Administration and Finance." *Asian Review of Public Administration* 6 (12): 33-91 (Reprinted in *Public Administration and Sustainable Development*, eds. M.J.E. Jafari, R.P. De Guzman, and M.A. Reforma. Tehrain, IR: State Organization for Administrative and Employment Affairs under the Auspices of the Eastern Regional Organization for Public Administration.

Dixon, J., and A. Kouzmin. 1994b. "The Commercialisation of the Australian Public Sector: Competence, Elitism or Default in Management Education?" *International Journal of Public Sector Management* 7 (6): 52-73.

Dixon, J., and P.P.-S. Wong. 2015. "Organization Traits under Conditions of Relational Dominance: The Archetypal Confucian Organization." *AFBE Journal* 8 (1): 41-55.

Dixon, J., A. Kouzmin, and N. Korac-Kakabadse. 1997. "Managerialism— Something Old, Something Borrowed, and Little New: Prescription Versus Effective Organizational Change in Public Agencies." *International Journal of Public Sector Management* 11: 164-179.

Dixon, J., G. Davis, and A. Kouzmin. 2004. "Achieving Civil Service Reform: The Threats, Challenges and Opportunities." In *Verändertes Denken—Bessere ÖffentlicheDienste!? [Alternativ Thinking—Better Public Services?]*, eds. R. Koch, and P. Conrad. Weisbaden: DE Gabler-Verlag.

Dixon, J., R. Dogan, and A. Kouzmin. 2004. "The Dilemma of Privatized Public Services: Philosophical Frames in Understanding Failure and Managing Partnership Terminations." *Public Organization Review* 4 (1): 25-46.

Dixon, J., R. Dogan, and K. Carrier. 2005. "On Investigating the 'Underclass': Contending Philosophical Perspectives." *Social Policy & Society* 4 (1): 21-30.

Dixon, J., A. Sanderson, and S. Tripathi. 2006. "Ethics, Trust and the Public Interest: The Contending Modes of Societal Governance." In *Governance, Strategy and Policy: Seven Critical Essays*, eds. N. Korac-Kakabadse, and A. Kakabadse. Basingstoke Hamp., UK: Palgrave Macmillan.

Dixon, J., A. Sanderson, and S. Tripathi. 2007. "Governance and the Public Interest: The Challenges for Public Sector Leaders." In *Public Governance and Leadership*, eds. R. Koch, and J. Dixon. Weisbaden, DM: Gabler-Verlag.

Dixon, J., R. Dogan, and A. Sanderson. 2009. *Situational Logic of Social Actions*. New York: Nova Science.

Dolan, T.E. 2010. "Revisiting Adhocracy: From Rhetorical Revisionism to Smart Mobs." *Journal of Futures Studies* 15 (2): 33-50.

Domahidy, M.R., and J.F. Gilsinan. 1992. "The Back Stage is not the Back Room: How Spatial Arrangements Affect the Administration of Public Affairs." *Public Administration Review* 52 (6): 588-593.

Donagan, A. 1987. *Choice: The Essential Element of Human Action*. London: Routledge & Kegan Paul.

Donahue, R. 1989. *The Privatization Decision: Public Ends, Private Means.* New York: Basic. Books

Doron, G. 1992. "Rational Choice and the Policy Sciences." *Policy Studies Review* 11 (3): 359-369.

Douglas, M. 1970. *Natural Symbols: Explorations in Cosmology.* London: Barry and Rockliff.

Douglas, M. 1982. "Cultural Bias." In *In the Active Voice*, ed. M. Douglas. London: Routledge & Kegan Paul.

Douglas, M. 1994. *Risk and Blame: Essays in Culture Theory.* London: Routledge.

Douglas, M., and B. Isherwood. 1979. *The World of Goods: Towards an Anthropology of Consumption.* London: Allen Lane.

Douglas, M., and S. Ney. 1998. *Missing Persons: A Critique of the Social Sciences.* Berkeley and Los Angeles, CA: University of California Press.

Downs, A. 1957. *The Economic Theory of Democracy.* New York: Harper & Row.

Downs, A. 1967. *Inside Bureaucracy.* Boston, MA: Little, Brown.

Doyal, L., and I. Gough. 1991. *A Theory of Human Need.* Bassingstoke, Hants, UK: Macmillan.

Druckman, J.N. 2001. "Evaluating Framing Effects." *Economic Psychology* 22: 91-101.

Dugan, M.A. 2003. "Empowerment." Posted on *Beyond Intractability*, eds. G. Burgess, and H. Burgess. Boulder, CO: Conflict Information Consortium, University of Colorado. http://www.beyondintractability.org/essay/empowerment (retrieved June 26, 2005).

du Gay, P. 2000. *In Praise of Bureaucracy: Weber—Organization—Ethics.* London: Sage.

Dulles, A. 1983. *Models of Revelation.* Garden City, NY: Doubleday.

Dummett, M. A. E. 1963. "Realism." In *Truth and Other Enigmas*, ed. M.A.E. Dummett. London: Duckworth.

Dumont, L. 1970. *Homo Hierarchus.* Chicago, IL: University of Chicago Press.

Dunsire, A. 1988. "Organizational Status and Performance: A Conceptual Framework for Testing Public Choice Theories." *Public Administration* 66 (4): 363-388.

Dunsire, A. 1996. "Tipping the Balance: Autopoiesis and Governance." *Administration and Society* 28 (3): 299-334.

Durkheim, E. [1895] 1982. *The Rules of Sociological Method and Selected Texts on Sociology and Its Method*, ed. S. Lukes, tran. W.D. Halls. London: Macmillan.

Durkheim, E. [1912] 2001. *The Elementary Forms of Religious Life*, trans. C. Cosman. Oxford: Oxford University Press.

Durkin, K. 1995. *Developmental Social Psychology: From Infancy to Old Age*. Oxford: Blackwell.

Dworkin, R. 1981a. "What is Equality? Part 1: Equality of Resources." *Philosophy and Public Affairs* 10: 185-246.

Dworkin, R. 1981b. "What is Equality? Part 2: Equality of Welfare." *Philosophy and Public Affairs* 10: 283-345.

Dworkin, G. 1988. *The Theory and Practice of Autonomy*. Cambridge: Cambridge University Press.

Earman, J. 1986. *A Primer on Determinism*. Dordrecht, NL: Reidel.

Eccles, J.C. 1994. *How the Self Controls its Brain*. Berlin: Springer.

Eckhoff, T. 1974. *Justice: Its Determinants in Social Interaction*. Rotterdam, NL: Rotterdam University Press.

Edgeworth, F.Y. 1881. *Mathematical Psychics: An Essay on the Application of Mathematics to the Moral Sciences*. London: C. K. Paul. https://archive.org/details/mathematicalpsyc00edge (accessed June 17, 2014).

Elder, N., A. Thomas, and D. Arter. 1982. *The Consensular Democracies? The Government and Politics of Scandinavian States*. Oxford: Martin Robertson.

Ellis, R.J. 1992. "Radical Locheanism in American Political Culture." *Western Political Quarterly* 45 (4): 825-850.

Elster, J. 1979. *Ulysses and the Sirens*. Cambridge: Cambridge University Press.

Elster, J. 1982. "The Case for Methodological Individualism." *Theory and*

Society 11: 453-482.

Elster, J. 1985. *Sour Frapes: Studies in the Subversion of Rationality.* Cambridge: Cambridge University Press.

Elster, J. 1986. "Introduction." In *Rational Choice*, ed. J. Elster. Oxford: Basil Blackwell.

Elster, J. 1989. *Nuts and Bolts for the Social Sciences.* Cambridge: Cambridge University Press.

Elster, J. 1991. "The Possibility of Rational Politics." In *Political Theory Today*, ed. D. Held. Oxford: Oxford University Press.

Elster, J. 1999a. *Alchemies of the Mind.* Cambridge: Cambridge University Press.

Elster, J. 1999b. *Strong Feelings.* Cambridge, MA: MIT Press.

Embree, L., E.A. Behnke, D. Carr, J.C. Evans, J. Huertas-Jourda, J.J. Kockelmans, W. Mckenna, *et al.* 1996. *The Encyclopedia of Phenomenology.* Dordrecht, NL: Kluwer.

Emery, F.E., and E.L. Trist. 1965. "The Causal Texture of Organizational Environments." *Human Relations* 18 (1): 21-32.

Epstein, R.A. 1985. *Takings: Private Property and the Power of Eminent Domain.* Chicago, IL: University of Chicago Press.

Erikson, E.H. 1963. *Childhood and Society.* Second Edition. New York: Norton.

Erikson, E.H. 1964. *Insight and Responsibility.* New York: Norton.

Esping-Andersen, G. 1990. *The Three Worlds of Welfare Capitalism.* Cambridge: Polity Press.

Etzioni, A. 1961. *A Comparative Analysis of Complex Organizations.* New York: Free Press.

Etzioni, A. 1993. *The Spirit of Community: Rights, Responsibilities and the Communitarian Agenda.* New York: Crown Publishers.

Etzioni, A. 1995. *New Communitarian Thinking: Persons, Virtues, Institutions, and Communities.* Charlottesville, VA: University of Virginia Press.

Etzioni, A., ed. 1998. *The Essential Communitarian Reader.* Lanham, MD: Rowman & Littlefield.

Fama, E.F. 1980. "Agency Problems and the Theory of the Firm." *Journal of Political Economy* 88 (2): 288-307.

Fama, E.F., and M. Jensen. 1983a. "Separation of Ownership and Control." *Journal of Law and Economics* 26: 301-326.

Fama, E.F., and M. Jensen. 1983b. "Agency Problems and Residual Claims." *Journal of Law and Economics* 26: 327-349.

Farmer, D.J. 2005. *To Kill the King: Post-Traditional Governance and Bureaucracy.* Armonk, NY: M.E. Sharpe.

Farmer, D.J. 2007. "Invited Essay: Epistemic Pluralism and Neuroscience." *Administrative Theory & Praxis* 30 (3): 285-295.

Farmer, D.J. 2010. *Public Administration in Perspective: Theory and Practice through Multiple Lenses.* Armonk, NY: M.E. Sharpe.

Fayol, H. [1916] 1949. *General and Industrial Management*, trans. C. Stoors. Boston, MA: Pitman.

Feinberg, J. 1970. *Doing and Deserving.* Princeton, NJ: Princeton University Press.

Feldman, F. 1992. *Confrontations with the Reaper.* Oxford: Oxford University Press.

Feldman, F. 1995a. "Adjusting Utility for Justice: A Consequentialist Reply to the Objection from Justice." *Philosophy and Phenomenological Research* 55: 567-585.

Feldman, F. 1995b. "Desert: Reconsideration of Some Received Wisdom." *Mind* 104: 63-77.

Feldman, F. 1995c. "Justice, Desert, and the Repugnant Conclusion." *Utilitas* 7: 189-206.

Feldman, F. 1996. "Responsibility as a Condition for Desert." *Mind* 105: 165-168.

Feldman, R., and E. Conee. 2004. *Evidentialism: Essays in Epistemology.* Oxford: Oxford University Press.

Feldman, M.S., and A.M. Khademain. 2000. "Managing for Inclusion: Balancing Control and Participation." *International Public Management Journal* 3 (2): 149-167.

Ferguson, A. [1767] 1782. *An Essay on the History of Civil Society*. Fifth Edition. London: T. Cadell. http://oll.libertyfund.org/titles/ferguson-an-essay-on-the-history-of-civil-society (retrieved March 13, 2010).

Ferguson, A. [1776] 1792. *Principles of Moral and Political Science: Being Chiefly a Retrospect of Lectures Delivered in the College of Edinburgh*, 2 vols. London and Edinburgh, SCT, UK: A. Strahan and T. Cadell, and W. Creech. https://books.google.com.tr/books?id=f8oLAAAAIAAJ&source=gbs_similarbooks (retrieved March, 13 2010) and https://books.google.com.tr/books?id=3mlYAAAAcAAJ&source=gbs_similarbooks (retrieved March 13, 2010).

Ferguson, K. [1994] 2004. *Fire in the Equations: Science, Religion and the Search for God*. Philadelphia, PA and London: Templeton Foundation Press.

Ferlie, E., L. Ashburner, L. Fitzgerald, and A. Pettigrew. 1996. *New Public Management in Action*. Oxford: Oxford University Press.

Festinger, L. 1957. *A Theory of Cognitive Dissonance*. Evanston, IL: Row, Peterson.

Feyerabend, P. 1963. "Mental Events and the Brain." *Journal of Philosophy* 60: 295-296.

Fine, B., and A. Saad-Filho. 2016. "Thirteen Things You Need to Know About Neoliberalism." *Critical Sociology*, forthcoming. http://eprints.soas.ac.uk/22614/1/Fine_Saad-Filho_22614.pdf

Finer, H. [1941] 1966. "Administrative Responsibility in Democratic Government." *Administration and Policy: Selected Essays*, ed. P. Woll. New York: Harper Torch.

Fingerette, H. 1969. *Self-Deception*. London: Routledge & Kegan Paul.

Firth, C. 2007. *Making up the Mind: How the Brain Creates Our Mental World*. Oxford: Blackwell.

Fischel, W.A. 1995. *Regulatory Takings: Law, Economics, and Politics*. Cambridge, MA: Harvard University Press.

Fischer, F., and J. Forester. 1993. "Introduction." In *The Argumentative Turn in Policy Analysis and Planning*, eds. F. Fischer, and J. Forester. London: UCL Press.

Fishburn, P.C. 1982. *The Foundations of Expected Utility*. Dordrecht, NL: D. Reidel.

Fiskin, J. 1991. *Democracy and Deliberation*. New Haven, CT: Yale University Press.

Flam, H. 1990. "Emotional Man 2: Corporate Actors as Emotion-Motivated, Emotion Managers." *Intermational Sociology* 5 (2): 225-242.

Fletcher, J. 1966. *Situational Ethics*. Philadelphia, PA: Westminster Press.

Fletcher, J. 1997. *Situation Ethics: The New Morality*. Louisville, KY: Westminster John Knox Press.

Fodor, J. 1980. "Methodological Solipsism Considered as a Research Strategy in Cognitive Science." *Behavioral and Brain Sciences* 3: 63-73.

Fodor, J. 1987. *Psychosemantics*. Cambridge, MA: MIT Press.

Fodor, J. 1991. "A Modal Argument for Narrow Content." *Journal of Philosophy* 88: 5-26.

Foot, P. 1978. *Moral Relativism*. Lawrence, KS: University of Kansas Press.

Foucault, M. [1966] 1989. *The Order of Things. An Archaeology of the Human Sciences*. London and New York: Routledge. http://booksgoogle.co.uk/s?id=7z0nXi4R8m4C&printsec=titlepage&vq=Foucault+1966+The+Order+of+Things&source=gbs_toc_s&cad=1#PPR12,M1 (retrieved February 16, 2016).

Foucault, M. [1969] 2002. *The Archaeology of Knowledge*, trans. A.M. Sheriden Smith. London and New York: Routledge.

Foucault, M. 1978. *The History of Sexuality, Vol. 1: An Introduction*, trans. R. Hurle. New York: Pantheon.

Foucault, M. 1983. "Discourse and Truth: The Problematization of Parrhesia: Six Lectures Given by Michel Foucault at the University of California at Berkeley, October–November 1983," ed. J. Pearson. http://foucault.info/documents/parrhesia/ (retrieved September 19, 2003).

Foy, N. 1980. *The Yin and Yang of Organizations: A Scintillating Guide to the Best in Current Management Thinking*. London: Grant McIntyre.

Frank, P. 1949. *Modern Science and its Philosophy*. Cambridge: MA: Harvard University Press.

Frankfurt, H. [1971] 2002. "Freedom of the Will and the Concept of a Person." In *Free Will*, ed. R. Kane. Malden, MA: Blackwell.

Frankl, V.E. [1946] 2000. *Man's Search for Meaning: An Introduction to Logotherapy*, pref. S. Hunt. New York: Washington Square Press.

Frankl, V. E. [1948] 2000. *Man's Search for Ultimate Meaning*, Rev. Paperback Edition, for. S. Hunt. New York: Perseus.

Frege, G. [1918] 1997. "Der Gedanke [Thoughts]." *Beiträge zur Philosophie des deutschen Idealismus* 1 (1918-9): 58-77. Reprinted in *The Frege Reader*, ed. M. Beany. Oxford: Blackwell.

Freire, P. 1983. *Pedagogy of the Oppressed*. New York: Continuum.

French, J.R.P., and B. Raven. 1959. "The Bases of Social Power." In *Studies in Social Power*, ed. R. Cartwright. Ann Arbor, MI: University of Michigan Press.

Freud, S. [1912] 1959. "The Dynamics of the Transference." In *Collected Papers of Sigmund Freud*, vol. 2, ed. E. Jones, trans. J. Riviere. New York: Basic Books.

Freud, S. [1929] 1971. *The Complete Introductory Lectures on Psychoanalysis*. London: Allen & Unwin.

Fundación para las Relaciones Internacionales y el Diálogo Exterior (FRIDE). 2006. *Empowerment* (Development Backgrounder, O1). Madrid, ES: FRIDE. http://fride.org/download/BGR_Empowerment_ENG_may06.pdf (retrieved March 14, 2012).

Fried, C. 1978. *Right and Wrong*. Cambridge, MA: Harvard University Press.

Friedman, D.D. [1986] 1990. *Price Theory: An Intermediate Text*. Second Edition. Nashville, TN: South-Western Publishing Co. http://www.daviddfriedman.com/Academic/Price_Theory/PThy_ToC.html (retrieved July 17, 2016).

Friedrich, C.J. [1940] 1966. "Public Policy and the Nature of Administrative Responsibility." In *Public Policy*, eds. C.J. Friedrich, and E.S. Mason. Cambridge: Harvard University Press. https://archive.org/stream/publicpolicy032464mbp/publicpolicy032464mbp_djvu.txt (retrieved May 25, 2014).

Furnham, A. 1984. "Many Sides of the Coin: The Psychology of Money Usage." *Personality and Individual Differences* 5: 501-509.

Fuss, D. 1989. *Essentially Speaking: Feminism, Nature and Difference*. New York: Routledge.

Gambetta, D. 1988. "Can We Trust?" In *Trust: Making and Breaking*, ed. D. Gambetta. Oxford: Oxford University Press.

Garfinkel, H. [1967] 1984. *Studies in Ethnomethodology*. Oxford: Blackwell.

Geertz, C. 1983. "The Way We Think Now: Towards an Ethnography of Modern Thought." In *Local Knowledge*, ed. C. Geertz. New York: Basic Books.

Gellerman, S.W. 1968. *Management by Motivation*. New York: American Management Association.

Gergen, K.J., and T.J. Thatchenkey. 1998. "Organizational Science in Postmodern Context." In *In the Realm of Organization: Essays for Robert Cooper*, ed. R.C.H. Chia. London: Routledge.

Gibbard, A. 1990. *Wise Choice, Apt Feelings: A Theory of Normative Judgment*. Cambridge, MA: Harvard University Press.

Giddens, A. 2001. *Sociology*. Fourth Edition. Cambridge: Polity Press.

Gigerenzer, G. 1991. "How to Make Cognitive Illusions Disappear: Beyond 'Heuristics and Biases.'" In *European Review of Social Psychology*, vol. 2, eds. W. Stroebe, and M. Heewstone. Chichester, ESuss, UK: Wiley.

Gigerenzer, G., and D.G. Goldstein. 1996. "Reasoning the Fast and Frugal Way: Models of Bounded Rationality." *Psychological Review* 103: 650-669.

Gilbert, N., and D. Gilbert. 1989. *The Enabling State*. Oxford: Oxford University Press.

Goffman, E. 1959. *The Presentation of Self in Everyday Life*. New York: Doubleday.

Goffman, E. 1961. *Encounters: Two Studies in the Sociology of Interaction*. Indianapolis, IN: Bobbs-Merrill.

Goffman, E. 1963. *Behavior in Public Places*. New York: Free Press.

Goffman, E. 1974. *Frame Analysis*. Cambridge, MA: Harvard University Press.

Goldman, A.I. 1986. *Epistemology and Cognition*. Cambridge, MA: Harvard University Press.

Goodsell, C.T. 1989. "Administration as Ritual." *Public Administration Review* 49 (2): 161-166.

Goodsell, C.T. 1983. *The Case for Bureaucracy: A Public Administration Polemic*. Washington, DC: CQ Press.

Gorovitz, S. [1977] 1978. "Bioethics and Social Responsibility." *The Monist*, 60 (1). Reprinted in *Contemporary Issues in Bioethics*, eds. T.L. Beauchamp, and L. Walters; Encino, CA: Dickenson.

Gossen, H.H. [1854] 1983. *The Laws of Human Relations and the Rules of Human Action Derived*, ed. and trans. G. Georgescu-Roegen. Cambridge, MA: MIT Press.

Gouinlock, J. 1972. *John Dewey's Philosophy of Value*. New York: Humanities Press.

Grave, S.A. 1960. *The Scottish Philosophy of Common Sense*. Oxford: Clarendon.

Gray, J. 2002. *Straw Dogs: Thoughts on Humans and Other Animals*. London: Granta.

Graziano, W.G., and N. Eisenberg. 1997. "Agreeableness: A Dimension of Personality." In *Handbook of Personality Psychology*, eds. J. Hogan, J. Johnson, and S. Briggs. San Diego, CA: Academic Press.

Green, T.H. [1895] 2006. *Lectures on the Principles of Political Obligation*. New York: Antiquarian Booksellers' Association of America.

Green, D.P., and I. Shapiro. 1994. *Pathologies of Rational Choice Theory: A Critique of Applications in Political Science*. New Haven, CT: Yale University Press.

Greenberg, J. 1993. "Stealing in the Name of Justice: Informational and Interpersonal Moderators of Theft Reactions to Underpayment Inequity." *Organizational Behavior and Human Decision Processes* 54 (1): 81-103.

Gribbin, J. 2005. *The Fellowship: The Story of a Revolution*. London: Allen Lane.

Gross, B.M. 1964. *The Managing of Organizations: The Administrative Struggle*, vol. II. London: The Free Press of Glencoe.

Gross, K. 2008. "Framing Persuasive Appeals: Episodic and Thematic Framing, Emotional Response, and Policy Opinion." *Political Psychology* 29 (2): 169-192.

Guignon, C.B. 2004. *On Being Authentic*. New York: Routledge.

Habermas, J. 1968. *Knowledge and Human Interest*. Boston, MA: Beacon Press.

Habermas, J. 1971. *Towards a Rational Society*. Boston, MA: Beacon Press.

Habermas, J. 1975. *Legitimation Crisis*. Boston, MA: Beacon Press.

Habermas, J. [1981] 1984. *The Theory of Communicative Action, 1: Reason and the Rationalization of Society*, trans. T. McCarthy. Boston, MA: Beacon Press.

Habermas, J. [1981] 1987. *The Theory of Communicative Action, 2: Lifeworld and Systems: A Critique of Functionalist Reason*, trans. T. McCarthy. Boston, MA: Beacon Press.

Habermas, J. 1986. "Hannah Arnedt's Communications Concept of Power." In *Power*, ed. S. Lukes. New York: New York University Press.

Habermas, J. 1996. *Between Facts and Norms: Contributions to a Discourse Theory of Law and Democracy*. Cambridge: Polity Press.

Hägerström, A. 1964. *Philosophy and Religion*, trans. R.T. Sandin. London: Allen and Unwin.

Hague, H. 1978. *The Organic Organization and How to Manage It*. London: Associated Business Press.

Hahn, F., and F. Petri. 2004. *General Equilibrium: Problems and Prospects*. London and New York: Routledge.

Haidt, J. 2003. "The Moral Emotions." In *Handbook of Affective Sciences*, ed. R.J. Davidson. New York: Oxford University Press.

Hales, C. 2001. *Managing Through Organization: The Management Process, Forms of Organisation and the Work of Managers*. London: Business Press.

Hallett, G.L. 1991. *Essentialism: A Wittgensteinian Critique*. New York: SUNY Press.

Hammond, M., J. Howarth, and R. Keat. 1991. *Understanding Phenomenology*. Oxford: Blackwell.

Hampshire, S. 2005. *Spinoza and Spinozism*. Oxford: Clarendon.

Hampton, J. 1986. *Hobbes and the Social Contract. Tradition*. Cambridge and New York: Cambridge University Press.

Handy, C. [1976] 1993. *Understanding Organisations*. Fourth Edition. Harmondsworth, Gt. Lon., UK: Penguin.

Harding, S. 1986. *The Science Question in Feminism*. New York: Cornell University.

Harding, S. 1991. *Whose Science? Whose Knowledge? Thinking from Women's Lives*. Ithica, NY: Cornell University Press.

Harding, S. 2005. "Rethinking Standpoint Epistemology: What is 'Strong Objectivity?'" In *Feminist Theory: A Philosophical Anthology*, ed. A.E. Cudd, and R.O. Andreasen. Oxford: Blackwell.

Harman, G. 1989. "Some Philosophical Issues in Cognitive Science." In *Foundations of Cognitive Science*, ed. M.I. Posner. Cambridge, MA: MIT Press.

Harré, R. 1980. "Social Being and Social Change." In *The Structure of Action*, ed. M. Brenner. Oxford: Blackwell.

Harré , R. 1983. *Personal Being*. Oxford: Basil Blackwell.

Harré, R. 1988. *The Singular Self: An Introduction to the Psychology of Self*. London: Sage.

Harré, R., and G. Gillett. 1994. *The Discursive Mind*. London: Sage.

Harris, M. 1979. *Cultural Materialism: The Struggle for a Science of Culture*. New York: Random House.

Harvey, D. 2005. *A Brief History of Neoliberalism*. Oxford: Oxford University Press.

Harvey, J.T. 2012. "Why Government Should Not Be Run Like A Business." *Forbes Leadership* (October 5). http://www.forbes.com/sites/johntharvey/2012/10/05/government-vs-business/#5918e4932685 (retrieved May 30, 2016).

Haselbach, A. 1994. "On Ways and Patterns of Thinking 'Identity.'" In *The Multiple Identity: What is it and How does it Work*, ed. S. Novak-Lukanovic. Ljubljana, SL: Slovenian National Commission for UNESCO and Institute for Ethnic Studies (European Project:

Overlapping Cultures and Plural Identities/Cultures Partielles et Identités Multiple).

Hawking, S., and L. Mlodinow. 2011. *The Grand Design*. London: Bantam.

Hayek, F.A. 1948. *Individualism and Economic Order*. Chicago, IL: University of Chicago Press.

Hayek, F.A. 1960. *The Constitution of Liberty*. London: Routledge & Kegan Paul.

Hayek, F.A. 1991. *Economic Freedom*. London: Basil Blackwell.

Haymes, S., M. Vidal de Haymes, and R. Miller. 2015. "Introduction." In *The Routledge Handbook of Poverty in the United States*, eds. Haymes, S., M. Vidal de Haymes, and R. Miller. London and New York: Routledge.

Heath, J. 2015. "Methodological Individualism." In *The Stanford Encyclopedia of Philosophy*. Spring Edition, ed. E.N. Zalta. http://plato.stanford.edu/archives/spr2015/entries/methodological-individualism/ (retrieved April 15, 2016).

Heckscher, C., and A. Donnellon, eds. 1994. *The Post-Bureaucratic Organization: New Perspectives on Organizational Change*. New York: Sage.

Hegel, G.W.F. [1806] 1998. "Independence and Dependence of Self-Consciousness Lordship and Bondage." In *Hegel Reader*, ed. S. Houlgate. Oxford: Blackwell.

Hegel, G.W.F. [1807] 1977. *Phenomenology of Spirit*, trans. A.V. Miller. Oxford: Oxford University Press.

Hegel, G.F.W. [1821] 1991. *Elements of the Philosophy of Right*, ed. A.W. Wood, tran. H.B. Nisbet. Cambridge: Cambridge University Press.

Heider, F. [1958] 1982. *The Psychology of Interpersonal Relations*. Hillsdale, NJ: Lawrence Erlbaum.

Held, D. 1980. *Introduction to Critical Theory*. Berkeley and Los Angeles, CA: University of California Press.

Held, D. 1987. *Models of Democracy*. Cambridge: Cambridge University Press.

Held, V. 1984. *Rights and Goods: Justifying Social Action*. New York and London: Free Press.

Heller, J. 1961. *Catch-22*. New York: Simon & Schuster.

Hempel, C.G. 1966. *Philosophy of Natural Science*. Englewood Cliffs, NJ: Prentice Hall.

Hempel, C.G. 1980. "The Logical Analysis of Psychology." In *Readings in the Philosophy of Psychology*, vol. 1, ed. N. Block. Cambridge, MA: Harvard University Press.

Hendriks, F., and S. Zouridis. 1999. "Cultural Biases and New Media for the Public Domain: Cui Bono." In *Cultural Theory as Political Science*, eds. M. Thompson, G. Grendstat, and P. Selle. London: Routledge.

Hermans, H.J.M. 2004. "The Dialogical Self: Between Exchange and Power." In *The Dialogical Self in Psychotherapy: An Introduction*, eds. H.J.M. Hermans, and G.F. Dimaggio. Hove, ESuss., UK/New York: Brunner-Routledge.

Hershey, P., and K.H. Blanchard. 1969. "Life Cycles Theory of Leadership." *Training and Development Journal* 23 (5): 26-34.

Hershey, P., and K.H. Blanchard. 1993. *Management of Organizational Behavior*. Sixth Edition. Englewood Cliffs, NJ: Prentice-Hall.

Herzberg, F. [1966] 1974. *Work and the Nature of Man*. London: Crosby, Lockwood, Staples.

Herzberg, F., B. Mausner, and B. Snyderman. 1959. *The Motivation to Work*. New York: Wiley.

Hicks, J. 1939. "The Foundations of Welfare Economics." *Economic Journal* 49: 696-712.

Higgins, K., and R. Solomon. 1993. *The Age of German Idealism*. London and New York: Routledge.

Hirshleifer, J. 1977. "Economics from a Biological Viewpoint." *Journal of l`awand Economics* 20; 1-52.

Hirst, P. 1994. *Associative Democracy: New Forms of Economic and Social Governance*. Cambridge: Polity.

Hitchcock, C. [1997] 2002. "Probabilistic Causation." In *The Stanford Encyclopedia of Philosophy*, ed. E.N. Zelta. http://plato.stanford.edu/entries/causation-probabilistic/ (retrieved July 7, 2007).

Ho, D.Y.F. 1998. "Social Relationships and Relationship Dominance: An

Analysis Based on Methodological Relationalism." *Asian Journal of Social Psychology* 1 (1): 1-16.

Ho, D.Y.F., S.F. Chan, and Z.X. Zhang. 2001. "Metarelational Analysis: An Answer to 'What's Asian about Asian Social Psychology.'" *Journal of Psychology in Chinese Societies* 2 (1): 7-26.

Ho, D.Y.F., and C.Y. Chiu. 1998. "Collective Representations as a Metaconstruct: An Analysis Based on Methodological Relationalism." *Culture and Psychology* 4 (3): 349-369.

Ho, D.Y.F., S.Q. Peng, A.C. Lai, and S.F. Chan. 2001. "Indigenization and Beyond: Methodological Relationalism in the Study of Personality across Cultural Traditions." *Journal of Personality* 69 (6): 925-953.

Hobbes, T. [1642] 1949. *De Cive, or On the Citizen*. New York: Appelton-Century-Crofts.

Hobbes, T. [1651] 1948. *Leviathan*, ed. M. Oakeshott. Oxford: Cambridge: Blackwell.

Hobbes, T. [1651] 1962. *Leviathan*, ed. J.P. Plamenatz. London: Collins.

Hobsbawm, E. 1997. *On History*. London: Weidenfeld & Nicolson.

Hoffer, E. [1951] 1989. *The True Believer: Thoughts on the Nature of Mass Movements*. Perennial Library Edition. New York: Harper & Row.

Hofstede, G. 1980. *Culture's Consequences*. Newbury Park, CA: Sage.

Hofstede, G. 1991. *Cultures and Organizations: Software of the Mind*. New York: McGraw-Hill.

Hogarth, R.M., and M.W. Reder, eds. 1987. *Rational Choice: The Contrast between Economics and Psychology*. Chicago, IL: University of Chicago Press.

Hogben. L. 1933. *Nature and Nurture*. New York: W. W. Norton.

Hollingsworth, J.R., and L. Lindberg. 1985. "The Role of Markets, Clans, Hierarchies, and Associative Behavior." In *Private Interest Government: Beyond Market and State*, eds. W. Streeck, and P. Schmitter. London and Beverly Hills, CA: Sage.

Hollis, M. 1977. *Models of Man: Philosophical Thoughts on Social Action*. Cambridge: Cambridge University Press.

Hollis, M. 1989. "Honour among Thieves." *Proceedings of the British Academy* l75: 165-187.

Hollis, M. 1994. *The Philosophy of Social Science*. Cambridge: Cambridge University Press.

Hollis, M., and S. Lukes, eds. 1982. *Rationality and Relativism*. Cambridge, MA: MIT Press.

Hollis, M., and E.J. Nell. 1975. *Rational Economic Man: A Philosophical Critique of Neoclassical Economics*. Cambridge: Cambridge University Press.

Hood, C. 1991. "A Public Management for All Seasons?" *Public Administration* 69 (1): 3-19.

Hood, C. 1998. *The Art of the State: Culture, Rhetoric, and Public Management*. Oxford: Clarendon.

Hood, C. 2000. "Paradoxes of Public-Sector Managerialism, Old Public Management and Public Service Bargains." *International Public Management Journal* 3 (1): 1-22.

Horney, K. 1937. *The Neurotic Personality of our Times*. New York: Norton.

Horney, K. 1945. *Our Inner Conflicts*. New York: Norton.

Horton, R.D. 1987. "Expenditures, Services and Public Management." *Public Administration Review* 47 (5): 378-384.

How, A. 2003. *Critical Theory*. Basingstoke Hamp., UK: Palgrave Macmillan.

Humbolt, W. von. [1791] 1969. *The Limits of State Action*, ed. and trans. J.W. Burrow. Cambridge: Cambridge University Press.

Hume, D. [1739-1740] 1978. *A Treatise of Human Nature*, orig. ed. L.A. Selby-Biggs, rev. ed. P.P. Nidditch. Oxford: Clarendon.

Hume, D. [1748] 1975. *An Enquiry Concerning Human Understanding*. Third Edition, orig. ed. L.A. Selby-Bigge, rev. ed. P.H. Nidditch. Oxford: Clarendon.

Hume, D. [1751] 1998. *An Enquiry Concerning the Principles of Morals*, ed. T.L. Beauchamp. Oxford: Oxford University Press

Hume, D. [1748/1751/1777] 1902. *An Enquiry Concerning Human*

Understanding [1748] *and Concerning the Principles of Morals* [1751]. Second Edition, ed. L.A. Selby-Biggs. Oxford: Clarendon.

Hurka, T. 1993. *Perfectionism*. New York: Oxford University Press.

Husak, D. 1992. "Why Punish the Deserving?" *Nous* 26: 447-464.

Husserl, E. [1907] 1966. *The Idea of Phenomenology*, trans. W.P. Alston, and G. Nakhnikian. The Hague, NL: Martinus Nijhoff.

Husserl, E. [1928] 1931. *Ideas*. Third Edition, trans. W.R.B. Gibson, London: Allen and Unwin.

Husserl, E. [1928] 1964. *On the Phenomenology of the Consciousness of Internal Time*, trans. J.S. Churchill, ed. M. Heidegger. Bloomington: Indiana University Press.

Husserl, E. [1929] 1981. *Husserl: Shorter Work*, eds. P. McCormick, and F.A. Elliston. Notre Dame, IN: University of Notre Dame Press.

Husserl, E. [1931] 1960. *Cartesian Meditations: An Introduction to Phenomenology*, trans. D. Cairns. The Hague, NL: Martinus Nijhoff.

Huxham, C., and S. Vangen. 2005. *Managing to Collaborate: The Theory and Practice of Collaborative Advantage*. London: Routledge.

Ingrao, B., and G. Israel. 1990. *The Invisible Hand: Economic Equilibrium in the History of Science*. Cambridge, MA: The MIT Press.

International Monetary Fund. 2000. "Globalization: Threats or Opportunity." Issue Brief 00/01, 12 April, corrected January 2002. Washington, DC: International Monetary Fund. http://www.imf.org/external/np/exr/ib/2000/041200to.htm (retrieved July 15, 2006).

Iversen, R.R., and A.L. Armstrong. 2006. *Toward a New Economic Mobility for Low-Income Families*. Philadelphia, PA: Temple University Press.

Jackson, M. 1987. "On Ethnographic Truth." *Canberra Anthropology* 10 (2): 1-31.

Jager, R. 1972. *The Development of Bertrand Russell's Philosophy*. London: Alan & Unwin.

James, W. [1897] 1979. *The Will to Believe and Other Essays in Popular Philosophy*. Cambridge, MA and London: Harvard University Press.

James, W. [1907] 1995. *Pragmatism [a New Name for Some Old Ways of*

Thinking]. Toronto, ONT, CA: General Publishing.

James, W. [1909] 1979. *The Meaning of Truth*. Cambridge, MA and London: Harvard University Press.

James, W. 1912. *Essays in Radical Empiricism*, ed. R.B. Perry. New York: Longman Green. http://spartan.ac.-brocku.ca/~lward/ James/ James_1912/ James_191-2_toc.html (retrieved January 3, 2007).

Janicaud, D. 2005. *The Human Condition*, trans. E. Brennan, intro. S. Critchley. London: Routledge.

Jaques, E. 1976. *A General Theory of Bureaucracy*. London: Heinemann.

Jensen, M.C., and W.H. Meckling. 1976. "Theory of the Firm: Managerial Behavior, Agency Costs and Ownership Structure." *Journal of Financial Economics* 3 (4): 305-360.

Jessop, B. 1997. "Capitalism and its Future: Remarks on Regulation, Government and Governance." *Review of International Political Economy* 4: 561-581.

Jevons, W.S. 1871/1888. *The Theory of Political Economy*. Second Edition. London: Machmillan. http://www.econlib.org/library/YPDBooks/ Jevons/jvnPE.html (accessed September 4, 2013).

Johnston, J., and A. Kouzmin. 1998. "From the Ideological Attack on Public Officials To the 'Pork Barrel' *Par Excellence*—Privatization and Out-Sourcing as Oligarchic Corruption." *Administrative Theory and Praxis* 20 (4): 478-507.

Jones, E.E., D.E. Kanouse, H.H. Kelley, R.E. Nisbet, S. Valins, and B. Weiner, eds. 1972. *Attribution: Perceiving the Causes of Behavior*. Morristown, NJ: General Leaning Press.

Jung, C.G. [1934] 1981. *The Archetypes and the Collective Unconscious*. Second Edition, trans. R.F.C. Hull. Princeton, NJ: Bollingen.

Kahneman, D., P. Slovic, and A. Tversky, eds. 1982. *Judgment under Uncertainty: Heuristics and Biases*. Cambridge: Cambridge University Press.

Kahneman, D., and A. Tversky. 1979. "Prospect Theory: An Analysis of Decision Theory Under Risk." *Econometrica* 47: 263-291.

Kajer, A.M. 2004. *Governance*. Cambridge: Polity Press.

Kaldor, N. 1939. "Speculation and Economic Stability." *Review of Economic Studies* 7 (1): 1-27.

Kaldor, N. 1985. *Economics Without Equilibrium*. Armonk, N.Y: M.E. Sharpe.

Kane, R. 1985. *Free Will and Values*. Albany, New York: State University of New York Press.

Kane, R. 1996. *The Significance of Free Will*. New York: Oxford University Press.

Kane, R. [2001] 2002. "Free Will: New Directions for an Ancient Problem." In *Free Will*, ed. R. Kane. Malden, MA: Blackwell.

Kane, R. 2005. *A Contemporary Introduction to Free Will*. Oxford and New York: Oxford University Press.

Kant, I. [1781–1787] 1956. *Critique of Pure Reason*, trans. L.W. Beck. Indianapolis, IN: Bobbs-Merrill.

Kant, I. [1788] 1906. *Critique of Practical Reason*, trans. T.K. Abbott. London: Longmans.

Kanter, R.M. 1984. *The Change Masters: Corporate Entrepreneurs at Work*. London: Allen & Unwin.

Kanter, R.M. 1989. *When Giants Learn to Dance: Master the Challenge of Strategy, Management, and Careers in the 1990s*. London: Simon & Schuster.

Kapitan, T. 1992. "Peirce and the Autonomy of Abductive Reasoning." *Erkenntnis (Historical Archive)* 37 (1): 1-26.

Katz, M.B. 2013. *The Undeserving Poor: America's Enduring Confrontation with Poverty*. Second Edition. New York: Oxford University Press.

Kaufman, H. 1976. *Are Governmental Organizations Immortal?* Washington, DC: Brooking Institution.

Kavka, G.S. 1982. "An Internal Critique of Nozick's Entitlement Theory." *Pacific Philosophical Quarterly* 63 (4):371-380.

Kekes, J. 1997. *Against Liberalism*. Ithaca, NY: Cornell University Press.

Kelley, H.H. 1967. "Attribution Theory in Social Psychology." In *Nebraska Symposium on Motivation*, ed. D. Levine. Lincoln, NE: University of Nebraska Press.

Kelley, H.H. 1972. "Causal Schema and the Attribution Process." In *Attribution: Perceiving the Causes of Behavior*, eds. E.E. Jones, D.E. Kanouse, H.H. Kelley, R.E. Nisbet, S. Valins, and B. Weiner. Morristown, NJ: General Learning Press.

Kelley, H.H. 1973. "The Processes of Causal Attribution." *American Psychologist* 28: 107-128.

Kelly, G.A. 1955. *The Psychology of Personal Constructs*. New York: Norton.

Kenis, P., and V. Schneider. 1991. "Policy Networks and Policy Analysis: Scrutinizing a New Analytical Toolbox." In *Policy Networks: Empirical Evidence and Theoretical Considerations*, eds. B. Marin, and R. Mayntz. Boulder, CO: Westview.

Kennedy, G. 2005. *Adam Smith's Lost Legacy*. Basingstoke Hamp., UK: Palgrave Macmillan.

Kernaghan, K. 2000. "The Post-Bureaucratic Organization and Public Service Values." *International Review of Administrative Sciences* 66 (1): 91-104.

Kettl, D.F. 1988. *Government by Proxy: (Mis?)Managing Federal Programs*. Washington, DC: CQ Press.

Kettl, D.F. 1993. *Sharing Power: Public Governance and Private Markets*. Washington, DC: Brooking Institution.

Kettl, D.F. 2000. *The Global Public Management Revolution: A Report on the Transformation of Governance*. Washington, DC: Brookings Institution.

Keynes, J.M. 1923. *A Tract on Monetary Reform*. London: Macmillan.

Keynes, J.M. [1936] 2007. *The General Theory of Employment, Interest and Money*. London: Macmillan.

Keynes, J.M. 1972. *The Collected Writings of John Maynard Keynes, Volume IX, Essays in Persuasion*. London: Macmillan.

Kickert, W.J. 1993. "Autopoiesis and the Science of (Public) Administration." *Organizational Studies* 14 (3): 261-278.

Kickert, W.J., J. Klijn, and J. Koppenjan. 1997. *Managing Complex Networks: Strategies for the Public Sector*. London: Sage.

Kim, J. 1993. *Supervenience and Mind.* Cambridge: Cambridge University Press.

Kim, J. 1998. *Mind in a Physical World.* Cambridge, MA: MIT Press.

Kinsbourne, M. 2008. "Integrated Cortical Field Model of Consciousness." In *Experimental and Theoretical Studies of Consciousness*, CIBA Foundation Symposium No. 174. Chichester, W. Sussex, UK: Wiley.

Kirchgässner, G. 2008. *Homo Oeconomicus: The Economic Model of Behaviour and Its Applications in Economics and Other Social Sciences.* New York: Springer Science.

Kirkham, R.L. 1992. *Theories of Truth: A Critical Introduction.* Cambridge, MA: MIT Press.

Klein, M. 1990. *Determinism, Blameworthiness and Deprivation.* Oxford: Oxford University Press.

Klein, N. 2007. *The Shock Doctrine: The Rise of Disaster Capitalism.* London: Allen Lane.

Kleinig, J. 1971. "The Concept of Desert." *American Philosophical Quarterly* 8 (1): 71-78.

Klijn, E.H., and J.F.M. Koppenjan. 2000. "Public Management and Policy Networks: Foundations of a Network Approach to Governance." *Public Management* 2 (2): 135-158.

Klijn, E.H., J.F.M. Koppenjan, and C.J.M. Terrier. 1995. "Managing Networks in the Public Sector." *Public Administration* 73 (3): 437-454.

Knight, C., and C. Stemplowska, eds. 2011. *Responsibility and Distributive Justice.* Oxford: Oxford University Press.

Knorr-Cetina, K.D. 1981. *The Manufacture of Knowledge: An Essay on the Constructivist and Contextual Nature of Science.* Oxford: Pergamon.

Kohut, H. 1971. *The Analysis of Self.* New York: International University Press.

Kohut, H., and E.S. Wolf. 1978. "The Disorders of Self and their Treatment." *International Journal of Psychoanalysis* 59: 413-426.

Komorita, S. S., and Parks, C. D. 1995. "Interpersonal Relations: Mixed-Motive Interaction." *Annual Review of Psychology* 46: 183–207.

Kooiman, J., ed. 1993. *Modern Governance: New Government–Society Interactions*. Newbury Park, CA: Sage.

Kooiman, J. 1997. "Social-Political Governance." Paper presented at the *Ross Priority Conference on the Theories of Governance*, University of Strathclyde, Glasgow, UK, October.

Kooiman, J. 1999. "Social–Political Governance: Overview, Reflection and Design." *Public Management* 1 (1): 67-92.

Kooiman, J. 2000. "Societal Governance: Levels, Modes and Orders of Social–Political Interaction." In *Debating Governance: Authority, Steering and Democracy*, ed. J. Pierre. Oxford: Oxford University Press.

Kooiman, J. 2001. *Interactive Governance*. London: Routledge.

Kooiman, J. 2003. *Governing as Governance*. London, Thousand Oaks, New Delhi: Sage.

Kooiman, J., and Associates 1997. *Social-Political Governance and Management*. (Report Series 33, 34 and 35). Rotterdam, NL: Erasmas University, Rotterdam School of Management.

Kooiman, J., and M. Van Vliet. 1995. "Riding Tandem: The Case of Co-governance." *Demos* 7: 44-45.

Kooiman, J., and M. van Vliet. 2001. "Self-governance as a Mode of Societal Governance." *Public Management* 2 (3): 360-377.

Kotz, D.K. 2015. *The Rise and Fall of Neoliberal Capitalism*. Cambridge, MA: Harvard University Press.

Kouzmin, A. 2002. "The New Political Economy of the "Smart State": Transitions in Governance Capacities: An Editorial." *Administrative Theory and Praxis* 24 (1): 25-30.

Kouzmin, A., and J. Dixon. 2003. "Public Domains, Organizations and Neo-Liberal Economics: From De-Regulation and Privatization to the Necessary 'Smart' State." In *Öffentlicher dienst als motor der staats- und verwaltungsmodernisierung [New Public Services]*, eds. R. Koch, and P. Conrad. Weisbaden, DE: Gabler-Verlag.

Kouzmin, A., and J. Dixon. 2005. "Neo-liberal Economics, Public Domains and Organizations: Is there any Organizational Design after Privatization?" In *Handbook of Organizational Theory and Management*. Second Edition, eds. T.D. Lynch, and T.J. Dicker. New York: Marcel Dekker.

Kouzmin, A., and J. Dixon. 2010. "Market Fundamentalism: From De-Regulation and privatizationation to Financial Fraud in the Criminogenic, Neo-Liberal State." In *Öffentlicher Dienst als Motor der Staats- und Verwaltungsmodernisierung [New Public Services]*. Second Edition, eds. R. Koch, P. Conrad, and W.H. Lorig. Weisbaden, DE: Gabler-Verlag.

Kouzmin, A., J. Dixon, and N. Korac-Kakabadse. 2001. "From Self-Referential Economics to Managerialism and the 'Economic Holocaust' of Downsizing/Re-Engineering: An Ethical Audit." *Titsmeikan Law Review* (Tokyo) 4 (cummulative. no. 278): 293-356 (in Japanese). Reprinted in Thorne, K., and G. Turner, eds. 2001. *Global Business Regulation: Some Research Perspectives*. Sydney: Prentice-Hall.

Kouzmin, A., R. Leivesley, and N. Korac-Kakabadse. 1997. "From Managerialism and Economic Rationalism: Toward 'Re-inventing' Economic Ideology and Administrative Diversity." *Administrative Theory & Praxis* 19 (1): 19-42.

Kraut, R. 2007. *What is Good and Why: The Ethics of Well-Being*. Cambridge, MA: Harvard University Press.

Kripke, S.A. 1979. "A Puzzle About Belief." In *Meaning and Use*, ed. A. Margalit. Dordrecht, NL: Reidel.

Krueger, A. 1974. "The Political Economy of the Rent-Seeking Society." *American Economic Review* 64 (3): 291-303

Lacan, J. 1968. *Speech and Language in Psychoanalysis*, trans. A. Wilden. Baltimore, MD: John Hopkins University Press.

Laing, R.D. 1960. *The Divided Self: An Existential Study in Sanity and Madness*. Harmondsworth, Gt. Lon., UK: Penguin.

Lakoff, G., and M. Johnston. 1999. *Philosophy in the Flesh*. New York: Basic Books.

Lamont, J. 1994. "The Concept of Desert in Distributive Justice." *The Philosophical Quarterly* 44: 45-64.

Lamont, J., and C. Favor. 2016. "Distributive Justice." In *The Stanford Encyclopedia of Philosophy*. Summer Edition, ed. E.N. Zalta. http://plato.stanford.edu/archives/sum2016/entries/justice-distributive/ (retrieved August 26, 2016).

Lane, J.-E. 2000. The New Public Management. London and New York: Routledge.

Lasch, C. [1979] 1991. The Culture of Narcissism: American Life in an Age of Diminishing Expectations. Second Edition. New York: Norton.

Lasswell, H.D. 1930. Psychopathology and Politics. Chicago, IL: University of Chicago Press.

Laumann, E.O., and D. Knoke. 1987. The Organizational State. Madison, WI: University of Wisconsin Press.

Lawson, T. 2012. "Mathematical Modeling and Ideology in the Economics Academy: Competing Explanations of the Failings in the Modern Discipline." Economic Thought: History, Philosophy and Methodology 1 (1): 3-22.

Leibniz, G.W. [1704/1764] 1996. New Essays on Human Understanding. Second Edition, trans. P. Remnant, and J. Bennet. New York: Cambridge University Press.

Leibniz, G.W. [1714] 1973. "The Monadology." In Leibniz: Philosophical Methods, ed. H.M. Lefcourt. Orlando, FL: Academic Press.

Levenson, H. 1981. "Differentiating among Internality, Powerful Others, and Chance." In Research with the Locus of Control Construct, 1: Assessment Methods, ed., H.M. Lefcourt. Orlando, FL: Academic Press.

Lévi-Strauss, C. [1958/1963] 1974. Structural Anthropology, vol. 1, trans. C. Jacobson, and B. Schoepf. London: Allen Lane/Penguin.

Lewis, C. I., 1946. An Analysis of Knowledge and Valuation (The Paul Carus Lectures, Series 8, 1946). La Salle, IL: Open Court.

Lewis, C.S. 1944. The Inner Ring, the Memorial Lecture at King's College, University of London. http://homepages.which.net/~radical.faith/misc/lewis.htm (retrieved January 3, 2002).

Ley, W.A.R., and C. Perry. 1959. Philosophy and the Public Interest. Chicago, IL: Committee to Advance Original Work in Philosophy.

Libet, B. 1985. "Unconscious Cerebral Initiative and the Role of Conscious Will in Voluntary Action." Behavioral and Brain Science 8: 529-566.

Libet, B., A. Freeman, and J.K.B. Sutherland, eds. 1999. The Volitional Brain: Towards a Neuroscience of Freewill. Charlottesville, VA: Imprint Academic.

Libet, B., C.A. Gleason, E.W. Wright, and D.K. Pearl. 1983. "Time of Conscious Intention to Act in Relation to Onset of Cerebral Activity (Readiness-Potential)." *Brain* 106: 623-642.

Liebowitz, S.E., and S.J. Margolis. 2000. "Path Dependence, Lock-In, and History." In *Encyclopedia of Law and Economics, vol I. The History and Methodology of Law and Economics*, eds. B. Bouckaert, and G. De Geest. Cheltenham, Glos., UK: Edward Elgar.

Lienhard, J.H. 1999. "Poets in the Industrial Revolution." *The Engines of Our Ingenuity* No. 1413. http://www.uh.edu/engines/epi1413.htm (retrieved May 12, 2016).

Likert, R. 1961. *New Patterns of Management*. London: McGraw-Hill.

Likert, R. 1967. *The Human Organization: Its Management and Value*. New York: McGraw-Hill.

Lin, N. 2001. *Social Capital: A Theory of Social Structure and Action*. Cambridge: Cambridge University Press.

Lipsey, RG., and K.A. Chrystal. [1953] 1995. *An Introduction to Positive Economics*. Eighth Edition. Oxford: Oxford University Press.

Lipsey, R.G., and K. Lancaster. 1956. "The General Theory of Second Best." *Review of Economic Studies* 24 (1): 11-32.

Lipton, P. [1991] 2004. *Inference to the Best Explanation*. Second Edition. London: Routledge.

Loar, B. 1988. "Social Content and Psychological Content." In *Contents of Thought*, eds, R. Grimm, and D. Merrill. Tucson, AR: University of Arizona Press.

Locke, J. [1688] 1960. "The First Treatise of Government." In *Two Treatises of Government*, ed. P. Laslett. Cambridge: Cambridge University Press.

Locke, J. [1689] 1960. "The Second Treatise of Government: An Essay Concerning the *True Original, Extent, and End* of Civil Government." In *Two Treatises of Government*, ed. P. Laslett. Cambridge: Cambridge University Press.

Locke, J. [1689-1690] 1824. *An Essay Concerning Human Understanding*. London: William Baynes and Son. https://books.google.com.tr/s?id=tWM9AAAAYAAJ&pg=PA202&lpg=PA202&dq=The+Mind+has+a+different+relish&source=bl&ots=pXHtuV

_N&sig=cdApQ05VPTJ7SPYyL1F2BopLIgU&hl=en&sa=X&ved=-6fiahsjOAhVC1RoKHVPBCWoQ6AEIIjAC#v=onepage&q=The%20Mind%20has%20a%20different%20relish&f=false (retrieved August 15, 2016).

Locke, J. [1689–1690] 2004. *An Essay Concerning Human Understanding.* http://www.arts.cuhk.edu.hk/Philosophy/8/echu/ (retrieved March 18, 2006).

Loux, M.J. 2002. *Metaphysics: A Contemporary Introduction.* Second Edition. London: Routledge.

Lucas, J.R. 1970. *The Freedom of Will.* Oxford: Oxford University Press.

Lucas, J.R. 1993. *Responsibility.* Oxford: Oxford University Press.

Lucey, K. 1996. *On Knowing and the Known.* Buffalo, NY: Prometheus.

Luhmann, N. 1979. *Trust and Power.* New York: Wiley.

Luhmann, N. 1988. "Familiarity, Confidence and Trust: Problems and Alternatives." In *Trust: Making and Breaking,* ed. D. Gambetta. Oxford: Oxford University Press.

Lukes, S. 1968. "Methodological Individualism Reconsidered." *British Journal of Sociology* 19 (2): 119-129.

Lycan, W., ed. 1990. *Mind and Cognition.* Oxford: Blackwell.

Lyotard, J.–F. 1979. *The Postmodern Condition: A Report on Knowledge,* trans. G. Bennington, and B. Massumi. Minneapolis, MN: University of Minnesota Press.

Macadam, R.D., and R.J. Bawden. 1986. "Challenge and Response: Developing a System for Educating More Effective Agriculturalists." *Prometheus* 18 (3): 125-137.

Machan, T.R. 2006. *Libertarianism Defenced.* New York: Ashgate.

MacIntyre, A. 1981. *After Virtue.* London: Duckworth.

Mack, E., and G. Gaus. 2004. "Classical Liberalism and Libertarianism: The Liberty Tradition." In *Handbook of Political Theory,* eds G. Gaus and C. Kukathas. London: Sage.

MacPherson, M.S. 1984. "On Shelling, Hirschman and Sen: Revisiting the Conception of the Self." *Partisan Review* 51 (2): 236-247.

MacPherson, S., and R. Silburn. 1998. "The Meaning and Measurement of Poverty." In *Poverty: A Persistent Global Reality*, eds. J. Dixon, and D. Macarov. London: Routledge.

Maiese, M. [2003] 2013. "Principles of Justice and Fairness", updated by H. Burgess. Posted (June) on *Beyond Intractability*, eds. G. Burgess, and H. Burgess. Boulder: Conflict Information Consortium, University of Colorado. http://www.beyondintractability.org/essay/principles-of-justice (retrieved March 17, 2016).

Mann, H. 1996. *The Origins of Humanism*. Cambridge: Cambridge University Press.

Marcel, G. 1952. *Men against Humanity*, trans. G.S. Fraser. London: Harvill.

Marcellino, P.A. 2006. "Scalar Principle." In *Encyclopedia of Educational Leadership and Administration*, ed. F.W. English. Thousand Oaks, CA: SAGE Knowledge. http://sk.sagepub.com/reference/edleadership/n504.xml (retrieved August 26, 2016).

March, J.G. 1988. *Decisions and Organizations*. Oxford: Blackwell.

March, J.G. 1994. *A Primer on Decision-Making*. New York: Free.

March, J.G., and J.R. Olsen. 1976. *Ambiguity and Change in Organizations*. Bergen, NO: Universitetsforlaget.

March, J.G., and J.R. Olsen. 1983. "Organizing Political Life: What Administrative Re-Organization Tells us about Government." *American Political Science Review* 77 (2): 281-296.

March, J.G., and J.R. Olsen. 1989. *Rediscovering Institutions: The Organizational Bias of Politics*. New York: Free Press.

Margolis, H. 1982. *Selfishness, Altruism and Rationality*. Cambridge: Cambridge University Press.

Marini, F. 1993. "Leaders in the Field: Dwight Waldo." *Public Administration Review* 53 (5): 409-418.

Markey, J. 1925–26. "A Redefinition of Social Phenomena: Giving a Basis for Comparative Sociology." *American Journal of Sociology* 31: 733-743. http://www.brocku.ca/MeadProject/Markey/Markey_1926.html (retrieved April 22, 2008).

Markova, I. 1983. "The Origin of the Social Psychology of Language in German Expressivism." *British Journal of Social Psychology* 22: 315-325.

Marshall, A. [1890] 1920. *Principles of Economics*. London: Macmillan. http://www.econlib.org/library/Marshall/marP.html (retrieved May 12, 2014).

Martin, R., and J. Barresi, eds. 2003. *Personal Identity*. Oxford: Blackwell.

Marx, K. [1845/1969] 2002. *Theses on Feuerbach*, trans. C. Smith, and D. Cuckson. http://www.marxists.org/archive/marx/works/1845/theses/index.htm (retrieved May 23, 2004).

Marx, K. 1852. *The Eighteenth Brumaire of Louis Bonaparte*. http://www.marxists.org/archive/marx/works/1852/18th-brumaire/ (retrieved May 24, 2016).

Marx [1859] 1977. *Contribution to the Critique of Political Economy*. Moscow: Progress Publishers. https://www.marxists.org/archive/marx/works/1859/critique-pol-economy/preface.htm (retrieved July 31, 2006).

Marx, K. [1867] 1993. *Capital: A Critique of Political Economy*. Harmondworth, Gt. Lon., UK: Penguin.

Marx, K., and F. Engels. [1848/1988] 2014. *Manifesto of the Communist Party*. http://ebooks.adelaide.edu.au/m/marx/karl/m39c/ (retrieved August 26, 2015).

Maslow, A.H. [1962] 1968. *Towards a Psychology of Being*. New York: Nostrand.

Maslow, A.H. 1970. *Motivation and Personality*. Second Edition. New York: Harper Row.

Maslow, A.H. 1971. *The Further Reaches of Human Nature*. New York: The Viking Press.

Mayer, R.C., J.H. Davis, and F.D. Schoorman. 1995. "An Integrative Model of Organizational Trust." *Academy of Management Review* 20 (3): 709-734.

Mayntz, R. 1993. "Governing Failure and the Problem of Governability: Some Comments on a Theoretical Paradigm." In *Modern Governance: New Government-Society Interactions*, ed. J. Kooiman. London: Sage.

McCallum. B.T. 2007. "Monetarism." In *The Encyclopedia of Economics.* Second Edition, ed. D.R. Henderson. Indianapolis, IN: Liberty Fund, Economics and Liberty. http://www.econlib.org/library/Enc/ Monetarism.html (retrieved June 23, 2016).

McCann, C.R. Jr. 2004. *Individualism and the Social Order.* New York: Routledge.

McClelland, D.C. 1961. *The Achieving Society.* Princeton, NJ: Van Nostrand.

McClelland, D.C., J.W. Atkinson, A. Clark, Russell, and E.L. Lowell. [1953] 1976. *The Achievement Motive.* Second Edition. Oxford: Irvington.

McCloskey, D.N. 1998. *The Rhetoric of Economics.* Second Edition. Madison, WI: University of Wisconsin Press.

McGregor, D. 1960. *The Human Side of Enterprise.* New York: McGraw-Hill.

McGregor, D. 1967. *Leadership and Motivation.* Cambridge, MA: MIT Press.

McGuire, W., and C. McGuire. 1982. "Significant Others in Self-space." In *Psychological Perspectives on the Self*, vol. 1, ed. J. Suls. Hillsdale, NJ: Erlbaum.

McLeod, O. 2013. "Desert." *The Stanford Encyclopedia of Philosophy.* Winter Edition, ed. E.N. Zalta. http://plato.stanford.edu/ archives/win2013/entries/desert/ (retrieved November 6, 2015).

Mead, G.H. 1925. "The Genesis of the Self and Social Control." *International Journal of Ethics* 35 (3): 251-277.

Mead, G.H. 1934. *Mind, Self, and Society.* Chicago, IL: University of Chicago Press.

Mead, G. H. 1938. *The Philosophy of the Act*, eds. A.M. Dunham, and C.W. Morris. Chicago, IL: University of Chicago Press.

Mead, M. [1935] 1963. *Sex and Temperament in Three Primitive Societies.* New York: Morrow Quill.

Meilaender, G.C. 1984. *The Theory and Practice of Virtue.* Notre Dame, IN: University of Notre Dame Press.

Mele, A.R. 2003. *Motivation and Agency.* New York: Oxford University Press.

Menger, C. [1871] 1994. *Principles of Economics [Grundsätze der*

Volkswirtschaftslehre], ed. L.M. Spadaro, trans. J. Digwell, and B.F. Hoselitz, intro. F.A. Hayek. http://www.mises.org/etexts/menger/principles.asp (accessed May 26, 2014).

Messner, D. 1997. *The Network Society: Economic Development and International Competitiveness as Problems of Social Governance*. London: Frank Cass.

Meyers, D.T. 1989. *Self, Society, and Personal Choice*. New York: Columbia University Press.

Midgley, M. 2003. *The Myths We Live By*. London: Routledge.

Miles, R.E., and C.C. Snow. 1978. *Organizational Strategy, Structure and Process*. New York: McGraw-Hill.

Milgram, S. 1963. "Behavioral Study of Obedience." *Journal of Abnormal and Social Psychology* 67: 371-378.

Milgram, S. 1974. *Obedience to Authority: An Experimental View*. New York: HarperCollins.

Mill, J.S. [1843] 1988. *A System of Logic*, ed. A.J. Ayer. London: Duckworth.

Mill, J.S. [1859] 1963. "On Liberty." In *The Collected Works of John Stuart Mill*, ed. J.M. Robson. Toronto, Ont., CA: University of Toronto Press.

Mill, J.S. [1863] 1968. *Utilitarianism, Liberty and Representative Government*. London: Everyman.

Miller, D. 1976. *Social Justice*. Oxford: Clarendon Press.

Miller, D. 1984. *Anarchism*. London and Melbourne, AU: J.M.Dent.

Miller, D. 1989. *Market, State, and Community*. Oxford: Clarendon Press.

Miller, D. 2000. *Principles of Social Justice*. Cambridge, MA: Harvard University Press.

Mills, J., and M.S. Clark. 1982. "Communal and Exchange Relationships." *Review of Personality and Social Psychology*, vol. 4, ed. L. Wheeler. Beverley Hills, CA: Sage.

Milne, H. 1986. "Desert, Effort and Equality." *Journal of Applied Philosophy* 3: 235-243.

Milton, J. [1644] 1949. "Aeropagitica: A Speech for the Liberty of Unlicensed Printing, to the Parliament of England." In *The Portable*

Milton, ed. D. Bush. New York: Viking Press.

Milward, H.B., K.G. Provan, and B.A. Else. 1993. "What Does the Hollow State Look Like?" In *Public Management: The State of the Art*, ed. B. Bozeman. San Francisco: Jossey-Bass.

Mintzberg, H. 1978. *The Structuring of Organizations*. Englewood Cliffs, NJ: Prentice Hall.

Mintzberg, H. 1989. *Mintzberg on Management*. New York: Free Press.

Mirowski, P, and D. Plehwe, eds. 2009. *The Road from Mont Pelerin: The Making of the Neoliberal Thought Collective*. Cambridge, MA: Harvard University Press.

Mises, L. von. 1944. *Bureaucracy*. New Haven, CT: Yale University Press.

Mises, L. von. [1949] 1996. *Human Action: Treatise on Economics*. Fourth Edition, trans. B.B. Greaves. Auburn, AL: Ludwig von Mises Institute. http://www.mises.org/humanaction/pdf/HumanActionScholars.pdf (retrieved September 19, 2001).

Moe, T.M. 1984. "The New Economics of Organization." *American Journal of Political Science* 28: 739-777.

Moe, T.M. 1991. "Politics and the Theory of Organization." *Jouranl of Law, Economics, and Organization* 7 (special issue): 106-129.

Moe, T.M. 1995. "The Politics of Structural Choice: Towards a Theory of Public Bureaucracy." In *Organizational Theory: From Chester Barnard to the Present and Beyond*. Expanded Edition, ed. O.E. Williamson. New York: Oxford University Press. https://www.researchgate.net/ profile/Terry_Moe/publication/247948583_The_Politics_of_ Structural_Choice_Toward_a_Theory_of_Public_Bureaucracy/links/ 55f1a59f08aedecb69017811.pdf (retrieved February 12, 2013).

Mohammadian, M. 2011. "Economics of the Thirds Way: Bioeconomics Ten Years On." *Journal of Interdisciplinary Economics* 23 (1): 289-334.

Mollon, P. 2000. *The Unconscious*. Cambridge: Icon.

Monbiot, G. 2016. "The Zombie Doctrine." The Guardian (UK) (April 15, 2016). http://www.monbiot.com/2016/04/15/the-zombie-doctrine/ (retrieved May 24, 2016).

Moore, G.E. 1903. *Principa Ethica*. Cambridge: Cambridge University Press.

Moore, G.E. 1959. *Philosophical Papers*. London: George Allen and Unwin.

Moran, D. 2000. *Introduction to Phenomenology*. London and New York: Routledge.

Morgan, G. 1986. *Images of Organizations*. Newbury Park, CA: Sage.

Morrow, P. 1983. "Concept Redundancy in Organizational Research: The Case of Work Commitment." *Academy of Management Review* 8: 486-500.

Moser, K.P. 1989. *Knowledge and Evidence*. Cambridge: Cambridge University Press.

Muirhead, J.H. 1932. *Rule and End in Morals*. Oxford: Oxford University Press.

Murray, A.J.H. 1997. *Reconstructing Realism: Between Power Politics and Cosmopolitan Ethics*. Edinburgh: Edinburgh University Press. http://books.google.com/books?id=UW0b6ABr9QEC&dq=bounded+realm+of+activi-ty (retrieved March 6, 2010).

Myrdal, G. 1963. *Challenge to Affluence*. New York: Random House.

Nadeau, R. 2013. "Neoclassical Economic Theory." In *The Encylopedia of Earth*. http://www.eoearth.org/vie w/article/154813 (retrieved May 5, 2014).

Nagel, T. 1979. "Subjective and Objective." In *Moral Questions*, ed. T. Nagel. Cambridge: Cambridge University Press.

Nagel, T. 1986. *The View from Nowhere*. New York: Oxford University Press.

Natanson, M., ed. 1963. *Philosophy of the Social Sciences*. New York: Random House.

Neilson, K. 2002. "The Compatibility of Freedom and Determinism." In *Free Will*, ed. R. Kane. Malden, MA: Blackwell.

Newsome, D. 1997. *The Victorian World Picture: Perceptions and Introspections in an Age of Change*. New Brunswick, NJ: Rutgers University Press.

Ney, S., and N. Molnaers. 1999. "Culture Theory as a Theory of Democracy." *Innovation* 12 (4): 489-509.

Nichols, J.R. 1986. "Congruent Leadership." *Leadership and Organizational Development Journal* 7 (1): 27-31.

Nietzsche, F. [1878] 1994. *Human, All Too Human,* trans. M. Faber. Harmondworth, Gt. Lon., UK: Penguin.

Nietzsche, F. [1883–1888/1895] 1967. *The Will to Power: Attempt at a Revaluation of all Values,* trans. W. Kaufmann. New York: Random House.

Nietzsche, F. [1886] 1998. *Beyond Good and Evil,* trans. M. Faber, intro. R.C. Holub. New York: Vintage.

Nietzche, F. 1887. *Genealogy of Morals,* trans. H.B. Samuel. New York: Boni and Liverright. https://archive.org/details/genealogyofmoral00nietuoft (retrieved October 16, 2004).

Nietzsche, F. [1888] 1969. *Twilight of the Idols and the Anti-Christ,* trans. R.J. Hollingdale. Harmondworth, Gt. Lon., UK: Penguin.

Nietzsche, F. [1983] 1967. "Thus Spoke Zarathustra." In *The Portable Nietzsche,* ed. and trans. W. Kaufmann. New York: Viking.

Nightingale, D.J., and J. Cromby. 1999. *Social Constructionist Psychology: A Critical Analysis of Theory and Practice.* Buckingham, Bucks., UK: Open University Press.

Niskanen, W.A. 1971. *Bureaucracy and Representative Government.* Chicago: Aldine Atherton.

Niskanen, W.A. 1973. *Bureaucracy: Servant or Master?* London: Institute for Economic Affairs.

Niskanen, W.A. 1975. "Bureaucrats and Politicians." *Journal of Law and Economics* 18 (3): 617-643.

Niskanen, W.A. 1994. *Bureaucracy and Public Economics.* Cheltenham, Glos., UK: Edward Elgar.

Nock, A.J. [1924] 1991. "On Doing the Right Thing." In *The State of the Union: Essays in Social Criticism by Albert Jay Nock,* ed. C.H. Hamilton. Indianapolis, IN. Liberty Fund.

Noll, R.G., and M.P. Fiorina. 1979. "Voters, Bureaucrats and Legislators: A Rational Perspective on the Growth of Bureaucracy." *Journal of Public Economics* 9 (3): 239-254.

Noonan, H.W. 2003. *Personal Identity.* Second Edition. London: Routledge.

Nozick, R. 1974. *Anarchy, State and Utopia*. New York: Basic Books.

Oakeshott, M.J. 1975. *On Human Conduct*. Oxford: Oxford University Press.

Ockham, W. [c 1329] 1974. *"Summa Logicae."* In Loux, M. J. (ed.), *Ockham's Theory of Terms*, ed., M.J. Loux. Notre Dame, IL: Notre Dame University Press.

Offe, C. 1999. "How We Can Trust our Fellow Citizens." In *Democracy and Trust*, ed. M.E. Warren. Cambridge: Cambridge University Press.

Oliner, S.P., and P.M. Oliner. 1988. *The Altruistic Personality: Rescuers of Jews in Nazi Europe*. New York: Free Press.

Olsaretti, S. ed., 2003. *Desert and Justice*, Oxford: Oxford University Press.

Olsaretti, S. 2004. *Liberty, Desert, and the Market*. Cambridge: Cambridge University Press.

Olsen, M. 1965. *The Logic of Collective Action*. Cambridge, MA: Harvard University Press.

O'Neill, O. 1989. *Constructions of Reason: Explorations of Kant's Practical Philosophy*. Cambridge: Cambridge University Press.

Onuf, N.G. 1989. *World of Our Making: Rules and Rule in Social Theory and International Relations*. Columbia, SC: University of South Carolina Press.

Organization of Economic Co-operation and Development (OECD). 2011. *Measuring Well-Being and Progress*. Paris: OECD. http://www.oecd.org/std/Measuring%20Well-Being%20and%20Progress%20Brochure.pdf (retrieved November 12, 2015).

Organization of Economic Co-operation and Development (OECD). 2013. *OECD Framework for Statistics on the Distribution of Household Income, Consumption and Wealth*. Paris: OECD. http://www.oecd.org/statistics/OECD-ICW-Framework-Chapter2.pdf (retrieved November 12, 2015).

Orlofsky, J.L. 1976. "Intimacy Status: Relationship to Interpersonal Perception." *Journal of Youth and Adolescence* 5 (1): 73-78.

Ortega y Gasset, J. [1929–31] 2002. *What is Knowledge?*, trans. J. García-Gómez. Albany, NY: State University of New York Press.

Ostrom, E., J. Walker, and R. Gardner. 1992. "Covenants with and without a Sword: Self-Governance is Possible." *American Political Science Review* 86: 404-417.

Otsuka, M. 2003. *Libertarianism without Inequality*. Oxford: Clarendon Press.

Ouchi, W.G. 1980. "Markets, Bureaucracies and Clans." *Administrative Science Quarterly* 25: 95-100.

Packard, V. 1959. *The Status Seekers*. New York: David Mackay.

Page, S.E. 2006. "Essay: Path Dependence." *Quarterly Journal of Political Science* 1: 87-115.

Panitch, L. 1977. "The Development of Corporatism in Liberal Democracies." *Comparative Political Studies* 10 (1): 61-90.

Panitch, L. 1980. "Recent Theorization of Corporatism." *British Journal of Sociology* 31 (2): 161-187.

Parducci, A. 1995. *Happiness, Pleasure, and Judgment: The Contextual Theory and Its Applications*. Hillsdale, NJ: Lawrence Erlbaum.

Pare, D. 1984. "On Nozick: A Critique of Entitlement." *Gnosis: A Journal of Philosophic Interest Montréal* 2 (3): 39-63.

Pareto, V. [1906/1927] 1971. *Manual of Political Economy*. trans. A.S. Schwier. New York: Augustus M. Kelly.

Parker, W.D. 2007. *Methodological Individualism vs Methodological Holism: Neoclassicism, Institutionalism and Socionomic Theory* (Discussion Paper). Gainsville, GA: Socionomic Foundation.

Parkes, C. 1971. "Psycho-social Transition: A Field for Study." *Social Science and Medicine* 5: 101-115.

Parrott, M. 2012. "Senses of First-Person Authority." http://philosophy. berkeley.edu/file/763/parrott.senses.1.2012.pdf (accessed December 12, 2012).

Parsons, T. 1937. *The Structure of Social Action*, vol. 2. New York: Free Press.

Parsons, T. 1951. *The Social System*. Glencoe, IL: Free Press.

Parsons, W. 1995. *Public Policy: An Introduction to the Theory and Practice of Policy Analysis*. Cheltenham, Glos., UK: Edward Elgar.

Peirce, C.S. 1877. "The Fixation of Belief." *Popular Science Monthly* 12 (November): 1–15. http://www.peirce.org/writings/p107.html (retrieved December 6, 2006).

Peirce, C.S. [1878] 1992. "How to Make our Ideas Clear." In *The Essential Peirce*, vol. 1, eds. N. Houser, and C. Kloesel. Bloomington IN: Indiana University Press.

Peirce, C.S. [1898] 1993. *Reasoning and the Logic or Things: The Cambridge Conference Lectures of 1898*, ed. K.L. Ketner, intro. H. Putman. Cambridge, MA: Harvard University Press.

Penner, L.A., B.A. Fritzsche, J.P. Craiger, and T.S. Freifeld. 1995. "Measuring the Prosocial Personality." In *Advances in Personality Assessment*, vol. 10, eds. J. Butcher, and C.D. Spielberger. Hillsdale, NJ: Lawrence Erlbaum.

Pereboom, D., ed. 1999. *The Rationalists: Critical Essays on Descartes, Spinoza, and Leibniz*. Blue Ridge Summit, PA: Rowman & Littlefield.

Perlman, M. 1976. "Party Politics and Bureaucracy in Economic Policy." In *The Vote Motive: An Essay in the Economics of Politics, With Applications to the British Economy*, ed. G. Tullock. London: Institute of Economic Affairs.

Perry, J. 1975. *Personal Identity*. Oakland, CA: University of California Press.

Peters, B.G. 1995. *The Politics of Bureaucracy*. Fourth Edition. New York: Longman.

Peters, B.G., and D.J. Savoie, eds. 1998. *Taking Stock: Assessing Public Sector Reforms* (Canadian Center for Management Development Series on Governance and Public Management, No. 2). Montreal: Canadian Center for Management Development and the McGill-Queen's University Press.

Peters, T.J. 1994. *The Pursuit of WOW*. New York: Macmillan.

Peters, T.J., and R.H. Waterman. 1982. *In Search of Excellence: Lessons from America's Best-Run Companies*. New York: Harper and Row.

Pettit, P. 2001. *A Theory of Freedom: From the Psychology to the Politics of Agency*. Cambridge: Polity Press.

Piaget, J. 1970. *Structuralism*, ed. and tran. C. Maschler. New York: Basic Books.

Pinker, S. 2002. *The Blank Slate: The Modern Denial of Human Nature.* London: Book Club Associates.

Place, U. T. 1956. "Is Consciousness a Brain Process." *British Journal of Psychology* 41 (1): 44–50.

Plato. [390s–347 BC] 1997. *Plato: Complete Works*, ed. J.M. Cooper. Indianapolis, IN: Hackett.

Plato. [c380 BCE] 1952. *Phaedras*, trans. R. Hackforth. Cambridge: Cambridge University Press.

Plato. [c360 BCE] 1955. *The Republic*, ed. H.P.D. Lee. Harmondworth, Gt. Lon. UK: Penguin.

Poincaré, H. [1905] 1907. "The Value of Science." In *The Foundations of Science*, trans. G.B. Haisted, pref. H. Poincare, intro. J. Royce. New York: Science Press.

Pojman, L., and O. McLeod, eds. 1999. *What Do We Deserve?* New York: Oxford University Press.

Poland, J. 1994. *Physicalism: The Philosophical Foundations.* New York: Oxford University Press.

Polanyi, K. 1957. *The Great Transformation: The Political and Economic Origins of our Time.* Boston, MA: Beacon Press.

Pollitt, C. 2000. "Is the Emperor in His Underwear?: An Analysis of the Impacts of Public Management Reform." *Public Management* 2 (2): 181-199.

Popper, K. [1935/1959] 2000. *The Logic of Scientific Discovery.* Second Edition. London: Routledge.

Popper, K.R. [1962] 1968. *Conjectures and Refutations.* New York: Harper and Row.

Popper, K. R. 1979. *Objective Knowledge.* Oxford: Clarendon.

Popper, K.R., and J.C. Eccles. 1977. *The Self and it Brain.* Berlin: Springer.

Portes, A. 1972. "Rationality in the Slum: An Essay on Interpretive Sociology." *Comparative Studies in Sociology and History*, 14: 668-686.

Powers, J. 1992. "Did God have any Choice in the Creation of the World: Symposium: Hawking's 'History of Time', Re-considered." The

Cambridge Review, March.

Prasser, S. 1990. "Reforming the Public Sector: Strategies for Change." In *Dynamics in Australian Public Management: Selected Essays*, eds. A. Kouzmin, and N. Scott. Melbourne, AU: Macmillan.

Price, H.H. 1932. *Perception*. London: Methuen.

Psillos, S. 1999. *Scientific Realism: How Science Tracks Truth*. London: Routledge.

Psillos, S. 2002. *Causation and Explanation*. Montreal, Ont., CA: McGill-Queens University Press.

Putman, H. 1980. "The Nature of Mental States." In *Readings in Philosophy of Psychology*, ed. N. Block. Cambridge, MA: Harvard University Press.

Putman, H. 1987. *The Many Faces of Realism*. La Salle, IL: Open Court.

Putman, H. 1988. *Representation and Reality*. Cambridge MA: MIT Press.

Pylyshyn, Z.W. 2007. *Things and Places: How the Mind Connects with the World*. Cambridge, MA: MIT Press.

Quade, E.S. 1976. *Analysis for Public Decisions*. Third Edition. New York: Elsevier.

Quine, W. van. 1951. "Two Dogmas of Empiricism." *The Philosophical Review* 60 (1): 20-43. ttp://www.ditext.com/quine/quine.html (retrieved September 16, 2008).

Radner, R. 1992. "Hierarchy: The Economics of Managing." *Journal of Economic Literature* 30: 1,282-1,315.

Rainey, H.G. 2014. *Understanding and Managing Public Organizations*. Fifth Edition. San Francisco, CA: Jossey-Bass.

Rainey, H.G., R. Backoff, and C. Levine. 1976. "Comparing Public and Private Organizations." *Public Administration Review* 36: 233-244.

Rainey, H.G., and B. Bozeman. 2000. "Comparing Public and Private Organizations: Empirical Research and the Power of A Priori." *Journal of Public Administration Research and Theory* 10 (2): 447-470.

Rainey, H.G., and Y.H. Chun. 2005. "Public and Private Management Compared." In *The Oxford Handbook of Public Management*, eds. E. Ferlie, L.E. Lynn, and C. Politt. Oxford: Oxford University Press.

Rand, A. 1957. *Atlas Shrugged*. New York: Random House.

Rand, A. 1965. *The Virtue of Selfishness: A New Concept of Egotism*. New York: American Library.

Rawls, J.A. 1971. *A Theory of Justice*. Oxford: Oxford University Press.

Reber, A.S. 1995. *Dictionary of Psychology*. Second Edition. Harmondsworth, Gt. Lon., UK: Penguin.

Redding, S.G., and G.Y.Y. Wong. 1992. "The Psychology of Chinese Organisational Behaviour." In *The Psychology of the Chinese People*, ed. M.H. Bond. Oxford: Oxford University Press.

Rein, M., and D.A. Schön. 1993. "Reframing Policy Discourse." In *The Argumentative Turn in Policy Analysis and Planning*, eds. F. Fischer, and J. Forester. London: UCL Press.

Rescher, N. [1983] 1994. *Risk: A Philosophical Introduction*. Washington DC: University Press of America.

Rey, G. 1997. *Contemporary Philosophy of Mind*. Oxford: Blackwell.

Rhodes, R.AW. 1994. "The Hollowing Out of the State: The Changing Nature of the Public Service in Britain." *Political Quarterly* 65: 138-151.

Rhodes, R.A.W. 1996. "The New Governance: Governing Without Government." *Political Studies* 44 (4): 652-657.

Ricoeur, P. 1981. *Hermeneutics and the Human Sciences: Essays on Language, Action and Interpretation*, ed. and tran. J.B. Thompson. Cambridge: Cambridge University Press.

Ridley, M., and R. Dawkins. 1981. "The Natural Selection of Altruism." In *Altruism and Helping Behavior: Social Personality and Developmental Perspectives*, eds. J.P. Rushton, and R.M. Sorrentino. Hillsdale, NJ: Lawrence Erlbaum.

Riesman, D. 1950. *The Lonely Crowd*. New Haven, CT: Yale University Press.

Riker, W.H. 1982. *Liberalism Against Populism: A Confrontation Between the Theory of Social Democracy and the Theory of Social Choice*. San Francisco, W.H. Freeman.

Riley, J. 1989. "Justice Under Capitalism." In *Markets and Justice*, ed. J.W. Chapman. New York: New York University Press.

Ring, P., and A. Van de Ven. 1992. "Structuring Cooperative Relationships between Organizations." *Strategic Management Journal* 13 (7): 483-498.

Ring, P., and A. Van de Ven. 1994. "Developmental Processes of Cooperative Interorganizational Relationships." *Academy of Management Review* 19 (1): 90-118.

Riso, D.R. 1987. *Personality Types: Using the Enneagram for Self-discovery.* Boston, MA: Houghton Mifflin.

Ritchie, D.G. 1896. *Principles of State Interference.* Second Edition. London: Swan Sonnenschein. https://archive.org/details/principlesstate01ritcgoog (accessed July 5, 2014).

Ritzer, G., and P. Gindoff. 1992. "Methodological Relationism: Lessons for and from Social Psychology." *Social Psychology Quarterly* 55 (2): 128-140.

Roberts Clark, W. 1998. "Agents and Structures: Two Views of Preferences, Two Views of Institutions." *International Studies Quarterly* 42: 245-270.

Robey, D., ed. 1973. *Structuralism: An Introduction.* Oxford: Oxford University Press.

Robinson, H. 2003. "Dualism." In *The Blackwell Guide to Philosophy of Mind*, eds. S. Stich, and T. Warfield. Oxford: Blackwell.

Rogers, C.R. 1961. *On Becoming a Person.* Boston, MA: Houghton Mifflin.

Rorty, R. 1971. "Mind–Body Identity, Privacy and Categories." In *Materialism and the Mind–Body Problem*, ed. D. Rosenthal. Englewood Cliffs, NJ: Prentice Hall.

Rorty, A. (ed.) 1976. *The Identities of Persons.* Berkeley and Los Angeles, CA: University of California Press.

Rorty, R. 1985. "Postmodern Bourgeois Liberalism." In *Hermeneutics and Praxis*, ed. R. Hollinger. Notre Dame, IL: Notre Dame University Press.

Rorty, R. 1986. "The Contingency of Selfhood." *London Review of Books* 8 (May): 15-17.

Rorty, R. 1997. "Realism, Antirealism, and Pragmatism: Comments on Alston, Chisholm, Davidson, Harman, and Searle." In *Realism/ Antirealism and Epistemology*, ed. C.B. Kulp. Totowa, NJ: Rowman & Littlefield.

Rose-Ackerman, S. 1978. "Bureaucratic Structure and Corruption." In *Corruption: A Study in Political Economy*, ed. S. Rose-Ackerman. New York: Academic Press.

Rosenberg, M. 1979. *Conceiving the Self.* New York: Basic Books.

Rosenthal, U. 1990. "Politics and Administration: Max Webber and the Quest for Democratic Order." In *Dynamics in Australian Public Management: Selected Essays*, eds. A. Kouzmin, and N. Scott. Melbourne, AU: Macmillan.

Ross, W.D. 1930. *The Right and the Good.* Oxford: Clarendon.

Rotter, J.B. 1966. "Generalized Expectancies of Internal Versus External Control of Reinforcement." *Psychology Monographs* 80 (609).

Rousseau, J.-J. [1762] 1973. *Du Contrat Social ou Principes du Droit Politique [The Social Contract]*. Reprinted in *The Social Contract and Discourses*, ed. and trans. G.D.H. Cole. London: Dent.

Rovane, C. 1998. *The Bounds of Agency: An Essay in Revisionary Metaphysics.* Princeton, NJ: Princeton University Press.

Rowley, C.K., R.D. Tollison, and G. Tullock, eds. 1988. *The Political Economy of Rent-Seeking.* Norwell, MA: Kluwer Academic.

Rubin, D.H. 1994. *Explanation.* Oxford: Oxford University Press.

Rúmi, J. 1956. *Rúmi, Poet and Mystic*, trans. and ed. R.A. Nicholson. London: George, Allen and Unwin.

Russell, B. [1910–1911] 1917. "Knowledge by Acquaintance and Knowledge by Description." In *Mysticism and Logic and Other Essays*. London: George Allen and Unwin. http://www.gutenberg.org/files/25447/25447-h/25447-h.htm (retrieved December 12, 2002).

Russell, B. 1912. *The Problems of Philosophy.* Oxford: Oxford University Press, Home University Library. http://www.gutenberg.org/files/5827/5827-h/5827-h.htm (retrieved Janury 4, 2003).

Russell, B. 1927. *An Outline of Philosophy.* London: George Allen & Unwin.

Russell, B. 1940. *An Inquiry into Meaning and Truth.* London: George Allen & Unwin.

Russell, B. 1946. *A History of Western Philosophy.* London: George Allen & Unwin.

Ryan, A. 1970. *The Philosophy of Social Explanation.* London: Macmillan.

Ryle, G. 1949. *The Concept of Mind.* London: Hutchinson.

Saad-Filho, A., and D. Johnston, eds. 2005. *Neoliberalism: A Critical Reader.* London: Pluto Press.

Sadurski, W. 1985. *Giving Desert its Due: Social Justice and Legal Theory.* Dordrecht, NL and Boston, MA: D. Reidel.

Salamon, L.M. 1981. "Rethinking Public Management: Third Party Government and Changing Forms of Public Action." *Public Policy* 29: 255-275.

Salamon, L.M. 1987. "Of Market Failure, Voluntary Failure, and Third Party Government: Towards a Theory of Government-Nonprofit Relations in the Modern Welfare State." *Journal of Voluntary Action Research* 16: 29-49.

Salamon, L.M. 1995. *Partners in Public Service: Government-Nonprofit Relations in the Modern Welfare State.* Baltimore, MD: Johns Hopkins University Press.

Samuelson, P.A. 1983. "Thünen at Two Hundred." *Journal of Economic Literature* 21: 1,468-1,488.

Samuelson, P.A. 1955. "Professor Samuelson on Operationalism in Economic Theory: Comment." *Quarterly Journal of Economics* 63: 310-314.

Sandel, M. 1982. *Liberalism and the Limits of Justice.* Cambridge: Cambridge University Press.

Sapir, E. 1958. *Selected Writing of Edward Sapir in Language, Culture and Personality,* ed. D.G. Mandelbaum. Berkeley and Los Angeles, CA: University of California Press.

Sartre, J.-P. [1943] 1957. *Being and Nothingness: An Essay of Phenomenological Ontology,* trans. H.E. Barnes. London: Methuen.

Sartre, J.-P. [1960] 1976. *Critique of Dialectical Reason,* vol. 1: Theory of Practical Ensembles, trans. A Sheridan-Smih. London: New Left Books.

Saul. J.R. [2005] 2009. *The Collapse of Globalism: And the Reinvention of the World*. Revised Edition. Toronto, ON: Penguin Canada.

Savage, L.J. 1954. *The Foundations of Statistics*. New York, NY: Wiley.

Scarre, G. 1996. *Utilitarianism*. London: Routledge.

Scharpf, F.W. 1994. "Games Real Actors Could Play: Positive and Negative Coordination in Embedded Negotiations." *Journal of Theoretical Politics* 6: 27-53.

Schatzki, T.R. 2002. *The Site of the Social: A Philosophical Account of the Constitution of Social Life and Change*. University Park, PA: Penn State University Press.

Scheffler, S. 1988. *Consequentialism and Its Critics*. Oxford: Oxford University Press.

Scheffler, S. 1992. *Human Morality*. Oxford: Oxford University Press.

Schein, E.H. 1980. *Organizational Psychology*. Third Edition. Englewood Cliffs, NJ: Prentice-Hall.

Schein, E.H. 1985. *Organizational Culture and Leadership*. San Francisco, CA: Jossey-Bass.

Schein, E.H. 1991. "What is Culture?" In *Reframing Organizational Culture*, ed. P.J. Frost. Newbury Park, CA: Sage.

Schiller, F.C.S. [1903] 1912. *Humanism: Philosophical Essays*. Second Edition. London and New York: Macmillan.

Schiller, F.C.S. [1907] 1912. *Studies in Humanism*. Second Edition. London and New York: Macmillan.

Schleiermacher, F.D.E. [1805–1810] 1977. *Hermeneutics: The Handwritten Manuscripts*, trans. J. Duke, and J. Forstman. Missoula, MT: Scholars Press.

Schmidtz, D., and R.E. Goodin. 1998. *Social Welfare and Individual Responsibility: For and Against*. Cambridge: Cambridge University Press.

Schmitter, P.C., and G. Lehmbruch, eds. 1979. *Trends Towards Corporatist Intermediation*. London: Sage.

Schofield, J. 2001. "The Old Ways are the Best? The Durability and Usefulness of Bureaucracy in Public Sector Management." *Organization* 8 (1): 77-96.

Schopenhauer, A. [1818/1844] 1969. *The World as Will and Representation*, 2 vols., trans. E.F.J. Payne. New York: Dover.

Schopenhauer, A. [1839] 1999. *Prize Essay on the Freedom of the Will*, ed. G. Zöller. http://books.google.com/books?hl=en&id=fW5DltU-SoC&dq=schopenhauer (retrieved May 9, 2001).

Schopenhauer, A. [1851] 1970. *Essays and Aphorisms*, trans. R.J. Hollingdale. London: Penguin.

Schütz, A. [1932] 1967. *The Phenomenology of the Social World*, trans. G. Walsh, and F. Lehnert. Evanston, IL: Northwestern University Press.

Schwartz, B. 2004. *The Paradox of Choice: Why More is Less*. New York: HarperCollins.

Schwarz, M., and M. Thompson. 1990. *Divided We Stand: Redefining Politics, Technology and Social Choice*. Philadelphia, PA: University of Pennsylvania Press.

Scitovsky, T.De. 1941. "A Note on Welfare Propositions in Economics." *Review of Economic Studies* 9 (1): 77-88. http://www.hujingbei.net/up-load/2007_11/07110714376633.pdf (retrieved June 23, 2015).

Scott, N., and J. Seglow. 2007. *Altruism*. New York: Open University Press.

Scruton, R. [1981] 1984. *A Short History of Modern Philosophy: From Descartes to Wittgenstein*. Second Edition. London: Routledge & Kegan Paul.

Scruton, R. 1985. *Thinkers of the New Left*. London: Longman.

Searle, J.R. 1983. *Intentionality*. Cambridge: Cambridge University Press.

Searle, J.R. 1995. *The Construction of Social Reality*. New York: Free Press.

Searle, J.R. 2004. *Mind: A Brief Introduction*. New York: Oxford University Press.

Seligman, M. 2003. *Authentic Happiness: Using the New Positive Psychology to Realize Your Potential for Lasting Fulfilment*. New York: Free Press.

Sen, A.K. 1970. "The Impossibility of a Paretian Liberal." *Journal of Political Economy* 78 (1): 152-157.

Sen, A.K. 1977. "Rational Fools: A Critique of the Behavioral Foundations of Economic Theory." *Philosophy and Public Affairs* 6 (4): 317-344.

Sen, A.K. 1980. "Description as Choice." *Oxford Economic Papers* 32 (3): 352-369.

Sen, A.K. 1985. "Commitment and Identity." *Journal of Law, Economics, & Organization* 1 (2): 341-355.

Sen, A.K. 1987. "Rational Behavior." In *The New Palgrave: A Dictionary of Economics*, eds. J. Eatwell, M. Millgate, and P. Newman. London: Macmillan.

Shand, J. 2002. *Philosophy and Philosophers: An Introduction to Western Philosophy.* Stocksfield, Nthumb., UK: Acumen.

Shepherd, L.J. 1993. *Lifting the Veil: The Feminine Face of Science.* Boston: Shambala.

Sher, G. 1987. *Desert.* Princeton, NJ: Princeton University Press.

Sher, G. 2010. "Real-World Luck Egalitarianism." *Social Philosophy and Policy* 27 (1): 218-232.

Shoemaker, S. 1963. *Self-Knowledge and Self-Identity.* Ithaca, NY: Cornell University Press.

Shope, R.K. 1983. *The Analysis of Knowing: A Decade of Research.* Princeton, NJ: Princeton University Press.

Shrader-Frechette, K. 1985. *Risk Analysis and Scientific Method.* Boston, MA: Kluwer.

Shweder, R.A. 1984. "Preview: A Colloquy of Culture Theorists." In *Culture Theory: Essays on Mind, Self, and Emotion*, eds. R.A. Shweder, and R.A. LeVine. New York: Cambridge University Press.

Siebers, T. 1994. *Heterotopia: Postmodern Utopia and the Body Politic.* Ann Arbor, MI: University of Michigan Press.

Silver, A. 1989. "Friendship and Trust as Moral Ideals: An Historical Approach." *European Journal of Sociology* 30: 274-297.

Silz, W. 1929. *Early German Romanticism.* Cambridge, MA: Harvard University Press.

Simmel, G. [1900] 2012. *The Philosophy of Money*, ed. D. Frisby, trans. T. Bottomore, D. Frisby, and K. Mengelberg, new for. C. Lemert. London and New York: Routledge.

Simmel, G. 1910–1911. "How is Society Possible?" *American Journal of Sociology* 16: 372-391.

Simmel, G. [1922] 1955. "The Web of Group Affiliations." In *Conflict and The Web of Group Affiliations*, ed. G. Simmel, trans. K.H. Wolff, and R. Bendix. Glencoe, IL: Free Press.

Simon, H.A. [1945] 1960. *Administrative Behavior*. Second Edition. New York: Macmillan.

Simon, H.A. [1945] 1976. *Administrative Behavior*. Third Edition. New York: Macmillan.

Simon, H.A. 1956. "Rational Choice and the Structure of the Environment." *Psychological Review* 63: 129-138.

Simon, H.A. 1957. *Models of Man: Social and Rational*. New York: Wiley.

Simon, H.A. 1982. *Models of Bounded Rationality*. Cambridge, MA: MIT Press.

Skinner, B.F. 1938. *The Behavior of Organisms*. New York: Appleton-Century-Crofts.

Skinner, B.F. 1953. *Science and Human Behavior*. New York: Macmillan.

Skinner, B.F. 1969. *Contingencies of Reinforcement*. New York: Appelton-Century-Crofts.

Skinner, B.F. 1971. *Beyond Freedom and Dignity*. New York: Knopf.

Skinner, B.F. 1973. *About Behaviorism: Radical Behaviorism for the Intelligent Layperson*. New York: Kopf.

Skinner, B.F. [1977]. 2002. "Walden Two: Freedom and the Behavioral Sciences." In *Free Will*, ed. R. Kane. Malden, MA: Blackwell.

Slimansky, S. 2002. *Free Will and Illusion*. Oxford: Oxford University Press.

Smart, J.J.C., and B. Williams. 1973. *Utilitarianism: For and Against*. Cambridge: Cambridge University Press.

Smith, A. 1755. "Adam Smith on the Need for 'Peace, Easy Taxes, and a Tolerable Administration of Justice." http://files.libertyfund.org/pll/quotes/436.html (accessed June 15, 2014).

Smith, A. [1759] 1976. *A Theory of the Moral Sentiments*. Oxford: Oxford University Press.

Smith, Adam ([1776] 1976. *An Inquiry into the Nature and Causes of the Wealth of Nations,* eds. R.H. Campbell, A.S. Skinner, and W.B. Todd. Oxford University Press.

Smith, K. K. and Berg, D. N. 1987. *Paradoxes of Group Life.* San Frncisco, CA: Jossey-Bass.

Sosa, E., ed. 1994. *Knowledge and Justification,* vol. 2. Brookfield, VT: Ashgate.

Spencer, W. [1851] 1995. *Social Statics.* New York: Robert Schalkenback Foundation.

Spiker, C.C. 1989. "Cognitive Psychology: Mentalistic or Behavioristic?" *Advanced Child Development Behavior* 21: 73-90.

Spinoza, B.de. [1677] 2009. *Ethics: Ethica Ordine Geometrico Demonstrata,* trans. R.H.M. Elwes. Portland, OR: The Floating Press.

Spreitzer, G.M. 1995. "Psychological Empowerment in the Workplace: Dimensions, Measurement and Validation." *Academy of Management Journal* 38: 1,442-1,465.

Staub, E. 1974. "Helping a Distressed Person: Social, Personality, and Stimulus Determinants." In *Advances in Experimental Social Psychology,* vol. 7, ed. L. Berkowitz. New York: Academic Press.

Steger, M.B., and R.K. Roy. 2010. *Neoliberalism: A Very Short Introduction.* Oxford: Oxford University Press.

Stevenson, R.L. [1879] 1909-1914. *Truth of Intercourse.* New York: P.F. Collier, The Harvard Classics. http://www.grtbooks.com/exitfram. asp?idx=3&yr=1886&aa=ST&at=DO&ref=stevenson&URL= http://www.bartleby.com/28/11.html (retrieved April 6, 2005).

Stevenson, C.L. 1944. *Ethics and Language.* New Haven, CT: Yale University Press.

Stevenson, C.L. 1963. *Facts and Values: Studies in Ethical Analysis.* New Haven, CT: Yale University Press.

Stewart, D. 1829. *The Works of Dugald Stewart,* Vol. V: *The Philosophy of the Active and Moral Powers of Man,* ed. W. Hamilton. Cambridge: Hilliard and Brown. https://books.google.com.tr/ books/about/The_Works_of_Dugald_Stewart_The_philosop. html?id=wVXJNcJ96BoC&redir_esc=y (retrieved May 22, 2016).

Stich, S. 1990. *The Fragmentation of Reason*. Cambridge, MA: MIT Press.

Stigler, G.J. 2007. "Monopoly." In The Concise Encyclopedia of Economics. In The Encyclopedia of Economics. Second Edition, ed. D.R. Henderson. Indianapolis, IN: Liberty Fund, Economics and Liberty. http://econlib.org/library/Enc/Monopoly.html (retrieved March 18, 2016).

Stogdill, R.M., and A. Coons, eds. 1957. *Leadership Behavior: Its Description and Measurement* (Research Monograph, 88). Columbus, OH: Ohio State University, Bureau of Business Research.

Stokey, E., and R. Zeckhauser. 1978. *A Primer for Policy Analysis*. New York: W. W. Norton.

Stoljar, N. 2000. "Autonomy and the Feminist Intuition." In *Relational Autonomy: Feminist Perspectives on Autonomy, Agency, and the Social Self*, eds. C. Mackenzie, and N. Stoljar. New York: Oxford University Press.

Strauss, A.L. 1959. *Mirrors and Masks: The Search for Identity*. Glencoe, IL: Free Press.

Streeck, W., and P.C. Schmitter. 1991. "Community, Market, State—and Associations? The Prospective Contribution of Interest Governance to Social Order." In *Markets, Hierarchies and Networks: The Coordination of Social Life*, eds. G. Thompson, J. Frances, R. Levacic, and J. Mitchell. London: Sage and Open University Press.

Stroll, A. 2006. *Did My Genes Make Me Do It and Other Philosophical Dilemmas*. Oxford: Oneworld.

Sunstein, C.R., and R.H. Thaler. 2003. *Libertarian Paternalism Is Not an Oxymoron*. Washington, DC: Brookings Joint Center for Regulatory Studies.

Swartz, R.J., ed. 1965. *Perceiving, Sensing, and Knowing*. New York: Doubleday.

Tajfel, H. 1981. *Human Groups and Social Categories*. Cambridge: Cambridge University Press.

Tajfel, H., ed. 1982. *Social Identity and Intergroup Relations*. Cambridge: Cambridge University Press.

Tajfel, H., and J.C. Turner. 1979. "An Integrative Theory of Intergroup

Conflict." In *The Social Psychology of Intergroup Relations*, eds. W.G. Austin, and S. Worchel. Monterey, CA: Brooks-Cole.

Tajfel, H., and J.C. Turner. 1986. "The Social Identity Theory of Intergroup Behavior." In *Psychology of Intergroup Relations*, eds. S. Worchel, and L.W. Austin. Chicago, IL: Nelson-Hall.

Taleb, N.N. 2007. *The Black Swan: The Impact of the Highly Improbable*. London: Allen Lane.

Tannenbaum, K. and W.H. Schmidt. 1958. "How to Choose a Leadership Pattern." *Harvard Business Review*, March–April: 95-102.

Tanner, M. 1996. *The End of Welfare: Fighting Poverty in Civil Society*. Washington, DC: Cato Institute.

Taylor, F.W. [1911] 1947. *Scientific Management*. New York: Harper and Row.

Taylor, C. 1975. *Hegel*. Cambridge: Cambridge University Press.

Taylor, G. 1985. *Pride, Shame and Guilt: Emotions of Self-Assessment*. Oxford: Clarendon.

Taylor, C.C.W., ed. and tran. 1999. *The Atomists: Leucippus and Democritus Fragments*. Toronto: University of Toronto Press.

Tegmark, M. [2014] 2015. *Our Mathematical Universe: My Quest for the Ultimate Nature of Reality*. London: Penguin Books.

Terrell, K. 1993. "Public-Private Wage Differentials in Haiti: Do Public Servants Earn a Rent?" *Journal of Development Economics* 12 (2): 293-314.

Teubner, G. 1993. *Law as an Autopoietic System*. Oxford: Blackwell.

Thelen, K. 2004. *How Institutions Evolve: The Political Economy of Skills in Germany, Britain, the United, and Japan*. Cambridge: Cambridge University Press.

Thévenaz, P. 1962. *What Is Phenomenology? and Other Essays*, ed. J.M. Edie, trans. C. Courtney, and J.M. Edie. Chicago, IL: Quadrangle Books.

Thiel, S.V., and F. Leeuw. 2002. "The Performance Paradox in The Public Sector." *Public Performance and Management Review* 25 (3): 267-281.

Thomas, W.I., and F. Znaniecki. 1918–20. *The Polish Peasant in Europe and America*, 2 vols. Second Edition. New York: Dover.

Thompson, G., J. Frances, R. Levacic, and J. Mitchell, eds. 1991. *Markets, Hierarchies and Networks: The Coordination of Social Life*. London: Sage and Open University Press.

Thompson, M., G. Grendstat, and P. Selle. 1999. "Cultural Theory as Political Science." In *Cultural Theory as Political Science*, eds. M. Thompson, G. Grendstat, and P. Selle. London: Routledge.

Thompson, M., and P. Taylor. 1986. *The Surprise Game: An Exploration of Constrained Relativism*. Warwick Papers in Management 1. London: University of Warwick, Institute for Management Research and Development.

Thorpe, W.H. 1962. *Biology and the Nature of Man*. London and New York: Oxford University Press.

Thucydides [401 BCE] 1972. *History of the Peloponnesian War*. Revised Edition, tran. R. Warner. Harmondsworth, Gt. Lon., UK: Penguin.

Thünen, J.H.von, [1826] 1966. *The Isolated State: an English Edition of Der Isolierte Staat*, ed. and intro. P. Hall, tran. C.M. Wartenberg. Oxford and New York, Pergamon.

Tickner, J.A. 1997. "You Just Don't Understand: Troubled Engagements between Feminists and IR Theorists." *International Studies Quarterly* 41 (4): 611-632.

Tilly, C. 1990. *Coercion, Capital and European States, AD 990–1990*. Cambridge, MA: Blackwell.

Titmuss, R.M. 1958. *Essays on the Welfare State*. London: Allen & Unwin.

Tobin, J. 2007. "Monetary Policy." In *Concise Encyclopedia of Economics*. Second Edition, ed. D.R. Henderson. Indianapolis, IN: Liberty Fund, The Economics and Liberty. http://www.econlib.org/library/Enc/MonetaryPolicy.html (retrieved June 23, 2016).

Tolman, E.C. 1922. "A New Formula for Behaviorism." *Psychological Review* 29: 44-53.

Tolman, E.C. 1932. *Purposive Behavior in Animal and Men*. New York: Appleton-Century-Crofts.

Torfing, J., and E. Sørensen. 2007. *Theories of Democratic Network*

Governance. London: Palgrave.

Tripathi, S., and J. Dixon. 2008. "Leadership in a Paradoxical Public-Sector Environment: The Challenges of Ambiguity." *International Journal of Leadership in Public Services* 4 (3): 1-16.

Tsoukas, H. 1998. "Forms of Knowledge and Forms of Life in Organized Contexts." In *In the Realm of Organization: Essays for Robert Cooper,* ed. R.C.H. Chia. London: Routledge.

Tullock, G. 1965. *The Politics of Bureaucracy.* Washington: Public Affairs Press.

Tullock, G. 1976. *The Vote Motive: An Essay in the Economics of Elites, with Applications to the British Economy.* London: Institute of Economic Affairs.

Tversky, A., and D. Kahneman. 1974. "Judgment under Uncertainty: Heuristics and Biases." *Science* 185 (1): 124-31.

Tversky, A., and D. Kahneman. 1981. "The Framing of Decisions and the Psychology of Choice." *Science* 211: 453-458.

Tversky, A., and D. Kahneman. 1986. "Rational Choice and the Framing of Decisions." *Journal of Business* 19 (4): 251-278.

Udehn, L. 1996. *The Limits of Public Choice: A Sociological Critique of the Economic Theory of Politics.* London and New York: Routledge.

Udehn, L. 2001. *Methodological Individualism.* London: Routledge.

Uhr, J. 1998. *Deliberative Democracy in Australia: The Changing Place of Parliament.* Melbourne: Cambridge University Press in association with, Australian National University, Research School of Social Sciences.

Urmson, J.O. 1968. *The Emotive Theory of Ethics.* London: Hutchinson.

Urry, J., R. Dingwall, I. Gough, P. Omerod, D. Massey, J. Scott, and N. Thrift. 2007. "What is 'Social' about Social Science?" *Twenty-first Century Society* 2 (1): 95-119.

Uslaner, E. 2002. *The Moral Foundations of Trust.* Cambridge: Cambridge University Press.

Vallentyne, P., ed. 1991. *Contractarianism and Rational Choice.* Cambridge: Cambridge University Press.

Vallentyne, P. 2001. "Introduction: Left-Libertarianism—A Primer." In *Left-Libertarianism and Its Critics: The Contemporary Debate*, eds. P. Vallentyne and H. Steiner. New York: Palgrave MacMillan.

Vangen, S., and C. Huxham. 1998. "The Role of Trust in the Achievement of Collaborative Advantage." Paper presented at the *14th European Group for Organizational Studies (EGOS) Colloquium*, Maastricht, NL, August.

Veblen, T. [1898] 1919. "Why Is Economics not an Evolutionary Science?" *Quarterly Journal of Economics* 12 (4): 373-397. Reprinted in *The Place of Science in Modern Civilization and other Essays*. ed. T. Veblin. New York: B. W. Huebsch.

Veblin, T. [1900] 2011. "The Preconceptions of Economic Science–III." *Quarterly Journal of Economics* 14 (2): 240-269. Reprinted in *Essential Writings of Thorstein Veblen*, eds. C. Camic, and G.M. Hodgson. London: Routledge.

Vigoda-Gadot, E. 2002. "From Responsiveness to Collaboration: Governance, Citizens, and the Next Generation of Public Administration." *Public Administration Review* 62 (5): 527-540.

Vigoda-Gadot, E. 2004. "Collaborative Public Administration: Some Lessons from the Israeli Experience." *Managerial Auditing Journal* 19 (6): 700-711.

von Sophilos 2012. *What is Simple Subjectivism? Explain and Evaluate the Two Most Prominent Arguments Against It.* https://sophilos.wordpress.com/2012/06/01/what-is-simple-subjectivism-explain-and-evaluate-the-two-most-prominent-arguments-against-it/ (retrieved May 24, 2016).

Vroom, V.H. 1964. *Work and Motivation*. New York: Wiley.

Vroom, V.H., and P.W. Yetton. 1973. *Leadership and Decision Making*. Pittsburgh, PA: University of Pittsburgh Press.

Wacquant, L. 2009. *The Neoliberal Government of Social Insecurity*. Durham, NC: Duke University Press.

Waldo, D. 1984. *The Administrative State: A Study of the Political Theory of American Public Administration*. New York: Holmes and Meier.

Walrus, L. [1874/1896] 2014. *Elements of Theoretical Economics or the*

Theory of Social Wealth, eds. and trans. D.A. Walker, and J.v. Daal. Cambridge: Cambridge University Press. http://digamo.free.fr/walras96.pdf (retreived 25 June 2016).

Walzer, M. 1983. *Spheres of Justice: A Defense of Pluralism and Justice*. New York: Basic.

Warnock, M. 1970. *Existentialism*. Oxford: Oxford University Press.

Watkins, J.W.N. 1952. "The Principles of Methodological Individualism." *The British Journal of the Philosophy of Science* 3: 186-189.

Watkins, J.W.N. 1957. "Historical Explanation in the Social Sciences." *British Journal of the Philosophy of Science* 8: 104-117.

Watkins, J.W.N. 1968. "Methodological Individualism and Social Tendencies." In *Reading in the Philosophy of the Social Sciences*, ed. M. Brodbeck. New York: Macmillan.

Watson, J.B. 1913. "Psychology as the Behaviorist Views It." *Psychological Review* 20: 158-177. http://psycnet.apa.org/index.cfm?fa=buy.optionToBuy&id=1926-03227-001 (retrieved September 11, 2007).

Watson, J.B. [1924] 1930. *Behaviorism: A Textbook of Comparative Psychology*. Revised Edition. Chicago, IL: University of Chicago Press.

Weber, M. [1903–1917/1949] 1997. *The Methodology of the Social Sciences*, trans. E.A. Shils, and H.A. Finch. New York: Free Press.

Weber, M. [1905/1930] 1992. *The Protestant Ethic and the Spirit of Capitalism*, trans. T. Parsons, intro. A. Giddens. London: Routledge.

Weber, M. [1914/1922] 1947. *The Theory of Social and Economic Organization*, trans. A.M. Henderson, and T. Parsons, intro. T. Parsons. New York: Free Press.

Weber, M. [1914/1922] 1968. *Economy and Society: An Outline of Interpretive Sociology*, eds. G. Roth, and C. Wittich, trans. E. Fischoff. New York: Bedminster Press.

Weber, M. [1948] 1998. *From Max Weber: Essays in Sociology*, eds., trans., for. H. Geeth, and C Wright Mills. London: Routledge and Kegan Paul.

Weick, K. E. 1979. *The Social Psychology of Organizing*. Reading, MA: Addison Wesley.

Weick, K.E. 1995. *Sensemaking in Organizations*. Newbury Park, CA: Sage.

Weimer, D.L. 1995. "Institutional Design: Overview." In *Institutional Design*, ed. Weimer, D.L. Dordrecht, NL: Springer. http://link.springer.com/chapter/10.1007/978-94-011-0641-2_1# page-2 (retrieved February 27, 2002).

Weimer, D.L., and A.R. Vining. 1992. *Policy Analysis: Concepts and Practice*. Second Edition. Englewood Cliffs, NJ: Prentice-Hall.

Weintraub, E.R. 1985. *General Equilibrium Analysis: Studies in Appraisal*. Cambridge: Cambridge University Press.

Weintraub, E.R. 2007. "Neoclassical Economics." In *The Concise Encyclopedia of Economics*. Second Edition, ed. D.R. Henderson. Indianapolis, IN: Liberty Fund, Economics and Liberty. http://www.econlib.org/library/Enc1/NeoclassicalEconomics.html (retrieved June 5, 2016).

Weissman, D. 2000. *A Social Ontology*. New Haven, CT and London: Yale University Press.

Welbourne, M. 2001. *Knowledge*. Stocksfield, Nthumb., UK: Acumen.

Weller, P., H. Bakvis, and R.A.W. Rhodes. 1997. *The Hollow Crown*. London: Macmillan.

Wertheimer, M. 1961. "Some Problems in the Theory of Ethics." In *Documents of Gestalt Psychology*, ed. M. Henle. Berkeley and Los Angeles, CA: University of California Press.

Whetten, D., and K. Cameron. 2002. *Developing Management Skills*. Upper Saddle River, NJ: Prentice-Hall International.

White, R.W. 1959. "Motivation Reconsidered: The Concept of Competence." *Psychological Review* 6 (5): 297-331.

White, S. 1991. "Narrow Content and Narrow Interpretation." In *The Unity of the Self*, ed. S. White. Cambridge, MA: MIT Press.

Whitehead, A.N. 1925. *Science and the Modern World*. New York: Macmillan.

Whitehead, T. N. 1936. *Leadership in a Democratic Society*. Cambridge, MA: Harvard University Press

Wholey, J.S. 1993. "Evaluation and Performance." *Australian Accountant* 63 (11): 28-33.

Whyte, W.F., ed. 1955. *Money and Motivation*. New York: Harper and Row.

Wicksteed, P.H. 1910. *The Common Sense of Political Economy: Including a Study of the Human Basis of Economic Law*, 2 vols. London: Macmillan. http://www.econlib.org/library/Wicksteed/wkCS.html (accessed August 17, 2014).

Widegren, O. 1997. "Social Solidarity and Social Exchange." *Sociology* 31 (4): 755-771.

Wiggins, D. 1991. *Needs, Values and Truth*. Oxford: Blackwell.

Wilde, O. ([1892]1917). *Lady Windermere's Fan: A Play about a Good Woman*, ed. D. Price. London: Methuen. http://archive.org/stream/ladywindermeresf00790gut/lwfan10.txt (retrieved November 2, 2008).

Wildavsky, A. 1994. "Why Self-interest Means Less Outside of a Social Context: Cultural Contributions to a Theory of Rational Choice." *Journal of Theoretical Politics* 6 (2): 131-159.

Wildavsky, A., and S.-K. Chai. 1994. "Cultural Change, Party Ideology and Electoral Outcomes." In *Politics, Policy and Culture*, eds. D.J. Coyle, and R.J. Ellis. Boulder, CO: Westview.

Wilkinson, A. 1998. "Empowerment Theory and Practice." *Personnel Review* 27 (1): 40-56.

Williams, P. 2012. *Collaboration in Public Policy and Practice: Perspectives on Boundary Spanners*. Bristol, UK: Policy Press.

Williams, M., and T. May. 1996. *An Introduction to the Philosophy of Social Research*. London: UCL Press.

Williamson, O.E. 1979. "Transaction Books Cost Economics: The Governance of Contractual Relations." *The Journal of Law and Economics* 22: 233-261.

Williamson, O.E., ed. 1985. *Organizational Theory: From Chester Barnard to the Present and Beyond*. Expanded Edition. New York: Oxford University Press.

Williamson, O.E. [1993] 1994. "Transaction Cost Economics and Organizational Theory." In *The Handbook of Economic Sociology*, eds. N. Smelzer, and R. Swedberg. Princeton, NJ: Princeton University Press.

Willke, H. and G. Willke (2012). *Political Governance of Capitalism: A Reassessment Beyond the Global Crisis*. Cheltenham, Glos., UK and Northampton, MA: Edward Elgar.

Wilson, C. [1956] 1957. *The Outsider*. Second Edition. London: Pheonix.

Wilson, E.O. 1975. *Sociobiology*. Cambridge, MA: Harvard University Press and Belknap.

Wilson, E.O. 1978. *On Human Nature*. Cambridge, MA: Harvard University Press.

Winch, P. [1958] 1990. *The Idea of Social Science and its Relation to Philosophy*. Second Edition. London: Routledge.

Wincott, D. 1996. "Subsidiarity." In *The Concise Oxford Dictionary of Politics*, ed. I. McLean. Oxford: Oxford University Press.

Wittgenstein, L. [1922] 1961. *Tractatus Logico-Philosophicus*, trans. D.F. Peters, and B.F. McGuiness. London: Routledge.

Wittgenstein, L. 1953. *Philosophical Investigations*, eds. G.E.M. Anscombe and R. Rhees, trans. G.E.M. Anscombe. Oxford: Blackwell.

Wittgenstein, L. [1956] 1978. *Remarks on the Foundations of Mathematics*. Revised Edition, eds. G.H. von Wright, R. Rhees, and G.E.M Anscombe, trans. G.E.M Anscombe. Oxford: Blackwell.

Wolch, J.R. 1990. *The Shadow State: Government and Voluntary Sector in Transition*. New York: The Foundation Center.

Wolf, E.S. 1988. *Treating the Self*. New York: Guildford.

Wolff, R.P. 1970. *In Defense of Anarchism*. New York: Harper & Row.

Wolff, J. 1991. *Robert Nozick: Property, Justice and the Minimal State*. Cambridge: Polity Press.

Woodcock, G. 1986. *Anarchism: A History of Libertarian Ideas and Movements*. Second Edition. Harmondsworth, Gt. Lon., UK: Penguin.

Woodfield, A. 1976. *Teleology*. Cambridge: Cambridge University Press.

Wright, C., B. Smith, and C. Macdonald, eds. 1998. *Knowing Our Own Minds*. Oxford: Clarendon Press.

Wright, C.J.G. 1987. *Realism, Meaning and Truth*. Oxford: Blackwell.

Wright, G.H. von. 1971. *Explanation and Understanding*. London: Routledge and Kegan Paul.

Wright, N.T. 2007. "Where Shall Wisdom be Found?" Homily [by the Bishop of Durham] at the 175th anniversary of the founding of the University of Durham. http://www.ntwrightpage.com (retrieved May 12, 2016).

Young, K. 1979. "Values in the Policy Process." *Policy and Politics* 5: 1-22.

Zahle, J. 2016. "Methodological Holism in the Social Sciences." In *The Stanford Encyclopedia of Philosophy*. Summer Edition, ed. E.N. Zalta. http://plato.stanford.edu/archives/sum2016/entries/holism-social/ (retrieved August 23, 2016).

Zaitchik, A. 1977. "On Deserving to Deserve." *Philosophy and Public Affairs* 6: 370-388.

Zimmerman, M.J. 1988. *An Essay on Moral Responsibility*. Totowa, NJ: Littlefield, Adams.

Zimmerman, M.J. 1996. *The Concept of Moral Obligation*. Cambridge: Cambridge University Press.

Zuriff, G.E. 1985. *Behaviorism: A Conceptual Reconstruction*. New York: Columbia University Press.

INDEX

living organism, 143
machine, 145
political system, 146
psychic prison, 148
structure
mechanistic, 145, 148
organic, 143, 147
public sector reform
civil service reform, 135
cognitive reform, 137
collaborative reform, 135
market-driven, 133
public services provision
state provision determined
by communities, 132
state provision determined
by end-users, 131
state provision determined
by independent professionals, 132
state provision determined
by politicians, 132
public-private partnerships, 133

R

rank-order equality, 71
rationalism, 26
realism
direct, naïve, or classical, 22
epistemological, 22, 23
inferential, 23
metaphysical, 22
scientific, 22
reasoning
bounded rationality, 63
communicative rationality, 64
sense making, 64
teleological, 63
regulatory instruments
command-and-control, 128, 129
economic, 128, 131
information, 128, 130
regulatory mode
hierarchical, 129
self-regulation, 128

voluntary network regulation, 130
rent-seeking behavior, 98,101
risk taking
avoidance, 66
entrepreneurial, 65
expert-driven, 65
politicized, 66

S

Scottish Enlightenment, 1, 2
self, the
autonomous
immaterial mind with
causal capacity, 36
lone self, 37
self-constructed, 37
superficial social
engagements, 38
neoliberal perspective, 36
neurological perspective, 36
relational, 41
neoliberal perspective, 41
self-determinism, 10
individual authenticity, 11
self-rule, 11
self-governance, 112
self-interest, 16, 39, 73
social action attribution
agential-causation, 5
expected utility of
consequences, 8
intentional mental states, 18
self determined intentional
mental states, 8, 11, 14, 16
utility calculation, 17, 19
social-causation, 5, 44
structuralism, 46
cultural participation, 48
discourse participation, 49
dutiful social obligations, 49
economic participation, 46
linguistic participation, 48
social participation, 47
social alienation, 140, 171

ABOUT THE AUTHOR

Professor John Dixon, B Econ, M Econ, PhD (Public Management) AcSS, is a Professor of Public Administration in the Department of Political Science and Public Administration at the Middle East Technical University in Ankara, Turkey. He was previously the Distinguished Professor of Public Policy and Administration at KIMEP University (2009–2014) in Almaty, Kazkhstan, where he was concurrently Dean of the College of Social Science (2009–2012) and Dean of the Bang College of Business (2013–2014). He is the Emeritus Professor of Public Policy and Management at the University of Plymouth (United Kingdom), where he was Professor of International Social Policy (2000–2003), Professor of Public Management (2003–2005), and Professor of Public Policy and Management (2006–2008). Previously, he was an Associate Professor in Australia (University of Canberra (1982–1990) and Monash University (1991–1992) and Hong Kong (Lingnan College (1993–1997)). He is a fellow of the British Academy of the Social Sciences, nominated by the British Social Policy Association, and an honorary life member of the American Phi Beta Delta Honor Society for International Scholars, nominated by the American Political Science Association and the Policy Studies Organization. He has recently been a Visiting Professorial Fellow at the Graduate School of Business at the University of Wollongong (Australia) (2007–2010) and is a Visiting Professor in the School of Business at the University of Northampton (United Kingdom) (2013–2016). He has published very extensively (including 14 authored books, 22 edited books, 11 journal symposia, and over 90 referred articles) on public and social policy and administration.

www.ingramcontent.com/pod-product-compliance
Lightning Source LLC
Chambersburg PA
CBHW071535200326
41519CB00021BB/6500